Memoirs of a Foreign Service Arabist

ADST-DACOR Diplomats and Diplomacy Series

Series Editor: Margery Boichel Thompson

Since 1776, extraordinary men and women have represented the United States abroad under widely varying circumstances. What they did and how and why they did it remain little known to their compatriots. In 1995, the Association for Diplomatic Studies and Training (ADST) and DACOR – an organization of foreign affairs professionals – created the Diplomats and Diplomacy book series to increase public knowledge and appreciation of the professionalism of American diplomats and their involvement in world history. Ambassador RICHARD B. PARKER's autobiography, the 53rd volume in the series, tells the candid story, sprinkled with the author's fabled acerbic wit, of the sometimes parlous career of a leading twentieth-century Foreign Service Arabist.

Other Titles in the Series

Gordon Brown, *Toussaint's Clause: The Founding Fathers and the Haitian Revolution*

Charles T. Cross, *Born a Foreigner: A Memoir of the American Presence in Asia*

Parker T. Hart, *Saudi Arabia and the United States: Birth of a Security Partnership*

Dennis Kux, *The United States and Pakistan, 1947–2000: Disenchanted Allies*

Jane C. Loeffler, *The Architecture of Diplomacy: Building America's Embassies*

William B. Milam, *Bangladesh and Pakistan: Flirting with Failure in South Asia*

Robert H. Miller, *Vietnam and Beyond: A Diplomat's Cold War Education*

David D. Newsom, *Witness to a Changing World*

Richard B. Parker, ed., *The October War: A Retrospective*

Richard B. Parker, *Uncle Sam in Barbary: A Diplomatic History*

Nicholas Platt, *China Boys: How U.S. Relations with the PRC Began and Grew*

Howard B. Schaffer, *Ellsworth Bunker: Global Troubleshooter, Vietnam Hawk*

Ulrich Straus, *The Anguish of Surrender: Japanese POWs of World War II*

For a complete list of series titles, visit www.adst.org/publications

Memoirs of a Foreign Service Arabist

Richard B. Parker

An ADST-DACOR Diplomats and Diplomacy Book

NEW ACADEMIA PUBLISHING

VELLUM

Washington, DC

Library of Congress Control Number: 2013949829
ISBN 97809886376-6-5 paperback (alk. paper)

VELLUM An imprint of New Academia Publishing

NEW ACADEMIA
PUBLISHING

New Academia Publishing
PO Box 27420, Washington, DC 20038-7420
info@newacademia.com - www.newacademia.com

To all my Foreign Service colleagues
who helped me on my way

Contents

Part I

THE EARLY YEARS

1

Beginnings: Life as an Army Brat and College Student

I was an army brat. My father, Capt. Roscoe Stuart Parker, was a cavalry officer, born in Chicago in 1891, the son of a lawyer. My mother, Marguerite Blossom Parker, was born in Manassas, Virginia, on January 14, 1893. Her father, Edward Ebenezer Blossom, was a Union veteran from Indiana with clearly itchy feet. By 1890, he had married Elizabeth Bordeaux, a schoolteacher from Pennsylvania, and moved to Manassas. They had four children there: Earle, Marguerite, Raymond, and Rosamund.

The 1890 census listed E. E. Blossom as a "government clerk." He had prospered in Manassas, owning his own home and a building downtown and holding a seat on the town council. Soon after Rosamund's birth, he decided to move to some other place. He left by train and returned a year later to announce that he had found the place: Seattle. He took the family by the same route he had followed, passing through New Orleans, San Antonio, and San Francisco to show them the marvels he had seen.

In Seattle, E.E. went into the real estate business and bought a lumberyard. He was wiped out in a market crash, and the family was quite poor thereafter. The lumberyard somehow went to his partner, a man named Provine, who my mother said had been a Civil War acquaintance from Larned, Kansas, whom E.E. had picked up from the gutter and set up in business. The family legend is that Provine showed no gratitude and did not help E.E. when the crash came. Then some catastrophe at the lumberyard wiped out Provine, too. The Blossoms rejoiced.

Marguerite was a cheerleader at Lincoln High School in Seattle and graduated in the class of 1912. She apparently went to the University of Washington for a while but did not graduate. She worked as a secretary and knew how to type with the touch method, which later helped her find a job when my father died.

Where and when my parents first met I do not know. I was told that they renewed their acquaintance when he returned to Seattle on leave from training in Fort Leavenworth and ran into her on the street. When they married shortly thereafter, on New Year's Eve 1917, he had become a captain in the U.S. Cavalry and was assigned to the 9th Cavalry at Fort Huachuca, Arizona. They honeymooned en route to Huachuca, stopping at the Cliff House in San Francisco.

My brother, David S. Parker, better known as Bud or Buddy in his youth, was born at Fort Huachuca on March 22, 1919. A few years later the family moved to the Philippines, where Dad was assigned to the Philippine Scouts at Fort Stotsenburg and where I was born on July 3, 1923.

Soon after my birth the family returned to the United States, pausing briefly for a family visit at Seattle and then crossing the country to the Cavalry School at Fort Riley, Kansas, for a two-year stay. We next moved to Fort Clark, at Bracketville, Texas, where Dad commanded a troop of the Fifth Cavalry.

Fort Clark

My first memories are of Fort Clark, many connected with the bedroom I shared with Buddy, both of us sleeping on cast-iron quartermaster beds. One of these recollections is the reassuring sound of the sentry riding his horse up the road in back of our house at night. But I also remember the fun we had putting our fingers in the electric light socket that hung above my bed and experiencing a shock. There were less exciting incidents, like getting a nickel for an ice cream cone and having the ice cream fall on the ground, or going to horse races, with their colorful printed betting tickets.

And there was the rattlesnake. One day Dad brought a baby rabbit home from the rifle range. We kept it on the screened porch just outside our bedroom. In the middle of the night the rabbit screamed, and we discovered that a rattlesnake had entered the porch through the hole where water escaped. The snake had swallowed the rabbit but was now too large to exit through its entry hole. My father somehow killed the snake. Texas bedrooms were dangerous places; my mother bore for the rest of her life the vaccination-like scar of a tarantula bite on her nose received while making the bed one day.

There were many opportunities for getting into trouble at Fort Clark. Certain events stand out. One day when I was tagging along and probably bothering the older children playing cowboys and Indians, they held a mock trial and decided to hang me. They proceeded to carry out the judgment in a neighbor's woodshed, where I was tied up, with a manila rope around my neck. I could not move away and must have cried. I can remember the horrified look on the neighbor's face when she found me there and untied me.

Then there was the Maxwell boy. Among the papers my father saved is a penciled, undated note from General Elting, the post commander, which read as follows:

Dear Parker,
   This p.m. about 4:30 your boy and the Maxwell boy (Warren) were in the middle of the street in front of my house, to the danger of their lives from auto trafic [sic] and to the scandal of the community, engaged in an attempt to see which could urinate the fartherest [sic]. Thought you might as well know about it.
   Elting

I have no recollection of this incident but can imagine it.

Also in the official record is the account of an investigation of a fire in a garage that I was alleged to have fed. I can remember throwing a piece of burlap on it. I received corporal punishment for that.

In those days army officers on troop duty had orderlies called "strikers," enlisted men from the officer's unit whose title perhaps came from their duty of striking the officer's tent. The striker could be called on to perform various domestic duties as well. In our case, the striker was occasionally used as a babysitter. One evening I was left in the care of a striker, a bald-headed man who smelled strongly of horse. He promptly fell asleep in his chair, and I sneaked out and went to the movies, an open-air affair at one end of the parade ground. I sat in the front row and no one from my family saw me. I might have gone undetected had Buddy not heard me shout and turned me in.

We departed by train in August 1928 for Galveston, where we took the SS *Algonquin* for New York. The *Algonquin* was a passenger liner. I am sure it was comfortable and well run, but it was the first place I experienced rudeness from adults and where I had my first case of seasickness. After that, to me the dining room had a terrible smell that put me off milk and runny eggs semi-permanently. I became a finicky eater and a scrawny child. I tried to explain to my parents that this aversion had to do with the smell of the ship. They were never able to take me seriously, although they soon realized that I would not drink milk or eat fried eggs.

Disembarking in New York was a relief. Mother took me to see her girlhood friend, an opera singer from Seattle named Leonora Corona, and Dad took Buddy and me to the Bronx Zoo and Coney Island, where we had a wonderful time riding the roller coaster. From New York we traveled by train to Northfield, Vermont.

Northfield

Northfield was quite different from Fort Clark. Dad had been assigned as an assistant professor of military science and tactics at Norwich University, a cavalry ROTC school for men. Although it was a small town with not much to offer, Northfield was a great place for a boy to grow up in. It was here that we bought our first radio, a Majestic, and the first car we were able to keep, a 1929 Chevrolet with solid wheels. Dad bought a new Chevy every two years thereafter.

We soon moved to a large, red house on a corner. It was a gloomy place, drafty and cold in winter, and Mother hated it. The only pleasure I can remember her taking in it was the night she was able to freeze some chocolate mousse on the back porch, since we did not yet own a refrigerator. Another of her recipes that I remember fondly was her chocolate icebox cake, known more precisely as a charlotte, which she could make even before we had a refrigerator. It is still my favorite dessert.

In the fall I went to Mrs. Porter's kindergarten across the street. Her son built wonderful model airplanes and used Vaseline hair tonic, which I thought was pretty great. Buddy went to the grammar school across the railroad tracks and up the hill. He also began an industrious career selling candy bars to the workers at the knitting mill. The smell when he brought them home in their wooden basket was wonderful. I still recall that basket whenever I encounter that candy bar aroma. I don't know whether he ever ate any, but they were a terrible temptation to me. I quickly broke down and stole a couple, for which I was promptly spanked. That cemented an early relationship with Buddy; he was virtuous and I was not.

Later, Buddy gave up his candy route and began trapping muskrats, getting up before dawn in the middle of winter and trudging out to run his traps. He skinned the animals and stretched and dried their pelts in the basement, which always smelled bad as a result. He certainly earned his dollar per pelt. Emulating him seemed totally impossible, and I very sensibly did not try. I went with him once and found it difficult to get up so early and to walk so far in the cold. The disparity in our ages, and my relatively amoral outlook on life, must have made me an irritating little brother. We slept together in the same room until he went off to West Point in 1936; but as a child I never felt more than a certain grudging tolerance from him. I did not realize I loved him until he left home. After watching him board the train and leave San Antonio I went home and cried.

After a year in the gloomy old house with the rhubarb patch, we moved across town to a recently redecorated, university-owned house. It had an efficient coal-fired furnace and was wonderfully warm and tight in the winter. Adding to the marvels, it included our first refrigerator—a GE with a turret on top. To make our happiness complete, Mother found a way to make grilled cheese sandwiches in a new Toastmaster.

The stock market crash of 1929 must have occurred soon after we moved, but I was blissfully unaware and remember our three years in the new house as a happy period. There were woods to play in, a hayloft to jump out of, a clay cliff to dig in, and a swamp to play in. There were endless excursions to take and a couple of boys next door to play with. I did not enjoy the winter sports much because I was never any good at them, always getting snow in my

pants and freezing my feet and fingers and toes; but it was exhilarating to slide down the sidewalk at the grammar school, which I
began to attend when we moved.

First grade opened at Northfield Grammar School in the fall.
I walked nearly a mile to and from school four times a day, since
there were no lunch facilities at school, and did not think of it as
a particular hardship except when the air was very cold and it
snowed. Even then there were diversions such as catching a ride on
the back of the doctor's sleigh, which sometimes went down Main
Street at the right time of the morning.

Now began my first exposure to the life of the intellect. I already knew many of my classmates because we had gone to Mrs.
Porter's kindergarten together, and life in the classroom was congenial, although discipline was strict. We kept quiet and pinned to
our seats most of the time, only allowed to go to the bathroom at
designated times. I wet my pants twice because the teacher would
not let me go at an unauthorized time. Two traumatic occasions, I
guess, but they taught me not to pass up opportunities to pee—a
valuable lesson for later life.

Our first grade teacher was kind, and our second grade teacher
was strict. In the third grade we had Teresa Kingston, an angel who
was everyone's favorite and who taught generations of Northfield
children. The high point of the year was my appearance in the class
play as King Winter, opposite Minabel Chase as my queen. Minabel
had dark brown hair and I was very fond of her, although I had no
idea how to express that effectively. She sat in front of me for at
least one year. I don't know whether she reciprocated my admiration for her, and never saw her again after we left.

During this period I was introduced to the public library. The
first book I borrowed was by Burgess, about the animals around the
Smiling Pool. I would like to say that I devoured the books in the
library, but I fear that was not the case. I read some of the children's'
classics, and Aunt Rosamund, who was a librarian, always sent
me a book from the top of the current librarians' list at Christmas,
which I enjoyed. But I did not begin to read books seriously until I
was in high school.

My parents were not great readers, and our house was not full
of books. They subscribed to a number of magazines, including the

Saturday Evening Post, Colliers, and eventually *Time* and *Life.* Their favorite reading was the serial fiction in the *Saturday Evening Post*: stories about Fu Manchu; Mr. Glencannon and his favorite whiskey, Dugan's Dew of Kirkintilloch; Alexander Botts, the tractor salesman; Tugboat Annie; Dr. Moto; and others. Indeed, much of my own reading, perhaps a majority of it, was in magazines. It is remarkable to me how this source of light fiction has disappeared from our national life, and no one seems to miss it.

The climax of my Northfield career was my ninth birthday in 1932, the last such occasion on which I had a real party. I remember it as a great success. As my birthday fell on July 3rd, I was always likely to receive more money for fireworks than other kids, and so I began setting them off on the 3rd. We had two-inch and larger "salutes," which were very loud and would send a tin can spinning an enormous distance into the air. We all laughed when my father set off a salute under a can and was hit on the head by the can when it fell as he was running away. Everyone, including Dad, thought it was funny.

During this period I became aware of other members of our family, beyond our nucleus—my mother had two brothers and a sister, and I had cousins and a grandmother. (My father's parents were both dead, as was my mother's father.)

Buddy and I both had fond memories of Northfield. My only recollection of Grandmother Blossom is from when she came to visit us one summer. She seemed very old to me, though she was only in her mid-60s. I remember her descending from the train on arrival and telling Mother she had brought some Rocky Road candy that had melted in the heat. I can remember her ordering me in to dinner in spite of myself, and her reciting a poem about every cloud having a silver lining while pointing out the gleam around a cloud's edge.

The Northfield years were my last stage of freedom and innocence. I felt at home, and people were kind to me. I particularly remember Alson and Maude Edgerton. Remarkably worldly for Northfield, they had a house on Main Street with a porch on which they kept magazines and books during the summer. I would spend hours there reading the *National Geographic* and books about the outside world. They had an old farmhouse out in the country where we would go for picnics. No picnic since has ever matched those in my imagination. Vermont summers are so unthreatening compared to that of the southern United States–no chiggers or rattlesnakes or heatstroke, only clear brooks to wade in and reasonable trees to climb and sit in.

We left Northfield on July 23, 1932, for Fort Bliss, Texas, where Dad was assigned to command Troop B of the 7th Cavalry. This was the most memorable trip we ever had, a fitting climax to my birthday party. Dad had bought a 1932 Chevrolet with chrome-plated louvres and wire wheels, and Mother had a large, new suitcase (finally abandoned in Monterubbiano in 1996). Buddy had his graduation watch, and we were off on a new adventure.

We drove first to Washington and went to the Smithsonian, with Lindbergh's Spirit of St. Louis hanging from the ceiling and an unbelievable variety of other marvels beyond that. We saw everything: the Lincoln Memorial, the Washington Monument, Mt. Vernon, and the remnants of the bonus army. We visited the battlefields at Gettysburg and Manassas and ate grilled cheese sandwiches and did all sorts of wonderful things. In New York, we went to Coney Island again and did the rides, particularly the roller coaster.

From New York, we took the Army transport USS *Grant* for San Francisco via the Panama Canal. To my delight, its dining room did not smell like the *Algonquin*'s, there were lots of children my age on board, and the Filipino waiters served lovely French pastries at dinner. We had a stateroom that seemed nice to me, though far from luxurious; a "shower boy" named George notified you when one of the showers down the hall was free.

Panama was my first real sight of a foreign country, and I had never seen anything so exotic. There were strange smells and artifacts. We had fresh coconut juice; Mother happily bought some chinoiserie she had long wanted. I saw a shrunken head in a store window and it haunted me for years.

San Francisco was wonderful. After being on ship for ten days or so, everything on dry land seemed to move. We stayed for a few days at a nice hotel, the St. Francis, saw a great Harold Lloyd film set in Chinatown, went to the aquarium, and marveled at the cable cars. Then we took off in our Chevrolet, which had magically accompanied us on the ship. Mother, who had been homesick for the

West Coast ever since she left it, was particularly interested in orange juice, which must have been expensive in Vermont. At that point in the Depression, roadside stands in California were selling all you could drink for a few cents. I can't imagine that we stopped at more than one or two, but I'm sure she got her fill.

We went south to Los Angeles and then turned east on the old Route 66, passing through the Mojave Desert, Needles, and Flagstaff. We detoured to see the Grand Canyon, staying at the Bright Angel Lodge. The flat Painted Desert was a relief after the scary heights of the canyon, where I was afraid Dad would drive over the edge. We arrived in El Paso just in time for school and moved into a bungalow on the 7th Cavalry Officers' row.

Several months later I wrote the following account to Miss Kingston, my third grade teacher, who returned it to my parents for their amusement:

Qrs. 509
Fort Bliss Texas
Jan. 21, 1932

Dear Miss Kingston:
    We've been having a lot of bad weather. No snow but frost instead. So it's terrible. I didn't tell much about the trip we had last time [indicating that I had sent her an earlier letter] so I'll tell all about it now. We left July 15. Went to lake Champlain crossed in a ferry to port Arthur. Camped a little farther on. Went to Washington, D.C. Then we went to a hotel. We went to a museum and I saw the first airplane, Lindberg's plane (The Spirit of St. Louis) and a lot of other things. Then we went to Brooklyn, N.Y. Went in a boat. Got caught in a storm first day. Saw [the island of] San Salvador got to Panama Canal in a week. Bought rugs and dishes. set sail for old Panama got there in a day stayed half an hour. saw the ruins which were old roads, a great church and the other old buildings necessary, reached San Francisco in 3 days. Saw seals looked like dogs. went across the Mohave desert. saw volcano that erupted three years ago saw lava. Petrified wood all stone. Came to painted desert in 15 minutes looked like yellow, gray, red and purple. saw crystals.

went to grand canyon 15 miles wide purple and red. came to El Paso. stayed here for five months.

Yours truly
Richard Parker

Fort Bliss

Fort Bliss was much larger than Fort Clark. There were two regiments of cavalry, the 7th and the 8th, plus artillery and Air Corps units and Beaumont general hospital. The two cavalry regiments were billeted in barracks on one side of the parade ground, with the officers in individual quarters on the other. The officers of the 8th had substantial older houses while those of the 7th, including us, were housed in wooden bungalows put up as temporary structures in World War I. They were torn down and replaced by much larger, masonry structures in the mid-thirties. The bungalows were hot and close together, and we could hear much of what our neighbors said and did. My father used to delight in imitating the scolding by the officer's wife next door.

Between the post and El Paso was a stretch of empty desert, dotted with cactus and sagebrush and heavily populated with horned toads, lizards, and snakes. This was where the boys my age did much of our playing. It was a great place to explore, with cliffs and caves and no adults in sight.

The social climate at Fort Bliss was much different from that at Northfield. There was a swimming pool, where many of the kids spent the day in the weeks before school started. My inability to swim immediately set me apart. There were a lot of kids, all of whom also seemed much more sophisticated and knowledgeable than I, and most of whom were physically stronger and more aggressive. (I must have been the scrawniest kid there.) The boys reflected the climate of the Texas schoolyard, where the favorite pastime at that period was "frogging," hitting the playmate's upper arm in a way that produced pain and a welt. The girls were almost as terrifying as the boys. Ginnie, who was plump and outgoing, could outshout and outshove any of the boys. Abigail Robenson, whom I remembered as a tomboy in chaps at Fort Clark, had turned into a beautiful young woman who swam better than anyone else and obviously felt superior. Seeing her standing at the poolside made me feel even scrawnier. I eventually taught myself to dog paddle, and then my mother taught me the sidestroke.

Soon after our arrival, Charlie Booth and his family moved in on the other side of our bungalow. Charlie was another cavalry captain, and his wife Betty was a beautiful blonde Texas girl whose accent still rings softly in my ears. They had two sons, Charles and Jack.

Jack was my age and my closest friend at Bliss and later in San Antonio and was a terrible influence on me. He told me about sex, how to swear, and how to lie—the thing to do was to say "Sir" from time to time as you spoke. He was adventuresome and led me on many escapades I would never have dared try on my own. Once when I was sick in San Antonio, Jack brought me a flying model of a Fokker D-8 he had made from a 25-cent kit. I could never duplicate it.

One night we went across the road in back of the officers' row to the pumping station. The pumpkeeper had grapevines hanging from a trellis and was alleged to keep a shotgun loaded to use against intruders. Nevertheless, we sneaked into the grounds, stole as many grapes as we could carry, and then sneaked into the outdoor movie to eat them. The next morning I awoke with a stomachache and to my surprise was taken to the hospital, where I had my appendix cut out. I kept telling people about the grapes, but no one would listen. After the initial discomfort, the hospital stay was rather fun. People visited and brought me presents, which no one did when I was not in the hospital. It was during this stay, however, that my parents discovered that I had a depressed sternum, a malformation of the chest that in later years became a constant inhibition against appearing in public without a shirt.

School came as a great shock. Not only was my brother going off to a separate high school, but my new school was a far cry from the relatively intimate institution at Northfield. First of all, I had to ride a school bus, a 2.5-ton army truck with a canvas cover and bench seats full of hyperactive kids from the post. The school, Coldwell Elementary, had two or more homerooms per grade, a great change. But the biggest change was homework. I had never encountered that before, and its sudden imposition filled me with such despair that I had great difficulty doing it. My nightmares about unfilled or unmet obligations date from this period. (Were I in charge, there would never be any homework. I would keep the kids in class longer but leave them free at night.) As it was, I did poorly in class, was sent to the principal's office more than once, and was not sorry to leave when we did.

Santa Fe

Franklin Roosevelt and his team moved quickly after his inauguration in 1933 to attack the economic and social crisis. One of their more sensible initiatives was creation of the Civilian Conservation Corps, which took young men off the streets and sent them to camps throughout the country, where they planted trees, built roads, and received three square meals a day plus a small allowance. The army ran the program efficiently, and my father, still a captain, was one of the officers picked for that task. In May 1933 he was detailed to the Santa Fe subdistrict headquarters and found himself in charge of setting up camps throughout the state.

In early 1934, Mother, Bud, and I moved to Santa Fe, where we lived in what was then called a tourist camp and today would be a motel that the army had rented south of town. I went to a public school, Gormley, to which I insisted on wearing my Cub Scout uniform the first day. It was a Christmas present, and I had had no chance to wear it. No one in Santa Fe had ever heard of a Cub Scout, and I was too embarrassed ever to wear the uniform in public again.

Dad took me to school that morning. He strode into the fifth grade classroom and said, "Here's Dick," or something like that. Until then I had been Richard. To the teacher, a pleasant young woman named Beth Owen, I was Dick from then on. I found the new name vaguely unsettling, but put up with it. I became Richard again when we left the following summer for San Antonio.

In many respects Santa Fe was an ideal place to be a boy. Still a rather small town, it was friendly and open. There were Indians everywhere, and Ernest Thompson Seton, author of *Two Little Savages*, one of my favorite books, lived just outside of town and gave lectures on animals at the high school. There was much to see. In addition to romantic historic remains like the Spanish governor's palace, with the chair in which Lew Wallace wrote *Ben Hur*, and a house alleged to be the oldest in North America, there were wonderful places to explore, like Frijoles (Bandelier) Canyon, full of Indian ruins, arrowheads, and pottery. On the north rim of the canyon was a private school, Los Alamos, a place named for a grove of cottonwood trees. Bulky items were sent to the ranch in the canyon on a cable, down which a door-size platform slid on pulley wheels. One of the first acts of the CCC was to build a road down into the canyon and set up a camp there from which to work on the site of Bandelier National Monument. My brother got to spend the summer there, working in the canteen. I was only allowed to visit, but it was a wonderful place.

Santa Fe was a little rustic, however, or so it seemed to me. We did not live near any other children of my age, and my parents were busy; so I was largely left to my own devices. My chances to visit other CCC camps were limited, our camp had no library, the swimming pool was derelict, and most of my toys were still at Fort Bliss. We were only camping out in Santa Fe. I had a couple of friends at school, but they lived too far away for me to play with them much after school. I remember one from that period, David Salazar. We sometimes walked home together. Many years later, I encountered a Foreign Service officer who had also known David at Gormley, but neither of us had any reliable recollection of the other.

Some memorable events occurred during our brief stay, especially a pack trip of a week or two that we took with a forest ranger named Tom Buchanan. I do not know where it was, but we were in the woods out of touch with everyone for two weeks, each of us on a horse, with our tents and supplies on a couple of mules. I remember it as exciting but often uncomfortable. I was stung by nettles and worn out from riding all day, and I found the sleeping uncomfortable. I learned how to saddle a horse and tie a girth hitch, however. My father and Bud seemed to enjoy it greatly, but Mother found it a bit of a trial, I think

They must have made some concessions to my age, but I can't recall them. I had been taught to ride some time earlier and taken out regularly for early morning rides at Fort Bliss. It was assumed that I would stay on the horse and keep up.

Although Mother was full of admiration for Tom Buchanan's skill with a Dutch oven, I did not like the food very much, except for the hash. After a particularly long day in the rain, we arrived at our camp to have corned beef hash for dinner, and for the first time I realized how good it was. I have been fond of it ever since.

Considerably less successful was a fishing trip we took to a remote area on the Chama River in northern New Mexico, where there were supposed to be trout. It rained almost all the time we were there, living under a fly that Dad had quickly rigged on our arrival. The trout were not biting, and I evidently didn't enjoy fishing anyway. My desperate parents finally made me happy by buying me a set of Tootsie Toy cars at a general store in the vicinity. What a pill I must have been!

San Antonio

In the summer of 1934 Dad was promoted to Major. He bought a new Chevrolet, our first car with a trunk, and we moved to San Antonio, where he was in the CCC headquarters near a large installation at Fort Sam Houston. We lived just off the post in rented quarters across the street from the San Antonio Country Club, to which my parents belonged as a matter of course.

San Antonio was the big time. It was called the mother-in-law of the army because so many army officers married women from there. In addition to Fort Sam Houston were the Army Air Corps training fields at Randolph Field and Kelly Field, now closed. A constant flow of young officers moved through the town and many of them married there.

There was a lot to do in San Antonio outside of school. Though trite to say so, life in those days was a good deal simpler than it is today. There was no television and no stereo system, and we did not miss them at all. We had the Alamo and the Buckhorn Saloon and a museum and a nice zoo with a reptile garden where you could eat fried rattlesnake on Sunday afternoons. There was a Chinese store full of intriguing objects and a wonderful model airplane store where you bought airplane kits for 25 cents and balsa wood in all shapes and sizes. There were fancy drugstores and lovely air-conditioned movie houses. I bought ocarinas at the pawnshops and chocolate milkshakes all over town for 5 cents. Between my bicycle and the bus I could get any place in town on my own, and as far as I know no one worried much about my safety. San Antonio was a much safer place then than it is now.

Fort Sam Houston boasted all sorts of activities, too. I was aware of no great effort at organizing activities to keep me entertained or much effort to see to it that I was doing something improving, but I joined the Boy Scout troop when I turned twelve and emerged as an Eagle Scout three years later, somewhat to my parents' bemusement. Bud complained that they had made the merit badges too easy, and they had.

Mother liked to swim at the Salado, a large, tree-shaded swimming pool on the edge of the Fort Sam reservation, and we would go there frequently in the summer. I took swimming and boxing lessons at the Country Club and eventually dancing lessons at Bud Nash's studio. At this stage in San Antonio I was too shy to ever dance with a girl.

I was keen on a girl named Estelle, but I never dared even hold her hand, although I imagine she would not have minded if I had. Her name will be meaningless to readers, but remembering her is part of the mourning process with which one puts the past to rest.

San Antonio thought of itself as being western rather than southern. There was much talk of Texas pioneers, the Texas Rangers, and cattle drives. We were all taught what to do if bitten by a rattlesnake, and if we were lucky we could have a pair of cowboy boots. I finally got some for my fifteenth birthday and was very proud of them. Our links with the West were pretty ephemeral, but one common sight reminded us that we really weren't that far removed. Arizona Bill, a former Indian scout, had known Kit Carson and had helped capture someone. He was to be seen riding about town on a burro, a campaign hat on his head. At first glance he looked like a vagrant, but he was quite respectable and came to our scout troop to speak of his adventures. I last saw him riding down Broadway in the midst of traffic in about 1938. Today I marvel at the time span the two of us represented. To think that I knew someone who knew Kit Carson!

Our perception that we were on the frontier was supported by the terrors we coped with every day. There were the three-inch flying cockroaches mother called polo ponies, the scorpions and black widow spiders that were everywhere, the cattle ticks and chiggers we picked up in the tall grass, the extremes of weather with which we coped blithely, and the alligators in the San Antonio River. Of all these, the chiggers were the worst: a microscopic insect that burrows under your skin and itches terribly. They prefer the soft skin around the groin, and no insect repellent on the market worked for them. One morning as I pulled a shirt on over my head, I was stung by a scorpion. The bite was very painful, and mother took me to the post hospital for first aid. We were told that there was no treatment and not to worry. It was unlikely to be fatal. Citronella was effective against mosquitoes, but nothing daunted the chigger, although putting sulfur in your shoes and dusting it on your trousers and socks helped. We used to put fingernail polish on the bites in the belief that would smother the insect, but that was about as effective as calamine lotion. There were no miracle drugs.

We had no air-conditioning, as home air-conditioning was almost unheard of. Most workplaces were not air-conditioned either, but people did not seem to think a great deal of it. At home we had one Westinghouse electric fan, and that was all, to cope with the summer heat. It was also extremely humid, and prickly heat was a frequent affliction for which the only treatment was ineffective calamine lotion.

The army week was relatively relaxed. The landlords and gardeners tended to maintenance and mowing, so Dad did no housework at all except to tend the fireplace and the walks in winter. Mother did little housework of any kind and never did a wash. We had a maid to clean the house and do much of the cooking, and laundry was sent out. Thursday nights and Sundays the maid had off. Thursdays, we often went out for dinner at La Fonda, a Mexican restaurant run by two American ladies, and Mother cooked roast beef or pork and roast potatoes for Sunday dinner. Mother did most of her cooking with a can opener, but she did a wonderful job with baked ham, roast beef, and pineapple upside-down cake. Sunday dinner was followed by a long nap in the afternoon and a light supper. Wednesday and Saturday afternoons were free for sport, so Dad often played eighteen holes of golf with the men. Mother would play with the women at other times, and sometimes we would make a family foursome on Sunday mornings. I can remember beaning Bud with a sliced ball on one such occasion.

Mother used to dote on the Gulf breeze that came up every evening, which seemed to provide all the cooling she needed to permit a sound sleep. My parents rarely went out during the week,
and on summer evenings we would often sit out on the lawn, perhaps listening to Jack Benny and Bing Crosby or the Little Theatre
radio programs, or just talk and enjoy the breeze. We could hear
the dance music at the Fort Sam Officers Club, where my parents
often went on Friday or Saturday nights to drink and dance the
Varsoviana. We would drink lemonade or iced tea and have a most
pleasant time.

I went to Hawthorne Junior High School until 1937. Our home-
room teacher throughout the three years was Mrs. Willie J. Wick-
enhoefer, a middle-aged lady who was quite motherly to us and
who was addicted to Coca-Cola. Every day at 10:00 a.m. and 2:00
p.m. she would give one of the boys a nickel and send him across
the schoolyard to Sherry's to get her a coke. She drank it at her desk
while instructing us. I think she would have smoked a cigarette,
too, if it had been permitted. Our principal was an even older woman named Inez Huppertz, who informed us that she suffered from
dyspepsia because she had eaten too fast when she was our age,
and we should be careful not to bolt our food. She seemed a formidable woman. I don't recall her ever smiling, but she called me a
good student when we all went off to high school three years later,
so she must have known something about us and taken some pride
in our progress.

Until I was a junior in high school I was a rather erratic student.
I usually got As and Bs and was never in danger of failing, although
I once got a P for "Poor" in El Paso (but I was not working to capacity). Bud had an unblemished straight A record throughout twelve
years of school, and that was so hard to match that I didn't really
try. I learned early that some people shine more brightly than others and that those who are good-looking can get away with much
more than those who aren't. I was not ugly, but I was never what
one would call handsome, and girls and teachers did not fall for
me as they did for people like Johnny Donaldson at Fort Bliss, who
spat on the floor in class one day in the fifth grade. The two girls sitting next to him giggled, so I spat on the floor, too. They called the
teacher and I was sent to the principal's office. Johnny went on to

West Point and eventually became a general, but he got into trouble for shooting at civilians from his helicopter in Viet Nam.

Fort Leavenworth

In the summer of 1938, Bud had his "yearling" furlough, six weeks to recover from two grueling years at West Point. He drove to San Antonio with Hank Daniels, his roommate, in a 1934 Ford V-8 convertible he had bought for $250. Hank stayed with us for a couple of weeks before going to his own home in Memphis. I was not yet 15 but had my driver's license and was allowed to drive the rather sporty Ford. In the meantime Dad had gone off to Fort Leavenworth and a new job as Post Exchange Officer, a job he accepted because it was his only chance to get to Leavenworth, as he was too old for the Command and General Staff school. He left Mother to pack, pay, and follow.

In early August, Mother, Bud, and I took off in our 1938 Chevrolet for Kansas, stopping at Fort Worth for an open-air dinner, dancing, and a show at Billy Rose's Casino. The band was that of Wayne King, the Waltz King, who was bronzed and mellifluous in the style of Guy Lombardo and who oozed too much, I thought. But the nightclub setting fascinated me. We arrived at our new house in Fort Leavenworth late on a hot August afternoon. I was wearing my Nocona boots and Stetson hat and thought myself very Texan, whooping as I ran up the sidewalk to find Dad, who eventually came out of the shower. I'm not sure what the neighbors thought.

The officers' quarters were large, three-story Victorian duplexes, with five or six bedrooms. In the summer people spent much of the time out on the large screened porch, which tended to be the coolest place in the house. At one point our whole family slept there. Fort Leavenworth was even hotter than San Antonio in the summers of 1938 and 1939. Dad had bought a second fan, a GE pedestal model, and had been sleeping on the porch in his BVDs, a one-piece undergarment of light cotton rather like a loose one-piece bathing suit. One Sunday before our arrival, he had been napping on the porch in his BVDs, with the fan on, when some distant and stodgy cousins from Kansas City arrived unexpectedly to call on him. The porch was at the front of the house, and he had no alternative but to flee in his BVDs and get some pants on while his cousins gaped. I imagine they were people who did not nap and disapproved of those who did.

Fort Leavenworth held a rather compact assortment of different units. Its principal function had become the Command and General Staff School, where officers of the grade of major or thereabouts came for a year and studied military organization and tactics. The instructors and the permanent officer cadre of the post, people like my father, lived in the large, old quarters on the bluff above the river on the Missouri side, while the students lived in apartments of various sizes on the other side of the post. Infantry and cavalry regiments provided the garrison and service troops.

There were plenty of children on the post, and high school students were bused into town to either Immaculata, the Catholic school, or Leavenworth Senior High. Most army kids went to Immaculata, but I went to the public school. Although not favorably impressed at first, I came to enjoy the high school. It was much smaller and less sophisticated socially than Jefferson High School in San Antonio, but the classes were smaller and the instruction was more serious. I had to carry a heavy schedule and forgo electives but was accepted as a junior, even though I had only completed one year of high school. I liked my teachers and did well, splitting the scholarship prize with another boy at graduation.

There wasn't much going on in the town of Leavenworth, but there were lots of activities for kids on the post. A sergeant was detailed to the task of organizing events and could call upon a considerable infrastructure to put together riding classes, boys' football and basketball teams, bowling, gymnastics, swimming, and billiards. Most of these activities centered around the YMCA, so kids from town could join.

My experience with team sports at Leavenworth was not a successful one. I was persuaded to go out for the boys' football team but worked so hard at the first day's practice that I promptly fell ill and was in bed for a week. We decided that football was not for me and that I should try basketball. When basketball season came, my coordination was so poor that no one demurred when I quit after one practice. I took a course in gymnastics, which proved beneficial, but I obviously was not a team sports person. I did play a lot of golf, however, and eventually was good enough to lead the golf team to defeat against Wentworth Military Academy.

The most important activities for the high school kids were the dances, called hops. There was a program dance every Friday, with twenty sets of two or three dance numbers each, played by a band from the 17th Infantry. Each girl had a dance card with twenty spaces on it, which her date had to fill for her so that she would have someone to dance with every number and there would be no wallflowers. Obviously, if your date was considered attractive, you had little difficulty getting other boys to dance with her. If she wasn't, you might have to cash in some of your credits in the favor bank or otherwise you might have to dance with her all evening. That could be more fun at some times than at others, depending on who your date was.

Several dances during the year were invitational, and you were told whom you were to take. As I had shot up to 6' 2" by the time I was fifteen, I would be assigned a tall girl, who might not otherwise have had a date, and filling a program on such occasions could be difficult. If your peers did not like or sympathize with you, you had had it.

The proceedings at the dances were sedate. The band played popular melodic dance music, and there were no liquor, no drugs, and no unchaperoned activity. After the hop we would drive our fathers' cars down to Homer's drive-in, where we would sit in our cars and eat hamburgers and drink malted milks. Then, if you were lucky, you could go off somewhere and neck.

The first year I had no one to neck with. I was fond of a girl named Patsy Gardner, but never got beyond holding her hand in the movie. At the end of the year she and her family left and that was that. The second year was different. I found myself going steady with a very cute town girl, five foot two inches tall, named Peggy Schroeder. We did quite a bit of necking, but that was all. Nice girls did not go beyond that in those days, before we lost our moral compasses.

As time wore on there was talk about what I would do after graduation from high school in 1940. Like most army boys, I hoped to go to West Point. I could conceive of no other career than the army. The question was how to get a commission. Bud had taken and passed the West Point presidential exam in his senior year at high school and entered the academy three months after his seventeenth birthday, which was considered very early. He was at least a year younger than most of his classmates. It was agreed that I would have difficulty doing the same thing and should have a year of college somewhere else first.

We picked—I picked—someone picked Kansas State at Manhattan, because it was close and had a good engineering school, and engineering was my alternative career choice. The big career consideration in those Depression days was being reasonably sure of attaining permanent employment. You had to learn to do something practical. The luxury of majoring in an area of my interest, say, in English literature or history, never occurred to me, because one could not earn a living that way. Engineers graduating from good schools, however, were starting at $125 a month and having no trouble finding jobs if they were competent.

There was a tacit understanding that, after my first year at Kansas State, if I did not make it to West Point, I would be sent to some place more prestigious, perhaps Dartmouth, where we had a connection. This did not happen.

If the truth be told, I did not look forward to the West Point experience. I had a year of ROTC at Jefferson and a year at Leavenworth, but Bud's description of the physical demands made on the cadets at West Point was sobering. If he, who was much stronger physically than I, found them taxing, what would I find in the event I made it in? The physical component of the entrance exam already loomed as a major question mark: I had always been scrawny, weighing something like 125 pounds at 6′2″ and needed to gain another 25 or 30 pounds, which we hoped would come with an additional year or two, to pass the physical.

Meanwhile, I was having a good time in my senior year, getting good grades, and beginning to faintly perceive a wider world outside what I had known to date in the army environment. Several people were influential in this development. One, I realized many years later, was our British-American literature teacher, Minnimae Jones. Her speech and dress indicated experience in the world outside Kansas, and she opened our eyes to the wealth of literature, making us realize that there was a good deal of it we knew nothing about. Another influence was the musically talented Willie Burr, an army boy a year older than I who had graduated from Immaculata but was kept at home a year before trying for West Point. He was a wonderfully entertaining fellow and introduced me to hot jazz, beginning my lifelong interest in and enjoyment of the genre.

Jimmy Mans came to Leavenworth from Immaculata. Our classmate Nancy Todd and I rode to school in his Model A convertible. Nancy was always full of snappy responses. Jimmy was as combative as she was, so the ride to and from school was fun. For the first time I began to feel socially secure.

We had two years of compulsory ROTC at Leavenworth. I only had to take one because of my year at Jefferson. We were under the care of a rather ineffective major and a sergeant named Behnke. Once a year he would be on the program at a school assembly, why I cannot recall. I do recall vividly, however, his standing on the stage both years and telling the assembled students some morality story, the punch line of which was, "He flew the coop!" That was one of his favorite expressions, and I never hear it without thinking of him. Some six years later, in the officer's latrine at the Seattle port of embarkation, the officer sitting next to me turned and said, "Lieutenant, don't I know you from some place?" It was Sergeant Behnke, now a captain or major. He did not mention flying the coop.

Nineteen forty started as a magic number. The war in Europe seemed to be on permanent hold, both Bud and I were graduating from school, Dad had bought a new Chevrolet, and I was free for the summer. I broke up with my girlfriend when we returned to Leavenworth from West Point, however, and found myself spending most of the summer alone. Most of my friends on the post had left with their fathers at the end of the school year. The fall of France had suddenly awakened everyone to the danger we were in, although we had no idea of the magnitude of the changes we would encounter, and the summer became a disturbing and not altogether pleasant period, most of which I spent playing golf by myself.

Almost immediately after my graduation in 1940 we headed east to attend Bud's graduation at West Point. He was 14th in his class, considered remarkable for someone who had entered directly from high school. He had his choice of branches and had chosen the engineers.

We drove first to Washington, via Bowling Green, Kentucky, where we visited the Robensons. Abigail had just earned a certain fame by chasing a burglar away with her father's saber. She was on the dean's list and seemed very glamorous to me.

From Bowling Green we went to Fort Knox, Kentucky, which, as the center of U.S. armored corps development, was still considered a cavalry post, although the horse cavalry was about to disappear, over the strenuous objections of the cavalrymen. The smart ones among them were switching to armor, and the war in Europe was hastening that process. I suspect, in retrospect, that my father was probably scouting the opportunities for himself in this transition period and that was why we went to Knox. I do not know what he learned there.

In Washington we stayed at the Tangiers Hotel, which no longer exists as such. I recall being greatly embarrassed at my father's telling some noisy teenage boys down the hall to be quiet one night during our stay. My father also took me to see the doctors at Walter Reed Army Hospital for an examination and advice on my admissibility to West Point. They told us I would not make it, but did not explain to me exactly why—or if they did I suppressed the knowledge. I thought it was because I was so underweight, but can remember the doctor saying something about my posture that was not altogether unsympathetic. I realized much later that it was my chest deformity. Cadets were supposed to be physically sound and without deformities. I had no discussion with my father about it and do not know what he thought or planned to do. I was secretly relieved, and he must have been relieved that I seemed to be reconciled to a civilian career.

One other incident from this Washington visit remains in my memory. We went one evening to visit Maj. and Mrs. Gilbert Cheaves, who had been with us at Fort Bliss, where he had been the post-exchange officer. As we were coming down the steps from their house on our way home, Mother asked how much Dad thought Gilbert had paid for the house, which we thought very nice. Dad replied, "Ten thousand dollars." That was a lot of money for an army officer in those days, and my parents wondered where he got it. Years later I realized that the house in question was probably in Barnaby Woods, where we bought a house across the street from Gilbert's in 1967 for $37,500.

From Washington we drove up US 1 to New York and West Point, where we stayed at the Thayer Hotel along with all the other parents. June Week, as it is known, was glamorous, full of parties and parades witnessed by beautiful girls in floppy hats. There was no evident awareness that the military situation in Europe was about to change dramatically as the German blitzkrieg got under way. I can remember my father commenting that the legendary French 75th would stop the German tanks in their tracks. (Our standard antitank weapon at that point was a puny little 37 mm gun.)

Bud's graduation present was a 1940 Ford V8 convertible that cost $850. After a much-touted champagne breakfast we drove in two cars down to Scarsdale, Bud and I in the convertible with one of his girlfriends, Babs Garvey, whom I thought terribly sexy, between us. In Scarsdale we had lunch with Babs and her family, whom I thought attractive and personable, particularly her father, but I guess there was no serious romance there.

From there we drove to Northfield, where we stayed at Deborah Mayo's bed and breakfast and had a lovely picnic with the Edgertons at their farm. We then drove over to the pleasant Basin Harbor Club at Vergennes, where we were waited on by girls from the University of Vermont and had the use of a sailboat and a nice golf course. We would have liked to stay for a couple of weeks, but that was not to be. It was very expensive.

On leaving Vergennes, we split up. Our parents went one route, and Bud and I went another, stopping in Columbus, Ohio, to spend the night with another of Bud's girlfriends, Blanche Paige, and her family. It was great fun whizzing across the country with the top down, storing up solar keratoses for the future. I remember listening to the Republican convention. Bud was rooting for Wendell Willkie, who seemed a man of great promise who might be able to defeat Roosevelt; today he does not even rate a mention in the Columbia Encyclopedia (but he is searchable on Google).

Our parents moved in tandem with us across the country, but our paths did not cross. All the while, France was falling. We listened to the car radio avidly for some sign that it really wasn't quite happening as described and that the French had rallied at some point. That sign never came. At this remove I am uncertain about dates but think it was all over by the time we reached Fort Leavenworth.

It was the beginning of the end of life as we had lived it, but we did not realize it yet. We had been hearing Hitler's speeches ever since the seizure of Czechoslovakia—they would be broadcast over the school public address system—but nobody seemed to have taken the full measure of his evil, or of German intentions and power, and we were stunned by the collapse of the French and the British. It was a gloomy summer.

Bud had been assigned to a combat engineer battalion at Camp Ord, California, and had a brief leave en route. He stayed at Fort Leavenworth for a while and then drove off to California for a career that lasted some thirty-six years. I seem to recall our father telling him he really should order from London a pair of Peale boots, which every self-respecting cavalry officer wore, if he wanted to be properly uniformed. I can't remember whether he took the advice, but wonder if he ever got to use them if he did. (Just another question one waited too long to ask.)

Our neighbor across Meade Avenue was Lt. Col. Paul Goode. He had been a famous "Tac," or tactical officer, at West Point, responsible for checking on the activities and progress of cadets and given to sunrise visits and close, paternal supervision. A large, barrel-chested man, he was big on physical fitness. To keep himself winter hardy, he slept on the porch in a bedroll throughout the Kansas winter. His daughter Betsy, a year younger than I, also went to Leavenworth High School, and I was something of a big brother to her. When Jimmy Mans left in the middle of the year because his father was transferred to Washington and we no longer had his car to ride in, I used to ride the bus with Betsy. We would have serious conversations about life and love walking from the bus stop to our homes.

Willie Burr was fond of Betsy and at one point we did a good deal of double dating. On the first or second night after our return I was allowed to take Bud's car out and Peggy and Betsy and Willie and I did something exciting like going to a movie. I can remember our riding around, with the top down, listening to Glenn Miller's "Tuxedo Junction" (just released). It was sort of the realization of a teenager's dream—an early version of *American Graffiti*.

Then, suddenly and without explanation, I dropped Peggy. I had decided that I was in love with Nancy Todd, who was also going to Kansas State, and I felt it was time to break off the relationship with Peggy. It was very stupid and cruel on my part, and I've felt bad about it ever since. Betsy would no longer speak to me, and she and Peggy made catcalls across the street at me one afternoon. Meanwhile, Frank Sinatra was singing "I'll Never Smile Again," and I never hear that song without thinking of that summer.

I had not bothered to sound out Nancy on all this and was surprised to find that she did not return my affection for her, even though she had no real boyfriend at the time. So I spent the summer playing golf, mostly by myself. Willie had left and so had most of the other kids whose fathers had been students at the Command and General Staff School. I didn't feel like seeing anyone anyway.

Meanwhile, things were happening elsewhere. The Battle of Britain was on and it did not seem possible that a handful of British pilots could hold off the Luftwaffe with its vastly superior number of aircraft and pilots. We had no idea how well they were doing in their Spitfires, and we expected the invasion of Britain to start at any moment. The United States was still firmly neutral, but the armed services assumed that we would be involved sooner or later and were already beginning to put themselves in a state of readiness, to the extent they could with their limited resources. Units and individuals were moved, the draft began to call men up, and promotions suddenly happened. My father and most of his contemporaries were promoted to lieutenant colonel, somewhat to their surprise.

Kansas State

I continued to play golf and wonder a little about Kansas State. My father drove me over to Manhattan and we found a rooming house not far from the campus. With no dormitories for men, everyone lived in a rooming house, a boarding house, or a fraternity house. Full board cost something like $16.50 a month, while a room, or rather a bed, could be had for about $7.50. The house bill in a fraternity was $27.50 or thereabouts. I was to have $40 a month for expenses and allowance and did not know what I would do with all that money. My big concern was what I would do about laundry. This was before the day of the Laundromat, and I didn't know what

I was going to do about maintaining a supply of clean underwear and shirts. My parents assumed I would wind up in a fraternity, with laundry arrangements of some sort.

I went through Rush Week, was invited to join various fraternities, and chose Delta Tau Delta, primarily because of a laundry woman and two seniors I knew from Leavenworth. It was a great load off my mind. I never regretted the choice and found the fraternity a source of support and strength. The friends I made there are people for whom I still have a great affection, even if I do nothing about it. They were not all people I would choose to share a desert island with, but they were decent and supportive, and for the first time in my life I felt strength that comes from having people behind you.

About four weeks into the first semester I was summoned to the telephone one evening to be told by my father that he was going to Walter Reed for treatment of a stomach problem. I was not to worry. Mother was going with him, and they would probably be gone over Thanksgiving, which I was to spend with the Edmunds at Fort Leavenworth.

I knew it must be serious but assumed it was an ulcer. I received several cheerful letters from my father and did not worry unduly. Then, after ten days or so, someone called and told me that my father was very sick and my mother wanted me to come to Washington. Colonel Edmunds sent a car to bring me to Leavenworth, where I spent the night and was told that the doctors suspected cancer and were about to operate. The next morning I was taken to Kansas City and put on a TWA plane for Washington, with stops in St. Louis and Pittsburgh. We landed at the old Congressional Airport, where Mother met me and fretted that I had brought the wrong overcoat with me.

The operation was successful in the sense that they removed my father's stomach and thought he would survive, but he contracted postoperative pneumonia and died very quickly. This was before penicillin, which might have saved him (Bud survived a similar operation at about the same time in his life, some 25 years later.). They tried one of the new sulfa compounds, which were the miracle drugs of those times, but it did not work. An autopsy showed that the cancer had spread throughout his body, and he would not have lasted long in any event. The funeral was at Arlington Cemetery, where Bud was buried in 1990. Dad was something of a romantic and had requested that he be cremated and his ashes scattered over the Cascade Mountains in Washington State, of which he had fond memories from his Forest Service days. Bud managed to get an Air Corps pilot to fly him over the mountains in an Army plane and poured out the ashes as requested.

The fundamental assumptions of our lives changed immediately. Mother was now an army widow, entitled to a very modest pension and the proceeds of a couple of small insurance policies. She would be allowed a decent period in our quarters at Leavenworth after which she would have to move out. Our furniture and effects would be moved wherever she wanted or be held in storage for a fixed period, but that was the end. We were no longer in the army.

She moved temporarily to Carmel, where she had always wanted to go and where she could be near Bud. I would continue at K-State, which was cheap—I paid no tuition and my total costs were less than $500 a year—and where I was happy. In the spring she moved to San Antonio, where she took a duplex apartment at 127 Grant Avenue in Alamo Heights. She remained there for about ten years, eventually getting a job in the war censorship office after Pearl Harbor.

One of my early actions at Manhattan, before Dad's death, had been to buy a car—a Model T Ford—from Schmedeman's Sinclair station. There were two available—one for $10 and one for $15. The latter had a battery and self-starter, whereas the former had only a crank and a magneto. I decided to go whole hog and bought the more expensive model. Registration cost something like $5 and I was in business. I did not bother to tell my parents about this, but Nancy Todd told hers, who told Mother, after Dad was in the hospital. I did not think it was any of her business to do that.

Mother, Bud, and I returned to Fort Leavenworth for a few sad days. When I returned to Manhattan, I met with the dean of engineering. We agreed that I had missed so many class days of Surveying 1 that I should drop that course and switch from civil engineering to mechanical engineering, which did not require surveying. This was the first of several switches that led me on a checkered path through the academic jungle. Considerably sobered by my father's death, I studied hard and did well the first semester, winning the fraternity's scholarship prize of $25, with which I bought a gold ring that lasted until after the war.

K State was not all work, however. As fraternity pledges, we were required, among other things, to go out and find wooden barrel staves and fashion them into paddles, which were then used to beat us for infractions and sometimes for general principles. The search for barrels involved going down alleys late at night and stealing them from backyards. We thought this was exciting and great fun. I am sure the property owners did not and trust that the practice has long since been discontinued. I imagine wooden barrels are hard to find in today's backyards in any event, even in Kansas.

There were other pleasures, but not a great many. Engineering students were expected to carry 16 or 17 semester hours of courses, few of which were easy. Freshman engineering chemistry, taught by a German named Van Winkel, in particular flunked a substantial portion of the class every year, and those students switched to business administration or something similar, or left school. The survivors had to work hard and burn a great deal of midnight oil.

The weekends, however, often provided social entertainment, usually in the form of a fraternity dance. The grander occasions would be held in the college gymnasium or at the Avalon ballroom in Aggieville, which had a springy floor that responded to the dancers' feet and encouraged an exuberant dance style. More modest occasions were house dances, hosted at fraternity and sorority houses. They were sedate affairs, chaperoned by the housemother, whose performance was closely monitored by the dean of women. No drinking of alcoholic beverages was allowed, and social privileges were suspended for fraternities or sororities where drinking was known to have occurred. The lack of liquor was no real hardship, and people generally had a good time drinking nothing stronger than Coca-Cola.

On one such occasion at the Delt house in the fall of 1940 I met a town girl named Jeanne Jaccard. She had come with her childhood friend Virginia Howenstine on a double date. Virginia had refused to come out with my fellow pledge (and later best man) Gabe Sellers alone and stipulated that Jeanne must come as well. So Gabe fixed Jeanne up with one of our classmates, whose name we have all forgotten. I took Nancy Todd, about whom I still had some illusions. I was much taken, however, with Jeanne, who was very good looking (she would shortly be the runner-up in a beauty contest judged by Cary Grant) and who had a distinctly different personality. She was quite independent—not to say combative—and interested in exotic things. She did not fit the pattern of the usual Kansas State girl, who tended to be a home economics major. She was a speech major interested in the theater and wanted to make a career of it. After two years at Kansas State, she went off to Northwestern, where she graduated from the School of Speech in 1944. That she never had much chance to exercise her talent and education was the fault of the Foreign Service and the culture in which we raised our family, before it was respectable for married women to pursue careers like their husbands and leave their children to others. I will not go into the details of our courtship, except to say that it was long and ended in marriage some four years later, in June 1944. At this writing some sixty-five years later we are still married and have come to regard it as permanent.

The dizzying heights of my first semester performance were not attained again in my undergraduate career. The second semester, what with one distraction and another, I did not do nearly as well. That summer I went home to San Antonio, where Mother thought I looked puny and took me to see a doctor at the army hospital at Fort Sam Houston (dependents of officers who died while on active duty had the use of military medical facilities, the officers' club, and post exchange [PX]). There an internist named Caton told us that I had a heart murmur. He thought it was probably functional and that we need not worry too much, but I should take things easy for a while. I spent a quiet summer building model airplanes for the Jackson kids next door and riding a horse that belonged to a family friend who wanted it exercised, as he had no free time. It was a pinto stallion called Glory, kept at the small stables maintained at Fort Sam. I rode him almost every day for a couple of months and then went back to school, where I was excused from the second year of ROTC because of my heart and where I bent to learn calculus and descriptive geometry along with organic chemistry and quantitative analysis. By this point I had switched to chemical engineering in order to avoid engineering drawing, which I had decided was too much bending over a drawing board. Whatever my career plans, they came to naught on December 7, 1941.

It happened that I was not eating Sunday dinner at the Delt House that day but was sitting in the living room with a visitor from Fort Riley, a Delt from another school who had been drafted or called to active duty. Suddenly another boy came into the room and said excitedly that the Japanese had just attacked Pearl Harbor, wherever that was. (I knew where it was, but that was because I was an army boy. Few other boys did.) We didn't believe him and went to listen to the radio ourselves and then went into the dining room to tell the assembled company about it. We were at war at last. Life was never the same again.

None of us had paid much attention to the news up to that point, but from then on we were drawn to the radio, and a great deal of time that should have been spent studying was spent devouring news reports and talking about them and what they meant for us. The draft had been in effect since the fall of 1940 and boys who had been in reserve programs, like Gabe Sellers, had already been called to active duty. We realized that all of us were going to end up in one service or another, and most of us sought to postpone that day as long as possible. My heart had me sidelined momentarily, but in 1942, after spending the summer working as a rod man on a survey team at Kelly Field, San Antonio, I reentered the ROTC program at Kansas State in something called the Enlisted Reserve Corps. We were assured by the Adjutant General, a man named Julio who shall ever be remembered for keeping his word, that if we joined the ERC and were called to active duty we would eventually be sent to Officer Candidate School. That was what happened, but I am ahead of myself.

The draft began to hit the student body almost immediately, and by the spring semester of 1942 almost all the juniors in the Delt house were headed for one service or another by the end of the term. In these unusual circumstances, I, as a sophomore, was elected president of the chapter. Between my new duties and war fever and going off to Bud's wedding to Betty Augur in Washington in May, I did very poorly academically and barely escaped flunking integral calculus, a subject that I never fully understood and never shall. The one thing I did well in was scientific German, which chemical engineers were required to take. I discovered to my surprise that I had a gift for foreign languages, which most of my classmates did not, and the German teacher, Fritz Moore, encouraged me to take all the languages I could, which wasn't much, given the demands of my schedule, but I did manage to get in some Spanish as well as taking German well beyond the requirements of the engineering faculty.

In the summer of 1942, after my career as a rod man (earning a fat $106 a month), I returned to Kansas several weeks before school started in order to arrange a rush trip through eastern Kansas with Bill Rector, another boy from Leavenworth. Driving a Model A convertible I had bought for $65 from Kenny Palmer (a mild boy who had disappeared for an entire weekend once and was ever after called "Wildcat"), we drove from town to town looking for likely pledge prospects to invite to rush week. This was a good deal of fun and we ended up pledging forty-two freshmen, most of whom had disappeared into the armed services by June of 1943. By then fraternity life at Kansas State had pretty much shut down. Very few men remained on campus—so few that the Betas had had to close their dining room and move in to eat with us. When I went into the army in June 1943, I closed the chapter and gave the house keys to the alumnus who was chairman of our house committee. The house was soon in use as a dormitory for men sent to Kansas State under the Army Specialized Training Program, the ASTP. "Take down your service flag, Mother, your son's in the ASTP," we sang.

Jeanne had two older brothers, Bob and Dick. Bob, who had taken ROTC at Kansas State and had a reserve commission, was called to active duty very early on and remained in the army until his death in 1965. Dick had volunteered for a navy program that sent him to pilot training. He was one of the dive bomber pilots in the June 1942 battle of Midway, for which he was awarded the Navy Cross. In November 1942, however, he was reported missing in action, and we learned later that he had been one of the men who went down with the aircraft carrier *Wasp* at Guadalcanal. He was bright and personable (I met him only once).

It is illustrative of the war's impact that of the four men of military age in the Parker and Jaccard families, all four were in the service, three saw combat, two were declared missing in action, and one was killed.

I had one year of so-called senior ROTC in the Coast Artillery branch before being summoned to active duty at Dodd Field, Texas, on June 7, 1943. We had warning six months in advance that this would happen and, deciding that I would have one good-time semester, I gave up the thought of becoming a chemist and for my last semester took German, Spanish, public speaking, and spherical trigonometry, or navigation math, which is very easy. It was great, and I learned what a life of Riley all those humanities students were routinely leading.

Dodd Field has long since disappeared, but it was once the airfield of Fort Sam Houston. Before going there (by train), I spent a glorious week in Evanston with Jeanne and arrived for duty exhausted and weighing 134 pounds. After a week at Dodd Field, I was sent along with 100 or so others, by slow train to Camp Wallace, Texas, just south of Houston.

Here my youth ends and life begins to get serious.

Part II

THE WAR YEARS

2

The War: Stateside, Europe, and The Bulge

Camp Wallace was an antiaircraft artillery–replacement training center located south of Houston on a piece of filled-in marsh. The water table was at about one foot, easily reachable by digging with a bayonet. The legend was that the arch wheeler-dealer, Jesse Jones, had sold the property to the government. It was a hot, humid, treeless plain and most of us suffered badly from prickly heat, for which no effective remedy was available until just before our departure.

I never quite understood the system that brought us all—a very disparate group of men from around the country—to this particular place. I presumably was there because I had coast artillery ROTC training, an air defense responsibility. Some other men from Kansas State were there, but we also had men from Wisconsin, Ohio, and New York as well as Texas, who had no previous military training of any sort. Soon after our arrival we were classified into our training roles. We had already been assigned to battalions, which were broken down into batteries and platoons, and into gun crews within the platoons. Because of my ROTC background, I was designated a chief of section, or gun crew commander, and had about twelve men under my command during training exercises. It is still remarkable to me that the man who gave me that designation in that desolate place was the movie star Melvin Douglas, who had recently been taken into the Army and served briefly at Camp Wallace before going back to Hollywood to make training films.

Our training battalion was equipped with the 40mm Bofors gun, an admirably rugged and simple weapon first produced by the Swedes and still in use by armies around the world. It was a rapid-fire weapon fed by large clips of ammunition and was reasonably effective against low-flying aircraft of the sort in use in World War II. I cannot imagine it being much good against a fast-moving jet. The gun came with its own gasoline-powered generator and a director. The latter was a mechanical device that was connected to the gun by electric cables and gave commands to electric motors that moved the gun barrel. The director operators followed the aircraft target through telescopic sights and fed data into the machine that in theory assured that the barrel would be pointing sufficiently ahead of the target so that the projectile would intersect its trajectory. It was in fact quite inexact, but it was better than firing blindly, which I later saw the Russians do. I assume that radar and computers point today's 40mm guns much more effectively.

Our training seemed intense. No concessions were made to the climate, and we were worked very hard. We were not allowed to leave the post for the first six weeks or so, and there was nothing to do on the post itself. We were too tired to be bothered all that much. Sundays, our only day off, was spent washing our fatigues and underwear, writing letters, and trying to get some sleep, which is not easy in a barracks full of often noisy people.

I find I can remember very few people from this experience. Our platoon sergeant was a ferocious West Virginia coal miner. I had three Mexicans on the crew, one of whom, an older man, had been a cook. He was a gentle person and my Spanish improved a good deal talking to him. Then there were the two German American hooligans from Sheboygan. One was an accomplished shirker, melting away when there was work to be done. One day when he was loafing behind one of the sheds, a grass-cutting crew made up of Afrika Korps prisoners came along. Among them was a Sheboygan boy who had been taken to Germany by his grandmother on the eve of the war and been drafted into the army as a *volkdeutscher*, a person of German descent living abroad who was subject to military service if he returned to the homeland.

At the end of our seventeen-week training cycle most of the men were sent off as replacements, many to Anzio, which was still hotly contested. Those of us who had been in ROTC, however, were put on hold for about two weeks and then put on a train for Grinnell, Iowa, where we found a number of men housed in the Grinnell dormitories and waiting for instructions. We spent a pleasant couple of weeks hanging out at Grinnell, and I took the train to Chicago to see Jeanne for a while. Those of us from Kansas State were sent back and housed in a couple of lecture rooms in the agricultural science building around midterm. We were allowed to enroll in classes, so I took German. It was a rather pleasant interlude. We did not have to work very hard but did a lot of male bonding. Jeanne came home for Christmas and we saw a good deal of each other. We decided then to marry as soon as I graduated from Officer Candidate School. The ROTC Adjutant General had promised us we would go to OCS, and so we did.

Those of us who had taken coast artillery ROTC expected to be sent to Camp Davis, North Carolina, for coast artillery–antiaircraft OCS, but Camp Davis was being closed down because there was a surfeit of anti-aircraft officers and coastal defense was largely idle. There was a pressing need for more infantry officers, however, as the invasion of Europe loomed, so we were sent to Fort Benning, Georgia, for infantry OCS instead. I don't think any of us wanted to be in the infantry, but there we were. We were shipped off to Benning in mid-January and joined a group of men who had had similar ROTC basic training experiences.

There were two hundred of us in Officer Candidate Class 333. We had the rank and pay of corporal and were allowed to stay in the town of Columbus on the weekends. I was pleasantly surprised to find some old family friends on the main post who let me stay with them on weekends. The training was rigorous physically if not mentally. The Infantry School had put much thought and experience into designing and applying a training philosophy that worked. Certainly it was the most effective I ever experienced. I found the physical part of it difficult but persevered and graduated with the rest of the class on June 20, 1944. We were very pleased to have just missed D-Day.

Wedding

As soon as my second lieutenant bars were pinned on my collar at the end of the graduation ceremony, I raced with three other men in a rented taxi to Birmingham, where we caught the Louisville and Nashville train for St. Louis. We barely made it. The train was so crowded that there were no seats, and we had to stand up most of the way. I finally got a seat in the men's room but was pretty tired by the time we pulled into St. Louis some eighteen hours later. There we had to run through the station to catch the Union Pacific train to Manhattan. My suitcase fell open as we were in the middle of the station, but Jack Kilkenny, who was to be an usher at our wedding, picked up the other half and we kept moving.

We finally arrived in Manhattan late on the afternoon of June 21. Mother had come up from San Antonio, and she and Jeanne met me at the station. I was dead tired and was allowed to go to bed. The next day we went to the county clerk's office for a wedding license, which my mother had to sign for me since I was under 21. Then we went to Fort Riley for a rehearsal and were married on the following day, June 23, 1944, in the post chapel.

Those were heroic days. After the reception, we caught a ride to Nashville with a couple of officers on their way to Florida, spending our wedding night on the road before arriving at the Hermitage Hotel late the next afternoon. I had seven days left before I was to report to the 106th Infantry Division at Camp Atterbury, Indiana, enough time for a whirlwind honeymoon. We spent four or five days at the Hermitage, where we had managed to reserve the bridal suite, and then took another terrible Louisville and Nashville train to Indianapolis. There we stayed with the Jaccards' neighbors, Walter and Mary Elizabeth. The second night, Walter got drunk and tried to call a friend on the Normandy beachhead. He did not succeed, but we were fascinated by his effort and persistence. For a while we thought he might make it against all odds.

The 106th

I reported to the 106th on July 1. Jeanne and I immediately faced the problem of domestic arrangements. Married officers were on their own, and housing near every military installation in the country was extremely difficult to find and expensive when you found it. We moved first to a fleabag hotel in Columbus, almost literally on the railroad tracks. Then, acting on inspiration, Jeanne volunteered with a small organization trying to help military people find housing and soon learned of a suitable place for us. A Mrs. Keller, an older widow who while not very cuddly was suitably matriarchal, was renting the top floor of her farmhouse and giving kitchen privileges to a suitable couple, and we made the grade. We moved in, and Jeanne got a job to which she could go by bus, but I had to hitchhike to the base. The highway took a good deal of traffic by the front gate, and people stopped for men in uniform in those days, but it made us nervous nevertheless. I had to get up very early to ensure a ride and came home rather late. It was no wonder Jeanne reported that I snored.

The 106th had been one of the better units in the United States but had been stripped of all but a cadre of officers and noncoms in order to provide replacements for the Normandy landings. Of the seven officers who formed the normal complement of the company, five were new. Only the company commander and his executive officer were of the original unit. Some ten of us from my OCS class were sent as part of the process of building it back up to strength.

Morale in the division was not very good. There were a good many jokes about our being readied for Military Police duty in Germany or some other noncombatant role. The jokes were based on the fact that we were receiving a wild assortment of replacements, many of whom were not fit either by training or description for combat. I was given the first platoon of the antitank company of the 422nd infantry. I had a competent platoon sergeant and three well-trained squad leaders, but of my platoon, less than a third had had infantry basic training. One private was a carpenter who had spent the war making training aids and had risen to the rank of sergeant in the process. He had suddenly been plucked out of his job and put into the infantry, and been demoted in the process. His morale was as one would have imagined, and he knew nothing about the infantry. Another private had been a pastry cook in some military establishment until a month earlier, when he, too, had been drafted into the 106th. This story could be repeated over and over again through the Division. Fortunately, our noncoms were good, and we received an infusion of new infantry replacement training center graduates just before we sailed in October. Overall, the Division was not very effective, however.

We were equipped with three 57-mm antitank guns per platoon. The British, who developed it, called it the Six Pounder, referring to the weight of the projectile. It was a cumbersome weapon, hard to move, which fired an armor-piercing round at high velocity and had an effective range of about 1000 yards. It was of little use against the German Tiger tank, but could disable lesser vehicles. The story of antitank warfare in World War II was one of weapons trying to keep up with advances in armor. The U.S. Army had started with a 37-mm gun, which was quite mobile but far too light for use against the German tanks of that epoch. They were followed by the 57-mm and at war's end by a 90-mm gun mounted on a tank. We also had the rocket launcher, or bazooka, a piece of stovepipe through which a rocket-propelled antitank grenade was launched. It was named for the crude trombone composed of two pieces of pipe that was played by a comedian from Arkansas named Bob Burns in the thirties. I suspect that he in turn took the name from the Greek bouzouki or zither. The bazooka was more effective than an armor-piercing round of the same caliber but had a very short range. All in all, Allied antitank equipment was not as effective as it might have been. The Germans, on the other hand, had wisely opted for an 88-mm gun of very high muzzle velocity, which was about what was needed. They far outgunned us.

Fortunately, we did not realize just how undergunned we were and went about learning how to manipulate and fire the 57mm with enthusiasm. We were not informed where we were going and rather hoped the war would be over by the time we got there, but in case it wasn't, we thought we would give a good account of ourselves. Nevertheless, there was considerable skepticism about our combat role, since whipping the carpenters and pastry chefs into shape in a few months was a hopeless task. Division Commander Alan W. Jones, on the other hand, was reportedly eager to get us into combat and hoped to advance his own career thereby. He later got his wish, if not quite the way he wanted.

Late in the summer, we were each given a ten-day pre-embarkation leave. Jeanne and I took our second honeymoon at the hotel on Lake Wawasee in northern Indiana. There was a special rate for servicemen and people were very kind. When we returned, we still did not know exactly where the division was going, but it was clear we were going overseas. A final inspection was announced to determine whether we were fit to go. The inspection team was led by General "Yoo-Hoo" Ben Lear, who had made headlines by furiously disciplining a unit whose men had been making wolf calls at a group of girls, earning him his infamous nickname. My recollection is that he had also been my father's riding instructor at Fort Leavenworth in World War I and was famous then for his acerbic remarks to students.

Because of Commander Jones's anxiousness to get his unit overseas and into action, there was a certain amount of fudging about our readiness. Two small incidents indicate the atmosphere. One of my colleagues was given the job of testing units from another regiment on night patrolling. The first unit he tested performed abysmally. He gave it a failing grade but was summoned and told he could not do so. Secondly, we had in my platoon a 50-caliber machine gun that had long since fired more than enough rounds to be labeled Class X and replaced. We tried in vain to get this done before leaving but were told there wasn't time, so we went into combat with it. The gun fired perhaps a dozen rounds on the morning of December 16 before it broke down irreparably.

Some things we did do well, however. We tend to envision troops marching or riding off to war without giving much thought to the question of logistics, of how food and equipment keep up and arrive at the destination when the troops do. You cannot simply roll a 57-mm gun into your troop compartment on the ship. I was to learn about this when I was made packing and crating officer. I was given a small crew of men and a supply of lumber and nails and told to pack the company's enormous amount of loose equipment for loading onto the same transport we would be taking across some as yet unknown ocean. The big guns were the easiest. They simply had to be coated with Cosmoline, a very thick grease, and their muzzles and breechblocks wrapped in waterproof sheeting. Large crates had to be made for a great deal of other equipment, however, which had to be delivered at specified times and places, carefully marked and ready for shipment. We worked and swore until late at night, and we got everything correctly shipped off. This was an accomplishment that still fills me with a certain awe and of which I am still proud.

Europe

We sailed from Boston on the *Aquitania* on October 12, 1944. The *Aquitania* was an old four-stacker, faster than a submarine and therefore allowed to travel without a convoy. Narrow in beam, she rolled a good deal and did not stop doing so until we pulled into the harbor at Greenock, Scotland, ten days later. The enlisted men were in large, dark troop compartments, mostly below deck, with three-decker berths. The air was fetid, and we had to drive them out on deck to get them over their seasickness. There was nothing for it but lots of fresh air and movement. The officers were lodged in one of the considerably lighter and airier public rooms and were served meals at tables with tablecloths and napkins and a certain effort, remarkable in wartime, at first-class food. The British were less egalitarian than the Americans in such matters.

At Greenock we were put on trains and headed south, destination unknown. We traveled all day, getting a sandwich meal of sorts from a British Navy, Army and Air Force Institute canteen for lunch and K rations for dinner. We arrived that crisp autumn evening with a bright moon at Fairford, in the Cotswold Hills, west of Oxford. It was a charming village, famous for the stained glass in its Norman church, and it looked indescribably quaint to me as we marched through it. In a large park on the far side there was a large manor house for officers and a group of semicylindrical, corrugated steel Quonset huts for the men. There was no heat and barely any hot water in the manor house. My room had a coal grate and we managed to scrounge a little coal for a weak fire from time to time, but we would have been desolated had it not been for the bar and officers' club of the nearby general hospital, staffed with nurses who could look forward to tending to us when we got wounded. I learned years later that the Americans made such a mess of the manor house it had to be pulled down.

The Anti-Tank Company was billeted with the First Battalion of the 422nd. The first day after our arrival, the officers were assembled by Lieutenant Colonel Kent, commander of the First Battalion, who briefed us on our position, told us we should be careful about contact with the local women because the British only washed from the neck up, and said our first priority was to arrange for everyone in turn to be given leave to London. The rest of the time we would be training and equipping ourselves for eventually moving on to the mainland, exact destination undisclosed. We had an active training program, including firing our big guns, took long marches, and were in pretty good shape. I rented a bicycle in the village to ride around the countryside on Sundays. There was little traffic, the villages had quaint names like Stow-on-the-Wold, and the weather was bracing. All in all, it was very pleasant. The war was so far advanced that there was a general expectation we would never see combat. I caused a minor sensation by betting Lt. Herbert Johnson of the mines platoon two hundred dollars we would. He never paid me, although he did survive the war.

I was lodged with Carl Shapley and Donald Prell from my OCS class. Shapley was a tall, rather fundamentalist engineering student from Kansas State. Our relations were cordial but not warm. Prell, who was Jewish, was from California and had been very unpopular among the men in our platoon at Benning because he was a know-it-all. Prell and I got along all right, but Shapley did not like him and was quite overbearing to him. The three of us were persuaded that the other officers of the company, particularly the commanding officer, Capt. Edward Vitz, did not like us and treated us coldly. We complained about this one night after a poker game and obviously took Vitz and the others by surprise. Vitz seemed a cold fish and never did warm to us. In fact, there was something of a chasm between the older officers who had been with the division from the beginning and those of us who had joined it recently. This was a leadership failure, perhaps reflecting the personality of the regimental commander, Colonel Descheneaux, who was not liked by his men. Enlisted men are perceptive in judging the personalities of their leaders, since it is they who must bear the most consequences of the leaders' quirks. In this case, they called him "Dashing Balls."

Our relatively comfortable life at Fairford came to an end after about six weeks, late in November or early in December, when we were taken by train to Southampton and put on little channel steamers and taken across to Le Havre. The boat was so small I had to stand up at the top of the companionway and literally kick my men through the door to their compartment, it was so narrow. We spent ten days in the mud and rain on a hillside near Le Havre and then moved off across France in motorized column.

We drove across France in the rain, destination unknown. No one told those of us at the bottom what we were doing or where we were going. I guess it was the same in all units, but we seemed particularly ill informed. We passed towns and people, but had no idea where we were going until nightfall, when we arrived in St. Vith, Belgium, having traveled a distance of 420 kilometers as the crow flies.

The Bulge

On December 10 we replaced the 2nd Infantry Division along a 27-mile line, just over the Belgian border into Germany. The 422nd had as part of its sector the Schnee Eifel Ridge, which runs roughly northeast to southwest to Bleialf. This had been a quiet sector, and we were apparently being moved into the line at this spot to give us a gradual introduction to combat while the Second Division moved out for an attack to the south.

The 422nd relieved the 9th Infantry, and I inherited a very cozy position in the village of Schlausenbach, where I had the task of defending the regimental headquarters against tank attack. I had two 57 mm guns in position on the northeastern side of the village covering the approaches from Kobscheid and Auw. Our field of fire was admirable and we had just enough defilade to protect us effectively against flat trajectory fire. The gun on the left was commanded by Sergeant Michael Valovcin of Bridgeport, Connecticut, and that on the right by Sergeant William Chappello of Chicago. A third gun, under Sergeant Arthur Wiegert of Overland, Missouri, was detached from the platoon and set up near one of the Siegfried Line bunkers in the Schnee Eifel, near the elevation known as Schwarzer Mann. My platoon sergeant John Harrell of Bainbridge, Georgia, and driver Albert Kath of Janesville, Wisconsin, set up housekeeping in a little farmhouse on the very edge of the village, about fifty yards in front of our guns. We soon worked out a comfortable routine and looked forward to Christmas.

The division was spread out far too wide for even a battle-tested unit of that size to hold against a serious attack, but none was expected. The Germans may have been waiting for us, however. An officer from the 82nd Airborne who was captured a month or so earlier and whom I met later told me he had been asked by the Germans when the 106th Division was coming, but he had never heard of us. The only action was our division artillery's nightly shelling of distant German positions.

On the morning of the 16th of December, I pulled the three o'clock guard shift in our little farmhouse. I started a new pot of coffee and began a letter to Jeanne. After a little time had passed, the customary early morning barrage started. The artillery positions were just about a mile behind me, and by nature of the terrain, the shells came fairly low over the house. I could hear the very encouraging sound of outgoing mail and was happily thinking about the poor Germans who were getting killed with precision and finesse. Suddenly I realized that the shells passing overhead were coming in, not going out. The sound is distinctively different. I expected the firing to die down, believing it to be merely interdictory, but instead it increased in intensity, and soon shells were falling all over my little bailiwick. I took a look outside and saw the town of Kopfscheid, a mile to my left, a mass of flames and tracers, apparently a strong patrol action. I knew that there was a troop of the 14th Cavalry there and, very fond of the cavalry, figured that they would soon dispense with the nuisance.

The shelling ceased about daybreak and we went out to reconnoiter. It has been described as a heavy bombardment, but it did no real damage to the buildings of Schlausenbach and there were no casualties among the troops making up regimental headquarters. I was amazed to find that three shells, all of them duds, had landed within twenty yards of one position. The men were down in their holes, looking a little green around the gills. At the company CP (Command Post) we discussed the matter and decided it was excellent battle indoctrination. We found that a general attack had broken out along the entire front and that there were Germans running around all over the place, which was disturbing, to say the least. Later in the morning, we found that we were cut off from the Division. The 14th had pulled out without informing our regiment, exposing our left flank. Mine was the last unit on that flank because of the peculiar configuration of the line of defense. Soon we could see that the Germans were moving through the gap at Auw toward our rear. We were not being fired on, however, and had no idea of the scale of the attack being mounted. I got two of our men to bring up the platoon's 50-caliber machine gun and had them position it off to one side of our CP from which there was a clear view of Auw. It was extreme range, but they could still hit with fatal effect. Our Class X gun fired about twelve rounds and quit, never to fire again. That was just one of the details in a thoroughly mismanaged supply operation that contributed to our defeat.

Later in the day, when tanks began moving through the Auw gap I was ordered to fire on them, even though the effect was likely to be minimal. I stood beside the left gun, directing fire. Soon after we opened fire the Germans responded, and I could hear the sharp crack of their shells as they whizzed by; but our gun had been well sited in the defilade provided by a rise in the ground in front of us, so we presented a very small target. My gunners couldn't hit a thing, but neither could the Germans. We discovered after the battle, during which we used up a third of the gun's limited store of ammunition, that our gunner's vision was so poor that he could not see the target. Why we had not realized that before I will never know, but suspect it was because we never shot at moving targets during practice.

Subsequent events dissolve and reform in a haze of weariness that still overtakes me when I try to recall them. Only assorted details remain. One of our problems was a total lack of bazooka ammunition, another aspect of our supply fiasco. Our artillery was no more. Also, we had very little food or water.

On the evening of the 16th a displaced Tank Destroyer platoon appeared, equipped with halftracks mounting 75mm guns. It was most encouraging, because I was beginning to think that if any tanks ever attacked our positions, we wouldn't have much luck. I can still see the face of the platoon commander, name unknown: serious brown eyes in a rather distraught face. We invited him to stay with us and defend regimental headquarters, but after hesitating he decided he had better try to find the rest of his unit, wherever it was. We could not help him. Excited by the arrival of the

Tank Destroyers and their gift of bazooka ammunition, I went to regimental headquarters to report this encouraging development. I was ushered in to see Colonel Descheneaux, who was, on reflection, probably suffering from depression. He smiled faintly at my agitation, and I was ushered out. He had good reason to be depressed: communications were chaotic, there was no air support, our supply lines were cut, and we were caught in a massive pincer movement from which we had no realistic hope of escaping. We were all going to be either dead or POWs. People at my level did not realize this, however, and were quite prepared to fight. We did not know that there was a crisis of leadership.

The next morning I took two men out and posted them with a bazooka at a large foxhole from which they could command one of the roads leading into town. The two men were Lyman Peterson and Roy S. Sorenson. Peterson was from Utah, a taciturn Mormon who never smiled but was nevertheless a willing worker. Sorenson was also very quiet and retiring but cooperative and willing. Neither had basic infantry training. They were part of the flotsam that had been assigned to the division in the spring of 1944 and of whom we were supposed to make combat soldiers. I told them they were to fire at any German tank that came down the road. They nodded understanding, and I left them. I came back in the afternoon to see how they were doing and decided I should have them rehearse their roles. I asked who was going to load and who was going to fire. It transpired that they had never discussed that, and neither one knew how to do either. It also transpired that no German tank came down that road.

On the afternoon of the 17th a German horse-drawn artillery battalion pulled up and assembled in formation in a meadow about a thousand yards from us. It was a beautiful parade ground performance and they evidently were unaware of our presence. The commander of Cannon Company, Joel T. Broyhill, was called up to our little ridge and directed fire from his howitzers onto the Germans. It was a very professional job and the carnage among the men and horses was terrible. It was the only effective action taken by the 422nd that I was aware of. It also used up most of Cannon Company's ammunition. I can recall only one casualty at Schlausenbach, a lieutenant from Cannon Company who had been hit by a sniper and was in great pain. He was out in the middle of a field and no one could get to him because of the sniper. His face and the image of him out there will always be with me. A sniper almost got me later, the round whizzing past my head and smacking into a clay bank behind me. I remember watching a V-1 or "buzz bomb" pass over my head near the gun late one afternoon. V-1s were not rockets, but flying bombs that made a "put-put" sound as they flew by at subsonic speeds. It was hard to connect this rather strange looking apparatus with the dreadful damage it did on landing.

Meanwhile, the Germans made no move against our pocket. They were pushing on for a big breakthrough and would take care of us later. In our ignorance, my men and I were prepared to remain where we were and to fight off any eventual attackers. We were not worried a good deal as we had heard the Ninth Armored was to make a breakthrough, that ammunition and supplies would be dropped to us, and that Patton was on his way. Blissful ignorance.

On the morning of the 18th we were told that the rifle battalions were going to fight their way out of the trap, and we were going to follow them. I had an ant's eye view of the ensuing confusion, and my reconstruction of events is not to be taken as authoritative. The rifle battalions were most effectively stopped when they walked into a terrific nest of 88s, MG 42s, mortars, tanks, and everything else imaginable. We began to consider the situation desperate.

After dark we bivouacked in a field beside the road. Too tired to dig foxholes, we simply lay down and slept. The 19th was more of the same: very little movement and no information about anything. We had gone twenty-four hours without a regular meal and were terribly cold. The sun had not been out for days; the ground was covered with snow. We had been sent into the line with a third as much ammunition as would be required if any actual fighting was to be done. We briefly nourished the belief that the Air Corps would save the day by dropping some supplies, but it was grounded because of the weather.

At about midafternoon on the 19th, the motor elements with which my platoon and I were riding attempted to make a run for it and find some gap in the German lines. We moved through the village of Bleialf and up a ridge on the other side, only to run into a group of tanks that stopped us. Captain Vitz, who was ahead of us, turned around and came speeding back in the direction from which we had come, waving to me to follow. Vitz's Jeep stopped almost immediately. There was a waist-high wire across the road. Vitz got out and very gingerly approached the wire and cut it. Nothing happened and they set off up the road again. They had gone only a few yards when there was a tremendous explosion, and the jeep flew into the air, bodies hurtling in several directions, and stray bits of equipment littering the landscape. The wire had been put up as a warning that the road was mined. That stopped the whole column. They were hopelessly snarled up by that time, and we knew we didn't have time to clear any minefield. I ran up to the jeep, and we found everyone alive; the first sergeant and our radio operator were pretty badly hurt, but everyone else was doing fairly well. I can recall assuring one of them that his genitalia were intact. We began administering first aid and waited for developments.

At about this point Capt. Foster, the commander of Headquarters Company, appeared and said the column had been surrendered to the Germans. There was no way out. He was bordering on tears. We were going to run for the woods when night came, and that was not far off. However, we thought about the fact that we could see Germans all over the place and that we didn't have any idea where our lines were. We had no rations, most of us had sore feet, and the forest, a dark mass of geometrically planted pine trees, looked most inhospitable. We changed our minds, which was probably just as well. I opened the bottle of Harwood's Canadian whiskey I had been saving for Christmas. We all had a drink or two and felt much better. I decided that the Germans would probably give us some hot soup. That was a vision never to materialize fully. I have often regretted my decision to surrender as unheroic; but reading what happened to those who did hide out in the woods, I realize that my chances of surviving hiding out were very slim indeed.

About nightfall we loaded the wounded onto some trucks and took them to a German field hospital, a churchyard in the center of the village. Most of them were delirious, and I felt bad about leaving them, especially two of the boys from my platoon who had been shot in the leg. There was no soup or anything else. That night I slept on the ground in an enclosure with about five hundred prisoners and succeeded in doing a bang-up job of freezing my feet.

The next day was the 20th, and we were a sad-looking sight as we marched out on the road in columns of fives and started toward Germany, through Prum to Gerolstein. That day we marched for 32 miles. During the first hour we passed some of our artillery positions, surrounded by the frozen corpses of the gunners, but we saw few signs of battle after that. For most of the day I was marching with men from my platoon, and we joked that I would be the first officer across the Rhine with his platoon intact. We got no food or water but thought the sugar beets we occasionally found on the road most delicious. Passing one village, someone literally threw us a few pieces of bread from a window. Water we drank from the ditches. And I thanked God many a time that the United States Army gives you so many shots. Otherwise we all would have contracted something.

We reached the town of Gerolstein at 2 a.m. on the 21st, tired, hungry, and frozen. Here I ran into Johnson, Prell, and Shapley from my company, my entire platoon less the wounded, and a number of other officers from the regiment. Prell had attempted to escape but he ran full tilt into a German tent and was recaptured. We slept on the ground for a few hours, sharing my blanket. I slept soundly. In the morning I complained about my feet, which were very painful, and several people suggested I go to the aid station said to be in a large building on the edge of the field. I took about three steps when a Hauptmann came up to me, grabbed me and pushed me in another column. I found myself alongside Lt. Howard Alexander, our exec, and six other officers of the regiment just as the Germans passed out a handful of cheese and crackers to each of us. I asked what was going on and they said, "We're going to the train."

The guards marched us off; we loaded on 40-&-8 boxcars full of manure and pulled out for parts unknown. This was one of the last trains to leave Gerolstein, and if I hadn't gone to get my feet fixed, I never would have made it. Lady Luck had smiled again. The cars were called 40 & 8 because they were classified by the French military in World War I as large enough to accommodate forty men or eight horses My recollection is that there were fifty-six of us in our car. There was not room for everyone to lie down at once and we had to take turns. I ended up sitting next to two privates from the 28th division, who had apparently been south of us and to whom I had given cigarettes on the platform. There was a small opening up above our heads from which we could see the countryside as the train moved at a very leisurely pace to some unknown destination.

Answering the call of nature was a problem. We were given nothing to eat or drink, so the quantities involved were minimal, but no provisions were made for them. We could urinate through a crack in the door, although getting there involved clambering over protesting bodies, but there was no way one could get his buttocks through that crack. Someone sacrificed his blanket, and we defecated in that. After a day or two we came to Limburg, site of a large transient camp. We were allowed out of the cars once and emptied the blanket of its contents.

On the evening of the 23rd, the RAF came over to bomb the industrial and rail facilities at Limburg, and they succeeded in giving us a very bad night. The RAF's report of the raid called it a success, but in fact they missed the rail yard, thank God, or there would have been many casualties. One bomb fell on a barracks full of American officers at the camp and killed some sixty-seven officers. Jack Kilkenny, who was an usher at my wedding, was among these. We had about forty casualties on the train. Several of the cars broke open and the men rushed out into an open field running for an air raid shelter; a bomb hit in the field and caused a number of deaths and a larger number of wounded. I found a hole near the train and dived into it, finding myself on top of an American and a German soldier, both terrified. Nationality didn't seem to make much difference.

The raid was over in a few minutes. I pulled myself up out of the hole and went to see what happened. I discovered that some men from my platoon, from whom I had become separated at Gerolstein, had been in one of the other cars. One of them, Sergeant Wiegert, who was the commander of the third gun that had been up on the ridge at Schlausenbach, had been wounded. I went to where he lay, and all I could think of was Weigert's wife and child. He had been the oldest of my three squad leaders, very competent and rather sober. He was taken off, presumably to the POW hospital on the hill, where he died, we later learned.

There was a certain pandemonium in the air after the raid. I found myself wandering up and down the train, briefly considering the possibility of escaping but discarding that as unrealistic, particularly since I was overwhelmingly sleepy. I was drawn back to my little corner in the boxcar, as the others were to theirs. When I got there I promptly went to sleep. Later I realized that sleep was my reaction to shock or stress, and still is.

Christmas Eve came, and we sang "White Christmas" and "I'll be Home for Christmas" and similar sentimental songs with little belief that we would ever see home again. I can remember thinking ruefully of how Dutch Kaiser, a newly made general who had been a friend and colleague of my father, had asked my mother if I would like to be his aide and she had said no. How little she knew me.

Our overwhelming consideration was hunger; we hadn't had a meal for five days. The next day the Germans distributed Red Cross parcels to us, one for every five men. These parcels, from the United States, Britain, Australia, and New Zealand, were meant to supplement the German POW rations at the rate of one parcel per man per week. Typically, they contained a can of oatmeal, a can of powdered milk, a chocolate bar, some canned meat, vitamins, cigarettes, and instant coffee and/or cocoa. The total parcel was about the size of two shoeboxes. The best thing in it was the powdered milk, and Klim was the favorite brand. The oatmeal was also much appreciated, but hard to cook in a boxcar with no stove. Somehow I got a spoonful or two of oatmeal out of that package. Someone had managed to cook it, perhaps with a heat tab, a little cube of solid alcohol. I had no eating utensil, but I managed to make a very crude wooden spoon somehow. It served me through the boxcar journey, not that it had much food to deal with.

On or about the 27th the train moved out. We crept through Germany, stopping frequently and always moving slowly.

I might add at this point that it is extremely uncomfortable not to be able to lie down for nine days. Once during this leg of the journey I got about half a cup of hot yellow soup in my helmet liner, handed out by some charitable organization in the Stuttgart Bahnhof. I was almost sick from eating so much. That and the cheese at Gerolstein plus the one-fifth of a Red Cross parcel was my total nourishment for ten days.

But the greatest hardship of the journey was not physical but mental. It was like staring at a blank wall for a short eternity; when you're starving and cold, your mind doesn't function properly and you can't keep your mind on anything but food. My thoughts were of peanut butter and peach jam on bread. I could always see a plate of scrambled eggs and pancakes floating before my eyes, and it eclipsed all other mental activities. People told stories about their own favorite foods, of which the best was a description of a "poor-boy" sandwich from New Orleans. Such constant preoccupation with physical hardships reduces you to a kind of agonizing lethargy. It is perhaps remarkable that in the period of ten days that we spent in that boxcar, no leader of the group emerged, although there were four or five officers present. No one assumed charge. But there was no dissension or quarreling among the men, although I once suggested to someone that he had eaten something of mine. He denied it indignantly, but I am convinced to this day that he did. On New Year's Eve at about dusk, thirteen days after surrendering, we arrived at Stalag IVB at Muhlberg, south of Berlin.

3

Stalag IV B and Oflag 64

From the train we were marched to a large brick building behind an impressive wire fence to be deloused. After a superficial search, we were told to take off our clothes and herded into a large shower room. The water was hot but there was no soap. After a shower that was too short we passed in front of a man who sat behind a large bucket of brown disinfectant. He swabbed each of us in the groin and armpits with a rag dipped in the disinfectant and then gave each of us a typhus shot. Our clothes meanwhile were being gassed and we eventually met up with them. By that time we should have been dry but there were no towels, the building was not heated and some of us were still dripping wet when we were ushered outside into the frigid night air. I wondered why none of us got pneumonia from this experience.

Stalag is short for *Stamm Lager*, or "Base Camp." I suppose this refers to the fact that enlisted men, but not officers, were sent out on work parties, called *kommandos*, and periodically returned to the main camp. The author Kurt Vonnegut was evidently sent from IV B on a *kommando* to Dresden. He describes this experience in *Slaughterhouse Five*.

IV B had a mixture of French, Russian, and British prisoners. We were housed with the British, who were RAF noncommissioned officers who had been in the bag for a number of years. One man had been captured on the first day of the war in 1939. They had had plenty of time to organize and to learn how to make the best of their situation and had adjusted to survival stratagems that kept them whole. They had learned, for instance, how to make a small stove out of two tin cans of different sizes in which one burned bits of cardboard and paper when the Germans were not around (the Germans confiscated such stoves on discovery). Exploiting the Venturi effect, this so-called "smokeless heater" produced enough heat to make a pot of tea.

The British were very kind to us—taking us in and giving us their beds and offering us our first cup of "ersatz" or substitute coffee—a roasted barley confection reminiscent of Postum. They fed us a special New Year's Eve supper that night and entertained us with a theatrical skit involving a female impersonator who was unbelievably good. They also gave us valuable advice on how to conduct ourselves and whom to trust and whom not. The message, repeated a number of times for emphasis, was "Don't go to Jerry. He won't give you fuck-all." This was the first time I heard that expression, but not the last.

Here as at most of the German POW camps there was a cigarette economy. There were not many goods for sale, but whatever there was, the cigarette was the unit of currency. People would sell, for instance, items in their Red Cross parcels, delivery of which was often quite irregular. One man, we were told, had starved to death because he sold all his food for cigarettes.

The daily rations provided by the Germans were barbarously insufficient. A couple of slices of sour black bread that seemed to have a large component of sawdust, a thin soup, often rutabaga or turnip boiled with a little salt, an occasional special ration of sauerkraut, a very rare bit of meat or fish, for a daily average of 600 calories, whereas 900 were needed to keep a man alive in a heated room. Later we heard from prisoners at another camp that their contribution to the war effort was to urinate in the vats at the sauerkraut factory where they were sent on *kommando*.

The officers spent only two or three nights with the British and were then moved to another barracks where we were surprised to find the surgical team of the 101st Airborne and a few other officers who were not involved with the 106th or 28th divisions. We each received part of a Red Cross parcel and settled down to a new life as prisoners.

On the sixth of January, the officers were told to prepare to move out the next day for an officers' camp, by boxcar. All immediately perishable foods were eaten, and everyone made his own pitiful preparation for the ride. I toasted all my bread. There was nothing more I could do. An extra bread, sugar, and jam ration—a standard three-day supply—was issued and the group told to fall out the following morning at one o'clock.

We were deloused that afternoon—repeat of the previous performance. Upon falling out as scheduled, we were led to another search. This time it was more thorough. Pockets were searched, and everyone had to undress. My compass was found almost immediately. The possession of such an item was strictly *verboten,* and its appearance caused a little stir among the guards. But nothing was said to me about it. After further diligent searching I was cleared. My watch, which had been returned together with my wallet, was again in my trouser fly and was not found. Poor Captain Hollister was not so fortunate with his sleeping bag. The Germans were confiscating all blankets. He had rehearsed a little speech in atrocious German that was to inform the Germans that the bag was his and not United States government property and as such was not liable to confiscation under the Geneva Convention. The only effect of his speech was to provoke a few knowing grins from the guards, and he was summarily deprived of his prize possession. There followed an impassioned plea in the name of all decency and protestations of acute respiratory malfunction, to no avail.

Following the search we marched to Muhlberg, past the still dark cottages of German peasants and into the center of the silent town. There we squatted in the snow beside the Bahnhof and quietly began to freeze to death.

I asked a guard when the train would come.

"I don't know."

"It's cold here."

"Cold! You should be in Russia. Snow up to your neck! And a wind! My God how cold it is there."

"Where are we going?"

"To Poland."

"Poland?"

"Yes, to Oflag 64."

"How many days will it take?"

"Three or four."

"Is it a good camp?"

"They're all good."

Armed with this information, I went back to my seat in the snow and waited. By the time the train came, everyone was so stiff with cold we could hardly climb into the cars. Twenty-five went in each car, the middle of which was filled with a barbed wire barrier. Three guards moved into the other side, shifted the barrier so that no prisoner could get to the door, and then started a fire in the stove. I had fortunately grabbed a seat next to the wire and so was able to almost warm my hands and feet by the fire.

The journey proved to be less unpleasant than the previous one. The guards naturally kept a good fire going night and day and the prisoners profited thereby. Also the guards could apparently see the writing on the wall because they were almost kind. At most big stations they would go to their equivalent of the USO and return with hot ersatz or soup, some of which they would give to the prisoners. And at night they would allow some of the prisoners to climb over the wire and sleep on their side where there was more room.

Unfortunately, diarrhea reared its ugly head the first day, and its imminence waxed with every click of the wheels. The coming of this ailment in epidemic proportions had been expected for some time, and it did not fail to justify expectations. I was not a victim yet, but a number of the officers in the car were. As always in such cases, their affliction was characterized by a great urgency.

My job, as unofficial interpreter, was to intercede for the sufferers at every stop, providing someone was in need, which was always the case. The procedure was not easy. I would call, "*Posten, Posten, sin Mann scheissen!*" indicating to the guards that someone desired egress. If the guards gave their consent, the victim would be pushed up and over the barrier and let out of the car under the watchful eye of the guard.

This system worked fairly well until one fateful afternoon when the train stopped in Frankfurt an der Oder. It was fairly late in the day, but still light, and a beautiful snow was falling. The flakes looked as big as quarters—a regular Grimm's fairy tale snow. As the train pulled to a stop, one of the guards opened the door and looked out. The car was directly in front of the passenger loading platform, which was fairly crowded with travelers of both sexes, all of them looking at the train with idle curiosity.

As was to be expected, Francis Hesse, a boy from Wichita who was my "mucker" or buddy, called out, "Parker, tell him *ein Mann scheissen*. It's a matter of life or death!"

Realizing the difficulty of the situation, I spoke: *"Posten! Wir haben ein Mann krank. Sehr krank! Er muss scheissen."*

"Das geht nicht! Dieser is Deutchland! Und dieser ist der Bahnhof! Und dort heraus es gibt die Leute! Männer und Frauen! Dieser is keine Franzosischer Bahnhof."

"Aber, dieser Mann hat diarrhoe und er ist sehr krank. Er muss. Du kannst nicht nein sagen."

Despite the limping eloquence of my German, the guards were adamant. This was Germany and there would be no vulgarity in their railroad stations. Meanwhile, poor Hesse was grinding his teeth in agony.

It soon began to grow dark and the guards promised that when the cover of night was fairly complete, Hesse would be let out. But, just as the decision was handed down that it was dark enough, the train pulled out.

Hesse was beside himself with despair. The guards could see the critical nature of the matter and, after a hurried staff meeting, told the prisoners to hoist Hesse over the wire. When he had reached the other side they opened the door a couple of feet. Then, with a guard holding each wrist and his feet braced against the floor of the car, Hesse backed out into the snowy night and relieved himself as the train sped through the yards of Frankfurt. (We passed through Frankfurt on the way home from Zarnowiec in 1998 and I thought of Hesse again. I wished I had an address for him to let him know how immortal his experience was.)

The trip was without further incident. On January 10th, the train arrived at Szubin, Poland, north of Poznan. We scrambled from the cars, fell into column and marched through the town, which was small. I was impressed by the fact that we occasionally saw a smiling face, and some of the people looked almost friendly.

Still clutching the remnants of our Red Cross boxes, we were led into a low brick building.

Oflag 64

We entered a large, pleasantly warm room and faced a wide counter, behind which stood four Germans. An American Medical Corps captain sauntered up and passed out cigarettes by the pack. The room was immediately humming with expressions of wonder and delight and did not quiet down for some time.

Finally four queues formed up in front of the counter. Each man was searched, then inspected by the medical captain to ascertain if he had any diseases other than diarrhea. Next came a desk where we could file a free radiogram to the effect that we were well and happy and enjoying the benefits of a superior culture at Oflag (Offizier Lager) 64. After the radiograms, we went to the rear of the room and waited.

The searchers all spoke English. The one who searched me confiscated the papers from my wallet and seemed satisfied, except that he pounced on three dilapidated books picked up at IV B – *Northanger Abbey*, *Valley of the Sun*, and a Perry Mason thriller.

"Where did you get this?" Holding up *Northanger Abbey*.

"At Stalag IV B. It's been censored."

"It looks all right. How about this one?" pointing to *Valley of the Sun*.

"Same place. I use it for toilet paper."

"Hah! Very sensible. And this other—also toilet paper?"

"Yes."

"Okay."

I was then relieved of my field coat, which had nonmilitary buttons and could therefore be mistaken for a civilian coat. Its quick return with different buttons was promised.

The doctor found nothing seriously wrong with me, and after filing a radiogram, I went to chain smoke a couple of cigarettes, having smoked my last one the day before. It seemed there was no tobacco shortage here.

When the whole group had finished, we were taken outside, across a wide brick road, and into the camp proper, which was surrounded by a rather formidable barbed wire fence.

We were deloused in the basement of camp headquarters. The process was essentially the same as that at IV B except that there were no injections or disinfectant mops, and our clothes were baked, not gassed.

In the drying room we were approached by an American lieu-tenant who took our names and asked who wanted assignment to what barracks, explaining on the side the virtue of this or that building—one had wooden floors, another was close to the mess hall. It broke down into a matter of choosing which of your imme-diate companions you wished to accompany. Hesse and I decided to join forces and picked a building at random, Barracks 6A, with concrete floors.

After regaining our clothes we were taken to meet the senior American officer. I do not know which of us was the more sur-prised when I walked into the room to find that he was Pop Goode, Betsy Goode's father, from across the street at Ft. Leavenworth. (He later had me in for tea at his quarters in the administration building and gave me an extra wool shirt and a suit of long underwear.) The next-ranking officer was Col. Frederick Drury, an artillery officer whose son Fred was one of my playmates at Fort Bliss. The old army was a small family. Col. Goode gave us some fatherly advice and explained some of the rules and procedures of the camp.

We were then directed to our new home. The building was al-most identical to the compound at IV B, but it had been divided into eight-man cubicles through the expedient of using wooden lockers for walls, the lockers being a donation from the YMCA. We were quite pleased upon entering to receive two new G.I. blankets, a cup, knife, fork, spoon, razor, and a towel apiece. We were almost out of the woods—or so it seemed.

It was a particularly joyous occasion for Hesse, because an-other Wichita boy, Jim Ralston, greeted him as a long-lost brother. The two had gone through school together and had been intimate friends. It was entirely a matter of coincidence that the two had picked this barracks, and everyone marveled at the intricacies of fate.

We were both placed in Ralston's cubicle, and the next hour was spent in inquiries as to who had been where when what happened. All of the incoming men were given Christmas parcels and told they would receive a regular parcel the next week. The Christmas parcel contained goodies—plum pudding, dates, nuts, candies, and a few staples, not to mention a Currier and Ives print and a pocket game set. The meat cans were missing, however. These were withdrawn from all parcels and pooled, the meat being served with potatoes in the mess hall.

Oflag 64 was solely for American ground force officers, being filled to capacity at that time with about fifteen hundred. The routine was but slightly different from that of IV B. The most obvious difference was the tobacco supply. The Oflag had been established for two years, and enough prisoners had established contact with home to provide a fairly regular flow of packages. For some strange reason, Americans were allowed to receive a larger amount of tobacco than any other prisoners, so much larger as a matter of fact that the camp had now a large excess of cigarettes, pipe tobacco, and cigars. This excess was pooled and a record kept of every individual's stock. He could draw from his stock once a week.

As a natural result, there was no tobacco economy at the Oflag. Virtually the only trading was in food, which you could trade for other food. Also, the Germans occasionally paid you a small sum in Lager marks in accordance with the Geneva Convention. With these you could buy ashtrays and an inefficient sort of dentifrice at the camp store.

There was a brisk trade in food. Most traders specialized in certain items. One would try to collect cheese, another would buy your jam, and a third would have a locker full of bread. This bartering seemed more for the sake of satisfying the American urge for commerce rather than for any profit. The second biggest difference between the Oflag and IV B was the issuance of Red Cross parcels— one per man per week, this being a period of comparatively ample supplies, although the Oflag had also passed through the starvation period the preceding fall. The camp also had a fair library and a theater. I was quite happy about the whole thing. But my joy was marred by several events.

First, after eating the potatoes and corned beef provided at the first evening meal, I abruptly realized I had diarrhea—which was making up for lost time.

Secondly, I found that with all my clothes on, including two heavy sweaters and a field jacket with a pile lining, I weighed one hundred and thirty-four pounds. I was not corpulent. Despite this loss in weight I found that my trousers, which had previously been two inches too large around the waist, would no longer even start to button. Investigation revealed a tremendously bloated stomach.

Thirdly, my feet reacted most unfavorably to the concrete floors. If I was on my feet for more than fifteen minutes at a time they began to ache violently. I could not even keep them warm with two pairs of wool socks. On the second day, I went to the camp dispensary for some diarrhea medicine (totally ineffective). Later I was issued a suit of wool underwear, a wool shirt, and a wool knit cap, following which I drew a copy of *The Decline and Fall of the Roman Empire* from the library, put my new clothes on in addition to those I had originally, and climbed into bed to sweat the winter out—a procedure rendered difficult by the necessity for a constant state of alertness and a ready eye on the latrine.

This state of nervous tension had, by the fourth day, reduced me to a nervous hulk. I no longer cared about anything and was eating only a little bread and cheese. I was unable to concentrate on my book and, for the most part, stared at the ceiling pointlessly. Hesse had temporarily improved and was in a little more capable condition, which further exasperated me.

This gloomy picture was further darkened by Ralston's friendly but firm suggestion that I smelled bad and that everyone would appreciate it if I would wash all my clothes and my body. This was easier said than done. But the bother of washing did not trouble me; it was the implication that perhaps I was not as fastidious as I should have been.

The washing took the better part of a day. Hot water was almost unheard of, and it was only through much humiliating begging that I managed to secure a small bucket of lukewarm water. This served for washing my body and for soaking my old clothes. My new underwear and shirt were considered clean enough. It was necessary, however, to borrow another pair of pants. I was surprised to find that although they were seven inches larger in the waist they fit my new waistline perfectly.

I gained a fair conception of my complete debilitation when I found that I was miserably cold in only one suit of clothes; I needed two. My only solution was to crawl back into bed and await the interminable process of drying—which took two days. Even then I would have been cold if my coat hadn't been returned that day, with the same buttons, but with a small red triangle over the left breast.

By the time I was able to wear my quasi-laundered garments, my diarrhea had regulated itself to a predictable schedule and life began to improve. But here again there was no rest for the weary. The camp heard, via forbidden channels, that the Russians had jumped off across the Vistula and were now traveling at twenty-five or more miles a day toward Germany. This was heartening news in one respect—the war might end before too long—but also it meant that the Oflag would probably be evacuated. This would entail an uncomfortable journey by whatever the means, especially since the snow lay deep on the ground.

Corroboration of the rumors of Russian progress was given by an endless refugee column that appeared overnight, traveling by cart, bicycle, sled, and foot back to the Vaterland. Even the prisoners could feel sorry for these people, most of whom would die from exposure or Russian violence.

On the night of January 19th the prisoners were alerted to prepare for a long march. An extra parcel was given to each man, and the tobacco stores were distributed. Saturday, the 20th, was spent in feverish preparation. Everyone had accumulated an unbelievable pile of possessions. I was faced with the problem of discarding my cooking pans and consolidating my belongings. I made all of my free sugar, jam, powdered milk, and other odds and ends into an extremely rich, heavy pudding—to be carried as an iron ration. But I couldn't stand the suspense and had to eat it as soon as cooked. It was soggy but good.

The miscellaneous collection of officers who fell out on the morning of the 21st, prepared to march, would have put Cocksey's Army to shame. Here, one had sewn pockets from discarded trousers to the knees of those he was wearing. Another had made a small sled of bed slats, and his trifles were piled on it. Another carried an armload of books and little else. The mixture of uniforms was astounding—Polish, Danish, and Italian overcoats, American trench coats, field jackets, combat jackets, and overcoats; English battledress and boots; American combat boots, jump boots, shoes, and leggings, fatigues, O.D.s, greens, pinks, blouses, garrison caps, service caps, helmets, wool knit caps, berets, and knitted hoods. No two approached more than a rough similarity. Surely such a ragtag, bobtailed expeditionary force had never been seen assembled in one place before.

It was not without trepidation that this mob filed out upon the road to Germany. The weight of extra food, excess clothing, and miscellaneous claptrap made movement on the icy path strenuous. There was also the problem of traffic. The road was already clogged with refugees, and it was a communication line for the Wehrmacht. This meant a constant dodging back and forth and subjected everyone to the killing torture of the accordion—the alternate running and shuffling gait characteristic of all long, disorganized columns.

Under the influence of these factors, by the end of three hours marching, the column of fifteen hundred (1400 according to Fred Drury in a letter to the embassy in Moscow) men marching five abreast attained a length of two miles. At the end of the first hour men were already dropping their belongings by the way. One man stood in the middle of the road with a large tray of cigars, offering them to all comers. He had few takers.

Hesse and I were doubly encumbered. The unwonted exercise and excitement had reactivated our diarrhea, and we were constantly dashing into the fields to relieve ourselves, a feat demanding great dexterity when you are wearing two suits of long undergarments, two pairs of trousers, and numerous pieces of outer clothing and carrying blankets and food. As a result of these forays, we soon found themselves at the very end of the column and the objects of much displeasure on the part of the guards.

I almost collapsed from panic when, after one such excursion, I traveled a quarter of a mile down the road only to realize that I had left my priceless toilet paper in the field. My frantic gesticulations and broken German so amused the guards that they allowed me to retrieve my treasure. I did a thing which I thought impossible—I ran—my impedimenta flapping about me.

It was after returning from this chase and resuming my halting pace that I appreciated the true meaning of the term "rat race." Here were fifteen hundred prisoners and many more refugees scurrying about like so many rodents, each trying to retain the small fragment of life and pleasure that was his and each concentrating on surviving that particular minute—the next was a day to come.

The more enterprising prisoners were by now climbing on some of the refugee wagons—over the feeble protests of the guards and the baleful glances of the civilians. The column began to take on an international flavor—but there was no visible fraternization.

Towards noon we filed through the town of Exin (Znin), a county seat, to be greeted by the noncommittal stares of the villagers. One could almost sense a hidden sympathy for the prisoners, but these people had seen the tides of war before, and no one ventured to betray his feelings if he had any. The children were less inhibited. Some of the smaller boys even had the effrontery to run up and down the column begging for cigarettes, with little luck.

There was a Luftwaffe field at Znin. It had not been evacuated as yet, and some of the pilots, as easily recognizable as our own—clean-shaven, just sloppy enough to let you know they were fly boys—stood beside the road and watched.

Further along a group of schoolchildren, mostly girls, gathered on a small knoll and looked shy and cold. Their teacher looked stern and righteous, but not cold. The city fathers stood by, nodding wisely, indicating either approval or that they had known all the time that this would happen.

We left Znin, and the afternoon wore on slowly. There was a slight flicker of interest at the appearance of a shiny black coach pulled by two horses, which came through the crowd. I was able to see only a befurred female form. But it obviously could be nothing but the beautiful daughter of some nobleman, fleeing from the onrushing barbarians.

Nightfall came shortly after this glimpse into the romantic past. It was dark when Hesse and I, the rear guard, limped into a large barnyard, found the group we had started with, and dropped gratefully to the ground. Too tired to eat or to untie my blankets, I merely put my roll under my head and lay back to freeze to death as comfortably as possible.

My trance was cut short by the announcement that we could sleep in the barns. Certain groups were designated for each of the three barns. We were the last to enter ours, a large dairy barn with about seventy-five cows and with a charming litter of pigs just inside the door. There was a mad scramble for places everywhere but the pigsty. The preferred place seemed to be among the cows. And indeed, since their animal heat made the building warm, the best spot would be in close proximity to the source.

We had to be content with a ledge running along the wall which would barely accommodate us, but from which we could survey the scene. While I went in search of straw, Hesse, who knew about these things, headed for a likely cow and started milking. By the time I had returned with a great armload of hay, he had extracted a quart of milk. We settled down to a rustic feast, mixing the milk with cocoa powder and enjoying the most delicious chocolate shakes we had ever tasted.

The milk was so good that Hesse went back for more. In fact, he kept visiting the cow every fifteen minutes, until neither he nor the animal was capable of any more productive efforts. The beast was probably flattered by the attention but undoubtedly would have preferred to sleep.

The barn had electric lights, which lasted until early morning when the Germans demolished the power plant at Znin. I had difficulty going to sleep, with such a fascinating panorama spread out before me. The sudden intrusion had given the cows nervous diarrhea and the unfortunates in their midst were constantly dodging.

4

Wegheim

We found in the morning that we were at a large Polish estate that the Germans had seized and named Wegheim or "Road Home." There were no Germans in residence. The would-be lord of the manor had departed in the black coach mentioned above.

The Oflag column marched off early in the morning. Those who were lame or sick were allowed to remain behind and move into the manor house, which was large and slightly furnished but had no running water or electricity. We numbered about 120, I think. We were told that trucks would come back to take us to Germany, but they never came. Meanwhile the surgical team of the 101st Airborne set up a little aid station in the manor, and we tried to look wan in case the SS retreated down this road. They would shoot us if they thought we were malingering or trying to escape, which we were, in fact, hoping to do.

That night we heard a great clattering and cannon fire outside. The Russians had arrived. They came in and told us we were free. Trucks would come and take us to Moscow, where we would be shown the subway and other sights and then be sent home. The trucks never came. After a few days a young Russian lieutenant was introduced to us as a liaison officer who would help solve any problems we happened to have. He was housed in the village, where he was quartered on some unfortunate family and reportedly shacked up with one of the girls. The only manifestation of his presence that I can recall is the periodic delivery of spiritus, the 180-proof Russian or Polish alcohol. It was delivered in a large enameled pitcher of the type European hotels and pensions used for carrying hot water to your room. It was too strong for us to drink, but it worked in our Zippos.

Those among us who were in better physical shape lost no time in organizing life at Wegheim. A slit trench latrine was dug in the front lawn, much to the amusement of the girls from the nearby village who would pass by on their way to work as we strained to give our all to the gods of the underworld. There was no modesty on anyone's part.

Several officers from Texas constituted themselves a kitchen staff and providers and supervised the slaughter of a cow or two and a pig and began providing us with a nourishing soup and a porridge made of wheat.

Some of us went scrounging in the countryside, looking and begging for food or anything else useful, rewarding donors with cigarettes. The Poles, who were having very thin times themselves, were remarkably generous. All you had to do was say you were an American officer and you would be invited in and fed if there was any food to consume.

On one such excursion, Hesse, an officer named Scherer, and I came upon a hamlet with several households of Germans—descendants of the original settlers established there by Frederick the Great in the eighteenth century. The roads had been crowded with such people fleeing the Russians, and these Germans knew their days in the village were numbered. They were on the verge of leaving and were consuming everything they could not carry. One family had slaughtered a hog and were frying crullers in a large kettle full of fat. They welcomed us as saviors who would keep their Polish neighbors from attacking them and invited us in to lunch. We were uneasy about consorting with Germans, but were not going to pass up a meal. We sat around a big table in what had obviously been one of the more comfortable houses of the village. Our hosts bemoaned their fate. Their attractive blonde daughter had already been raped by Russian soldiers (the Russians were great rapists). They would be unable to take much with them. Everything was gone, the mother kept saying, "*Alles ist weg.*"

I do not remember what we ate, but there was a lot of it, and after we left Hesse and I both had violent bowel movements by the roadside, while a group of Polish teenagers looked at us with what might turn into hostility, I thought. We went back to Wegheim and didn't eat anything more for awhile.

By this time, Wegheim had become our home. Each of us had staked out positions on the wooden floor that were recognized by the others as ours. There were perhaps twelve men in the ground floor room where I slept. We had no beds or mattresses but slept on our blankets, of which we each had two or three. During daylight hours we talked and smoked and read. Pooling our individual holdings gave our room a stock of fifteen or twenty Armed Forces Editions paperbacks. I was the librarian and still have my record of who had what book, written on the backs of checks from the Army National Bank at Ft. Leavenworth.

One day the Polish owner of the property was introduced to us. He seemed somewhat shy and did not hang around. I never saw him again.

As the days went by, some officers disappeared, setting out for Warsaw and eventually Lublin, where a provisional government had been announced. Several made it as far as Moscow, where they gave the American military mission the first news it had of the existence of the POWs from Oflag 64 at Wegheim, which the mission took to be the name of a village and began calling a camp. Our senior American officer, Colonel Edgar Gans, who sported a handlebar mustache and had a wild look in his eyes, had issued orders that no one was allowed to leave. No one paid much attention to him, but we had no clear idea where to go. We thought of Danzig and Lublin, but had no map to tell us how to get there, and Warsaw seemed the most likely place to find an American official who would arrange our repatriation.

At the end of about three weeks Gans declared that we would leave the next day for Warsaw, marching to Znin and taking a train from there. By that time there were only about forty of us left, according to my recollection. The others had flown the coop. We all assembled the next morning and proceeded up the road in good order. As we entered the village of Znin three of us (Hesse, Anthony Sito, a Polish American boy from Detroit or Chicago, and I) noted a hotel that was open, the proprietor standing in the doorway. We quickly dropped out of the column and, after a little negotiating, were allowed in to spend the night. We slept in beds for the first time in months, paid for it with cigarettes, and discovered in the morning that the rest of the column had left by train while we slept.

We spent the second night sleeping on the floor of the railroad station. Sito became acquainted with the owner or manager of a creamery across the street from the station, and we were invited to spend the next night in his apartment above the creamery. Our host seemed to be doing well. He and his wife fed us and let us use their modern bathroom, where I did not know which was more delightful, use of a sit-down toilet or a hot bath in a tub. They had a radio, gave us the latest news, and promised to wake us when it became clear that a train was coming. There was no regular service, either freight or passenger. The trains were all going to the front with ammunition and supplies or coming back with no fixed schedule. There were no passenger cars, only boxcars or flat cars where one might find a place to sit or stand.

We were awakened at about 4:00 am, each given a pound of butter wrapped in wax paper, and sent on our way. I kept the butter in my coat pocket, which was sufficiently cold so that it would not melt. Together with a large round loaf of Polish brown bread, which each of us had been given at a bakery the previous day, it was my principal sustenance for some time. I still have a piece of the bread. The butter is all gone.

A train was in the station. The stationmaster put us on the coal car but we soon worked our way up to the firebox, where we could be warmer and chat with the engineer. Our first stop was Gniezno, the oldest city in Poland, where we had to change trains and where we encountered our first American enlisted men. They had been in a POW camp at Kustrin and were headed for Warsaw. From them we learned of rumors that there was an American presence in Lublin. The Poles told us that American planes were landing near Warsaw and taking away those who had preceded us. Some French prisoners we encountered said they had heard the same thing on Swiss radio. I commented at the time that no latrine ever boasted more gossip.

We rode on a flat car for several hours to Wrzeznia, where we spent two days in the station hoping to catch a train. We finally did

so, thanks to some French prisoners, one of whom I had befriend-
ed by giving him a Lucky Strike. The French were much better at
scrounging than we were. They quickly located a boxcar that was
reasonably clean and allowed us to join them. One of them stood
in the doorway directing two others to pick up a stove and some
fuel as we slowly moved out of the yard. In no time they had a fire
going and were cooking spaghetti, which they did not share with
us (and we did not ask them to, which would have been contrary to
prisoner etiquette.). They eventually got a girl on board and one of
them shared his bedding with her. We were too tired to watch and
too hungry to be much interested in sex.

Two or three days later we arrived in Warsaw. My recollection
has always been that it was the 22 of February, but a schedule I
wrote not long after said it was the 26th. In any case, the city lay
in ruins. We were told there were only eighty-six habitable dwell-
ing places left standing. That is, eighty-six apartments or individual houses. We walked down the main street toward the Vistula.
There was no building standing on either side of the road. The only
people we saw were a couple of miserable-looking women ped-
dling something. There was no noise and no sign of civic activity of
any sort. We walked across the bridge and arrived in the relatively
unscathed suburb of Praga. The Russians had stopped there and
stayed while the Germans systematically destroyed Warsaw.

In Praga we were directed to the Polish Red Cross, which occupied a small building with a soup kitchen and a few rooms where
one could sleep, but no running water. There were other American
prisoners already there, most of them enlisted men from Kustrin.
We were told that we should go to Lublin, but we heard that the
Russians were putting escaped prisoners in a concentration camp
there (Oswiecim?). We also learned that they were rounding up
prisoners in Praga and sending them out to the military academy
at Rembertow, where they were confined to the post.

Meanwhile, there were possibilities in Praga. A couple of GIs
came in the first night with a sack full of sausage (described as
"donkey dick"), cake, and doughnuts—items we had seen in shop
windows but been unable to buy because we had no money and
were running low on cigarettes. They had purchased these goods
with money they had received for the bicycles they had ridden

from Germany. They had gotten 9,000 zlotys for three bikes and spent three thousand of them on their food. They were very happy and gave me one of the doughnuts, which was delicious.

Then a man who spoke English came in and started buying clothes. He would pay 600 zlotys for a GI shirt. He would not buy the $200 worth of Belgian francs I had from a partial pay at Schlausenbach, but he suggested that I go into business with him. He had a phonograph and wanted to open an American bar. My job would be to buy the dollars and pounds sterling that prisoners were carrying and in which there was a black market. He claimed to be an American who had been long resident in France and been imprisoned by the Gestapo. He said he had begun with selling the coat on his back and had worked up to 3,000 zlotys and an apartment. I was intrigued by his offer. It sounded like an adventure that might be fun, but it would have been too imprudent. Besides, I had a wife to go home to.

Two days later, giving up on Hesse and Sito who could not decide what to do, I said I was going to hitchhike to Brest Litovsk, where we knew that American pilots were bringing in aircraft to turn over to the Russians. After some hesitation, they decided to come with me, and we walked over to a military police checkpoint about a mile away at an intersection where trucks going east would be stopped for inspection. The woman MP would, if you told her where you wanted to go, ask the driver of a truck headed in that direction to give you a ride. It was bitterly cold and after several hours at the intersection with no trucks, we gave up and went to a nearby church. Both Sito and Hesse were Catholics. The church was cold too, but the priest, after listening to our story, excused himself for ten or fifteen minutes and then came back and escorted us across the street to the tiny apartment of an elderly couple who were just getting ready to have supper. They offered to feed us, but we declined because we thought that would be too much. They suggested we sleep on the floor of their parlor, which we were preparing to do when two younger women entered. One was quite cute, the other less so. In any event, they invited us to come with them, saying they could take care of us much more easily than the elderly couple. We went with them to their apartment, which was not far away (the address was T Zana 6, m. 1).

The two women were sisters—Jadwiga and Lala Wierzbicka. There was a man in their apartment that we thought was Jadwiga's husband, but I later learned that they were not married. I do not recall the man's name, but he certainly acted like the head of the household. He had converted the bathroom into a distillery and was making spiritus, for which there was a ready market—the first enterprise to open in Praga after the Germans left was a bar—and the ménage did not lack money. We began each day with a shot of spiritus, which we found very strong but had to drink for the sake of America's reputation. There was plenty to eat, we had beds to sleep in, and we spent a pleasant week with Jadwiga and her sister. Then Hesse made a reconnaissance trip out to Rembertow and came back in a state of some agitation with the news that the Russians were readying a train for almost immediate departure for Odessa and were preparing to load all the American, British, and French prisoners on board. We ate a quick meal, grabbed our possessions, said goodbye and took off, arriving at Rembertow in time to be the next to the last men on the train (Col. Gans was the last man).

Our accommodations were in boxcars, but these were Russian broad-gauge cars, much larger than the tiny narrow gauge cars of most of the rest of Europe. The trip took about a week and was not unpleasant. Rough pine boards on which we could sit and sleep had been laid across the cars at intervals, and we could play cards and read and watch the countryside roll by. We stopped briefly in Lublin, where Scherer and Wright joined us and gave us our first word of the terrible massacre of Jews at Auschwitz. We also stopped briefly at Kiev, but we were not allowed off the train at any point except to answer the call of nature and to walk up to the flat car that was used as the kitchen, where we received a satisfying bowl of kasha flavored with mutton fat and a bowl of cabbage soup every day. I traded a pair of socks for two loaves of delicious bread, and we had some supplies from a captured German warehouse.

We arrived in Odessa about March and moved into a couple of large, abandoned mansions. There was no running water but an elaborate latrine had been dug in the side yard, and we had beds. The men who had gone to Lublin were there to meet us, and we had something of a reunion. There was also a major from the

Moscow military mission who had American cigarettes, corned beef, chocolate bars, Life Savers, preserved butter, pipe tobacco and other goodies to pass out. More important, he took our names and home addresses and reported them to Moscow, which informed Washington. At last our families learned that we were alive and safe.

We were told that a ship would pick us up in due course but had no idea that we were in effect being held as hostages until Russian prisoners taken on the western front were repatriated. Meanwhile, the Russians were doing their best to feed us, but they did not have a lot to offer. On one occasion they served us smoked fish, which they cut into three pieces and distributed around the table so that one man had the head, his neighbor had the middle, and the third man the tail. We did not like the idea of fish to begin with, and the men who got the head refused to eat it, while the rest of us only picked at ours. The Russians were very upset with us because we did not appreciate this delicacy—perhaps the Volga perch that was on the menu but never served when we were in Moscow in 1990.

At one point we were all deloused again. This time we emerged from the showers to find a very cute Russian woman doctor sitting on a stool and waiting to examine us while we turned around before her. It was a great sendoff. As at the Oflag, the Russians baked rather than gassed our clothes.

We were a motley crew. There were Frenchmen and a variety of other allied prisoners in addition to those of us from Oflag 64. One American, a boy from San Antonio named Gus Khruschevsky, was in pilot's fleece-lined leather and smoking Pall Malls, which none of us had seen for a long time. He had been shot down over Yugoslavia or Romania and exfiltrated by the partisans.

After about a week a British ship, the *Antenor*, arrived with a load of Russians. They debarked, and we embarked soon thereafter. We were escorted to the dock by a band that played while we boarded. Some twenty-nine years later, the Soviet ambassador in Rabat gave me a copy of Marshal Zhukov's memoirs, which has a photo of the Americans boarding the *Antenor*. He thought the tall man going up the gangplank was me, but I think it was "Sidi Bou," the lieutenant who was captured at the battle of Sidi Bou Zid in Tunisia and could talk of nothing else.

The crew of the *Antenor* welcomed us cordially and were amazed at our capacity for eating, particularly white bread, which we had not had for many months and which tasted like cake. The *Antenor* was a sleek, medium-sized vessel and moved very quickly. Our first stop was Istanbul, where someone stole my wallet with $200 worth of Belgian francs in it. I assumed it was one of the Frenchmen, but had no clue as to which one it might have been.

We spent the night on the Bosphorus. The sight of Istanbul was something I had never imagined. For one thing, there was no blackout, and the lights were all on, something we had not seen for many months. Then there were the walls and remains of Byzantium and the Ottoman Empire. I did not know such antique remnants existed in such quantity.

Very early in the voyage a poker game was established in the ship's salon and continued until we eventually arrived at Boston some weeks later, having changed ships at Port Said and Naples. I sat in briefly but soon realized that I was no match for the addicts around the table. On the very last day of our voyage the last pot went for something like a pair of fours.

The first thing that met our eyes at Port Said was a gigantic Johnny Walker sign. We were back in the British Empire at last. We were taken across to Port Fuad and immediately deloused with DDT powder, which was squirted down our necks and waists (with our clothes on). We were given clean uniforms, a Red Cross toilet kit (mine was from the ladies of Flint, Michigan) and a partial pay of $200 per officer. We were then allowed to take the ferry back to Port Said and do as we liked. We were the first "tourists" with money Port Said had seen in a long time, and the souvenir dealers did a land-office business. I bought cobra skin purses at Simon Arts for Mother and Jeanne and a bottle of alleged Chanel No. 5 perfume for Jeanne. But first we went to the Eastern Exchange Hotel and ate ice cream with whipped cream on top while being entertained by the street magicians. We did not know about the more exotic entertainments that Port Said offered.

After a few days we boarded another British ship (the *Moreton Bay*?) and left for Naples. The war was still on, but the Allies controlled the air and we did not worry about the Germans. On arrival in Naples we were taken to a hotel at Bagnoli, where we spent

about a week. Naples night life was booming with American soldiers. There was also a post exchange where we could buy uniform
items. I bought an "Eisenhower jacket" to wear in place of the dress
coat I had left in my footlocker at Schlausenbach. I was shaved by a
barber (the only time in my life) and had a meal of spaghetti at an
Italian restaurant. I didn't know that Bob Jaccard, Jeanne's brother
who was Mark Clark's aide, was at nearby Caserta, or I would have
tried to visit him.

In less than a week we were on one of the Matson liners (the
Mariposa) headed for Boston. We arrived there on April 12, the day
Franklin Roosevelt died. There was no band and no celebration to
mark our arrival. The town was in mourning, the bars were closed,
and although we were invited to a girls' party in Cambridge, we
spent a quiet evening. Most of us were eager to get to a telephone
and call home. We were shipped home by train rather quickly, given
sixty days' leave (disguised as "delay en route"), and told to report
to the Rest and Recuperation Center at Miami Beach by June 22.

Jeanne and Mother were at the station to meet me when we
arrived in San Antonio, and we had a joyous reunion. We took full
advantage of the sixty days, spending them in a leisurely fashion
except for a week spent at a dude ranch near Boerne, the home
town of Richard Reichenau, first sergeant of the antitank company
who had been injured in the blowing up of Capt. Vitz's jeep. On
arrival in Boerne I went directly to the barbershop and asked if anyone knew his parents. His father arrived in a matter of minutes,
very anxious for news. They had heard nothing. I told him what
had happened, and that his son had been alive but unconscious
when last I saw him. He was very grateful for the information. A
few weeks later he wrote to tell me that he had been informed that
his son had bled to death in a German hospital.

Thus ends my wartime saga, but I'm not finished with the army yet.

Epilogue

The above account (chapters 2 through 4) is an edited and somewhat expanded version of one I wrote in 1945 for a correspondence
course in short story writing at Kansas State. In any event, these
memories lived with me over the years, and I promised myself a

trip back to see what was left of Schlausenbach and try to get a better idea of what happened and why. The opportunity finally presented itself in early June 1971, when I attended a conference at Stuttgart and took time off afterward, to make a sentimental journey back. The following is my journal:

Schlausenbach, June 10, 1971

I can locate approximately Valovcin's and Chappello's gun positions, but there are new buildings and trees in the way so that I cannot be sure. I cannot decide where we put the 0.50 cal. machine gun that fired three shots and quit. The little stone farmhouse I slept in has been remodeled, added to, and stuccoed over so that it is almost unrecognizable.

I can still recognize the building in which the antitank company was headquartered, but it, too, is being remodeled. Behind it I can see clearly the clay bank I was standing against when a sniper almost got me. I cannot find the field where we laid the mines and where the lieutenant from Cannon Company was killed. There are too many trees.

There is an old church that I don't remember at all. Where regimental headquarters were, there is now an inn. There is another next to it, in which I am staying. There are two pensions up the street, both full. The Schnee Eifel has become a tourist center, and there are lots of elderly people out promenading in the rather chilly air. The countryside is green and picturesque, and I find that the hill in front of town, known as Schwarzer Mann, is some sort of attraction. I must investigate tomorrow.

The drive over from Koblenz was through a smiling countryside all the way. The villages were all decked out with flags, and the shops were closed, it being Ascension Day. Gerolstein turned out to be a very pretty town—not at all what I remembered. The railway station was unrecognizable, but I was told it was the same building that was there in 1944. I was very pleased to be able, after several false starts, to find the field where we slept those few hours the night of December 20 and to find the building where I

went to ask for first aid only to be shoved into another column and marched off to the railroad station. I also found
the row of houses from one of which an old lady emerged
and gave us water.

Prum, June 11, 1971

Some questions answered. Regimental headquarters were
in the lower of the two inns in lower Schlausenbach. The
name of the family that owns both inns is Scherberich.

I went to the farmhouse on the edge of town where I
lived for a week. The lady of the house was admiring her
window boxes. I explained my interest in the house and
asked if the original still stood within the stucco exterior.
She said it did and took me in. Everything was oilcloth and
plastic, but the three original rooms were there. She had
only lived in the house eleven years and was originally from
Brandscheid. She had never seen it in its original state (she
was nine in 1944). Her father-in-law, however, now eighty-
one (or was he her *grossvater*-in-law?), was there and was
the 1944 owner.

He was an old and feeble man, stretched out on a day
bed. He seemed pleased to see me, but communication was
difficult because he was deaf and I had trouble understanding his pronunciation. We all agreed 1944 had been a terrible time—they had all fled to the east until the war was
over. He said the clock on the wall was the same one that
had been in the house in 1944. It still ran. I told him it had
been running when I left, although, in point of fact, it had
stopped and we couldn't get it started again. He seemed
pleased. He had never heard of the footlocker I left in the
cellar. His son (or grandson) came in as I went out—a husky
man in his early thirties with a pleasant face. He was star-
tled at first, but when he heard the story was reassured and
friendly. His wife asked if I was on pension. She sounded
wistful.

I reconnoitered the lower road to Kobscheid and Auw.
I decided that's where Peterson and Sorenson sat with their

bazooka. From there I could look down into the lovely little valley where the battalion of German horse-drawn artillery had drawn up only to be caught unaware and smashed by Cannon Company. There was nothing in the scene to suggest the shambles of beasts and men that had been there. A Schlausenbacher was peacefully perambulating about in a tractor. . . .

The inn in Schlausenbach was very simple but not uncomfortable. My evening meal of goulash and bread was quite passable, and the young wife of the equally young proprietor gave me a great breakfast of ham omelet, bread, lard, and coffee. Lots of cholesterol in these parts. Tonight I find I left my raincoat there and must go back tomorrow.

The road we took to go up to the Schnee Eifel ridge when we evacuated Schlausenbach on December 18 is now passable only by jeep, or so a farmer told me. He said my rented VW couldn't make it. I therefore took another track, which could have been the original one for all I knew. The pine forests were just as dark and threatening as I had remembered. I don't know why they plant the trees so close together, but the effect is intimidating.

Near the summit I came across an old German bunker, partly demolished and surrounded by a fence. Had I not seen some of the originals, I would not have known what it was.

The road along the top of the ridge is now beautifully paved. About 3 km towards Bleialf from the point where I entered the ridge road is a ski lift, at the Schwarzer Mann. The ski lodge that was there burned down last winter, I am told by a USAF sergeant from Prum station, a nearby U.S. facility.

On to Bleialf, via a detour to Brandscheid. Bleialf doesn't look like the place, nor do Grosslangenfeld. Wiuterspelt, or Wintewscheid. I was certain, for some reason, that we surrendered at Bleialf, but after exploring every road in town, was sure it was not there. I consulted the map and decided that in terms of distance Schoenberg, just over the border in Belgium, was more likely. The magic figure was 32 miles we allegedly marched to Gerolstein on the 19th. I don't know how we knew it was 32, but think the Germans told us it was so many kilometers. Schoenberg is 23 km from Prum by the route I took, plus 20 to Gerolstein makes 43, or roughly 25 miles. Maybe we took a different route in 1944, which explains the difference in mileage, but I can't work it out on the map. We had to come via Bleialf.

In any event, off to Schoenberg. There is a long hill, which I seem to recall, and I remember the overweight medical officer who dropped out somewhere about here and wonder what happened to him. I thought I remembered the place where I found the sugar beet but could not find the town where someone threw bread to us, nor could I find the place where we passed the frozen bodies of a U.S. artillery battery. Schoenberg looks vaguely familiar, and its geography fits my recollections, but I won't swear to it.

There are so many new buildings and so much vegetation it is hard to tell, but I think I found the place where Captain Vitz's jeep blew up, on the hill above town, actually in the hamlet of Amelscheid, according to the map. It is green and peaceful looking. I was not sure which of two sites it was and took pictures of both.

Just outside Schoenberg I came across a farmer, about my age, herding his cows along the road. He was husky and vigorous-looking. I asked him if one spoke French or German here. He replied: "*Comme vous voulez, mon cher.*" I asked him about alternate routes to Prum, but he couldn't help. Finally, I explained what I was looking for. He was very sympathetic and said he had been a paratrooper in the Wehrmacht at the time of the December offensive and had been fighting at Remagen Bridge. He had never heard of the 106th. I left him and went on, or back, to Prum, where I checked into the Zum Goldenen Stern Hotel. Lunch at the hotel next door, not bad. Have changed my reservations and am leaving from Köln for Rabat tomorrow. Köln is 10 km from here.

Note: the surrender was at Bleialf.

5

Postwar Army

A stay at the Rest and Rehabilitation Center at Miami Beach was the last step in my cosseting phase following my wartime experiences. We were lodged in a nice hotel, given three meals a day, and subject to various dental and physical exams. After two or three weeks we were on our own, alerted to the possibility that under something called "Project Green" we might find ourselves involved in the landing in Japan, with the war still on and our POW experience not sparing us from further combat.

Initially I was assigned to the Infantry Replacement Training Center at Camp Blanding, north of Gainesville, Florida. We bought a Packard convertible that would not convert and had worn tires, which began falling apart by the time we reached Palm Beach. We limped into Gainesville three days later. I foolishly opted to take back my money from the dealer and put it down on a Chrysler which ran well but almost immediately had tire trouble as well. I later returned it to the dealer and lost most of my money. Memory of this transaction always flares in me when I contemplate the possibility of doing something to make money and leads me to decide I should not even think about it. We also had trouble finding housing, ending up at first in furnished rooms in the house of a maiden lady and later in a rustic apartment with a kerosene stove and an icebox. Not only were tires unavailable due to the war effort, there were no alarm clocks on the market either. We had to take turns staying awake to wake each other up in time to hitchhike to Camp

Blanding, where I was supposed to report at 6:30 each morning and Jeanne had a job that started at 7:30.

I was the executive officer of an antitank training company. We had 150 young men who understood that they would be fighting the Japanese, and we were very serious in our efforts to prepare them for what promised to be a nasty fight. Then came Hiroshima, Nagasaki and VJ day, along with orders transferring me to Camp Hood, an antitank training center in Texas. We squeezed in a week off at The Cloisters at Sea Island, Georgia, where there was a special wartime rate for the military of $16 a night. Those were the days. Our first priority at Camp Hood was to find a place to live, and the situation was even more dismal than it had been at Gainesville. We ended up in a furnished room in a converted barn that turned out to be tolerable, although the toilet and shower were outside.

At this point the army was beginning to demobilize and my training battalion went out of business by the end of the year. Officers had a choice of applying for immediate release from active duty, for a short indeterminate delay, or to remain indefinitely. I chose the latter, which was called "Category 1" because I was interested in obtaining a regular commission. I was enjoying army life with my promotion to First Lieutenant, and Jeanne was willing to go with me. I was also thinking about the Foreign Service after learning that I could apply to take a special written exam in 1946.

Meanwhile, on the army track, I applied for and was accepted for the Infantry Officer's Course at the Infantry School at Ft. Benning, Georgia. I went in January, and found a small apartment in Columbus, the original home of Coca Cola. It was not very exciting. The biggest thing that happened while we were there was that the entire town was sprayed with DDT by a crop duster airplane in order to get rid of the cockroaches, which were pretty bad. I don't know what the long term effects were. Rachel Carson had not yet alerted us to the dangers of DDT.

The Officer's Course was OCS all over again, but more fun because many of us had already been through the firing problems and enjoyed confounding the faculty by breaking records for number of targets hit. While I was in the course plans were announced for awarding permanent commissions to officers like me, and I applied to take that exam as well as the Foreign Service exam. The army's written exam was quite simple and I had what I thought was a satisfying oral interview with a panel of officers. No questions were raised when I took the physical exam so I assumed I had passed and had a good chance for a commission. I was not accepted, however, and when I applied again six months later I was rejected again. No explanation was given, but I assume it was because I had a heart murmur.

When the course ended late in the spring I was assigned to the Second Division at Ft. Lewis, Washington, near Seattle. We took the train to San Antonio, where we picked up Mother's 1940 Chevrolet and took off for California and up Route 101 to Seattle. It was a memorable trip, and we saw a lot of country. At one point, a state trooper stopped Jeanne for speeding but let her go with a warning when he saw me beside her, in uniform and asleep.

Mother had gone to Seattle to see off Betty, Bud's wife, who was going to join him in Tokyo where he had been since shortly after General McArthur's arrival. A lieutenant colonel of engineers, he had spent the war in the Pacific, eventually following McArthur up the chain of islands to Japan. We arrived in time to join in the general reunion. Housing was again an issue, and we finally found a cottage with an unsympathetic landlady near one of the many lakes in the region. It was not bad, but Jeanne had to row across the lake for groceries.

At Fort Lewis I was assigned to the reconnaissance troop of the Second Division. Technically a cavalry unit, the troop had no horses but rather small M-8 armored cars that mounted 37mm guns. I assumed I was picked for this noninfantry job because I had experience with antitank gunnery.

On two occasions when the troop commander was absent I had to take the troop on rather long journeys to Vancouver for a parade and to Yakima for target practice. Leading a convoy of 20 trucks and armored cars nearly 200 miles across country is a job requiring skills in which I had not been trained, but we survived both trips.

Then suddenly, because I was "Category 1," I was transferred to Japan. Jeanne would not be eligible to come with me until I had been there 18 months or so, mainly due to the housing shortage. Bud and Betty had a nice, western style house with central heating, but newcomers could expect to live in Quonset huts if they were lucky. On my arrival Bud mobilized the West Point mafia to find me an agreeable job. I turned down an offer to escort United Service Organization troupes around Asia and a job in McArthur's honor guard, but readily accepted a position with CIC, the Counter Intelligence Corps. I had no intelligence experience or training, but all they wanted was someone who could write. It sounded like fun and it was. My job was to write "letters of transmittal" summarizing and forwarding the reports of our intelligence agents, who at that point were concerned primarily with criminal activities centering around plots to steal from Japanese army warehouses.

The CIC unit was housed in the former compound of the Kempeitai, the Japanese secret police. Located across the road from the Royal Palace, there was a large, western-style building and a smaller, Japanese-style house with a charming garden. I was assigned to the very pleasant house. Indeed, the whole experience was pleasant. The first surprise was that the Japanese were remarkably cheerful and friendly. They did not seem to hold it against us that we had tried to bomb them into oblivion and much of their city lay in ruins around them. The contrast with the situation we find ourselves in with Baghdad today is night and day.

My roommate was Lieutenant Bruce Brown, whose father had been the Wrigley Gum representative in Japan before the war. Japanese industry in this period was not of highly regarded quality. The Japanese sometimes tried to get around this in the prewar American market by pretending that their products were made in America. They allegedly named a town USA, for example, so they could label their product "made in USA." Brown's father turned the tables on them by manufacturing tools in Japan under the name Brown and Sons, using the trademark B&S enclosed in a lozenge. The Japanese thought it stood for Brown and Sharpe, a highly regarded U.S. tool manufacturer, and bought his tools readily.

My CIC colleagues were an interesting bunch, some of them quite scholarly and all of them much more knowledgeable about Japan than I was. I had plenty of opportunities to explore the country in my Jeep, and we used to spend Sunday afternoons hunting for bargains in used cameras. I was discouraged from trying to learn much Japanese, but I absorbed enough to feel that Japan was a fascinating country and I wanted to remain there for awhile. I did have an opportunity to study Russian and learned enough to know that it would take a good deal more work before I could carry on a conversation.

Early in my tour I took the Foreign Service written exam. There were perhaps 15 or 20 of us and it lasted two or three days. I had no way to tell how I did. With no preparation other than trying to read Time religiously and finishing Gibbon's *Decline and Fall of the Roman Empire* on the transport from Seattle, I did not expect to pass. I assumed I would have to go to Georgetown for a year or two if I were serious about getting into the Service. Meanwhile, I was planning on remaining in Tokyo for some time.

I was quite surprised, therefore, when a few months later I received a letter telling me I had passed the exam and should hold myself in readiness to take the oral. I was even more surprised when the personnel office at General Headquarters agreed to let me leave the army and return to the United States to join the Foreign Service.

I was back in Manhattan by the end of March 1947. The dean of General Science cobbled together a program that allowed me to graduate with a BS from Kansas State in June 1947. Jeanne and I went to Chicago for my oral exam in July.

I had understood the oral to be primarily a test of demeanor and was surprised to be asked a number of substantive questions I could not answer. I did not know, for instance, who William Cullen Bryant was. When it was all over, the chairman of the review panel told me that while the panel liked my style, I did not know much about American history and should go back to college for a year before taking the exam again.

Somewhat crestfallen, Jeanne and I returned to Manhattan and considered alternatives. The head of the Department of Modern Languages had called his friends and had offers of graduate fellowships in German at Tulane, Northwestern, and Wisconsin, but we agreed that if I chose that route I should forget about the Foreign Service. I decided to enroll in the Institute of Citizenship, a novel organization set up under a grant from the Volker Foundation of St. Louis to teach "citizenship," whatever that meant. A group of four professors, none from Kansas, was brought in and began what amounted to a Great Books program organized around Socraticmethod seminars. It was delightfully unlike anything Kansas State had ever seen, and I had a thoroughly enjoyable year reading, writing about, and discussing books like John Locke's *Second Treatise* and Hobbes's *Leviathan*.

I wrote a Master's thesis on MacKinder's theory that who ruled the Heartland ruled the World Island and decided that this might or might not be true. I was awarded a Master of Science degree in June 1948 and went off to retake the Foreign Service oral examination at Washington in July. Jeanne, meanwhile, had been teaching speech at Kansas State and provided a substantial part of our income in addition to my $90 a month under the GI Bill of Rights. We also discovered that Jeanne was pregnant with our first baby, due in October.

The second oral was rather pro forma. I translated a passage from German, answered a simple question about the law of supply and demand, and was told that as a blue-eyed person I should wear sunglasses to avoid headaches if I went to a tropical post. The chairman of the Board of Examiners, an impressive figure named Joseph Coy Greene, said that the department would inform me when there was an opening for me. He did not know long it would take, but it would be months rather than weeks.

I immediately began looking for a job in Washington, but the State Department had nothing for me. One of the friends I was staying with came up with the telephone number of an agency that might be interested in my mathematical and linguistic background. They asked me to come for an interview; but I did not go, because the Institute of Citizenship had come through with a possible job at Kansas State. I later realized that the organization I turned down the interview with was the National Security Agency. The recently appointed president of Kansas State was Milton Eisenhower, younger brother of Dwight D. He was also chairman of the U.S. National Commission on UNESCO and thought that every state should have its own commission to stimulate local interest in and support for UNESCO and participate in intellectual activities with an international aspect.

Accordingly, he had established a Kansas State Commission on UNESCO and needed an executive secretary. The position paid $3,500 a year and came with a small office on the top floor of Anderson Hall, the center of college administration and home of the department of modern languages. I had a young secretary and a very limited budget. We put out a monthly bulletin and organized my first major conference. I did a certain amount of speaking on the radio and to groups in outlying towns and showed a film, "No Place to Hide", which imagined a nuclear war. I helped a forceful older woman named Rachel Carson organize a pageant at her tiny home town, Morganville, which wanted to celebrate its adoption of a French town. Rachel had been an editor at a well-known magazine in New York, and had come home to retire and stir up a greater interest in international affairs. The evening was a great success. People came from miles around and anyone with any talent was invited to perform. The high point was a woman singing an aria from *Madama Butterfly*.

Meanwhile, Jeanne's biological clock was ticking away and Alison was born on October 19, 1948. Our lives were changed immediately. We had a woman in to help for a few days but soon we were on our own, coping with the problems of diapers and midnight feedings and getting very little sleep. At one point when Alison was colicky we made a pancake and put it on her stomach, as the woman had recommended. It was too hot and Alison objected. She always was strong-willed.

About a month later I received a letter informing me that I was invited to join the new class of Foreign Service Officers to begin in January. This meant hasty rearrangement of responsibilities and obligations, and we decided that since I would probably be sent to Europe we should seize the opportunity to visit my mother and brother in California.

We were offered a ride by a Delt from Manhattan who was unmarried and had never been near a baby. We all piled into his Oldsmobile and took off for Route 66, which we sang all the way to San Bernardino. We had a pleasant Christmas with Mother and Bud and Betty and their two children. Soon after Christmas, Jeanne took the baby to Montana to spend some time with her brother Bob and his family. I set off for Washington for my Foreign Service training, beginning a thirty-one-year career.

Part III

DIPLOMACY

6

Junior Officer in the Foreign Service

On arrival in Washington I stayed initially with Russell Nixon and then, after a brief stay in a rented room in Chevy Chase, I soon found a small furnished apartment at the intersection of Lee Highway and Glebe Road in Virginia. The apartment building is still there, but the neighborhood is no longer recognizable.

I was sworn into the Foreign Service along with twenty-one other young men on January 6, 1949. The appointment of Dean Acheson as secretary of state to succeed George Marshall had just been announced. The swearing in took place in the Foreign Service Lounge in a temporary World War II building on 23d Street, in back of what was then known as "New State." We were then taken to a brick apartment building on C Street that stood about where the diplomatic entrance of the Department of State is today. This was the home of the Foreign Service Institute, a recently established training facility. The deputy director was Robert A. Walker, who had been director of the Institute of Citizenship at Kansas State.

We were assembled around a large table in a medium-sized classroom and asked to introduce ourselves to the rest of the class. Many of the others had educational backgrounds that sounded much more elegant than Kansas State, and I felt somewhat inhibited as a result, not realizing what I had to offer in the way of capabilities. I was particularly embarrassed by the class picture, in which I am wearing a double-breasted suit I had bought in Kansas City that I thought was not very becoming. Of the class, three of us went on to become chiefs of mission, and I was the only one to have more than one post in that capacity. At the start, and for many years thereafter, I had no inkling that would be the outcome.

The course lasted seventeen weeks or thereabouts. There was a good deal of emphasis on anthropology at the beginning, an introduction to linguistics, and a continuing emphasis on the rules and regulations of the Department of State. There was no diplomatic history to speak of and very little politics and economics, but there was a good deal of useful instruction on how to survive and cope with the problems peculiar to the service. The most memorable lecture was by a man from the Visa Office named Alexander who told us that every visa applicant was *ipso facto* a nonadmissible quota immigrant until he proved otherwise. We had a similar lecture from the Passport office, then run by a redoubtable woman named Ruth Shipley, who brooked no nonsense from young FSOs. Our headmaster was a very kind and pleasant officer named Robert Hale, who never went on to the top of the Service but who left with all of us an impression of a very decent human being who told us how to avoid the pitfalls that lay ahead.

My first question when the class started was whether there would be nursery facilities for our children so my wife could attend the class when she arrived. The answer was that they realized how useful that would be, but unfortunately there was no money for such facilities. In those days wives were expected to support their husbands and were often mentioned as assets or liabilities in the officers' annual fitness reports. In that case it was unjust that they were not able to benefit from the same instruction their husbands were receiving.

Jeanne arrived shortly after Harry Truman's inauguration in late January. I had gone to town on inauguration day to buy sheets and towels and had stood to watch Truman pass up Pennsylvania Avenue at 7th Street. I must have gone from there to the train station but have no memory of how I transported Jeanne and Alison to our Glebe Road hideaway, as we had no car. Perhaps Russell Nixon took us. Perhaps I hired a taxi. In any event, the two of them settled in quickly.

The biggest concern of the class was what our first posts would be and how we would cope with them. All of us were interviewed by the personnel people and asked where we wanted to go. I said my first preferences were Poland or Japan, but there were no suitable openings in either country. Apparently trying to at least put me in the same ball park with one of my desires, they assigned me to Seoul, Korea.

Seoul was a hardship post. The economy was in ruins, housing was short, and security was a problem. I remember the post report describing the audacity of the Koreans at stealing such items as the spare tires off a moving bus. But it sounded like an interesting place and we began preparing for it, actually studying Korean from an army manual and buying seersucker suits to wear in the semitropical summer, a pair of *Veldtschoen*, South African waterproof shoes to wear when it was wet, a wardrobe trunk to use on the ship, and I forget what else. We quickly ran through the $2,000 I had accumulated from my service in Tokyo.

The Foreign Service Association held a reception for the class, and there I met John Muccio, the ambassador to Korea. We had a very brief chat. He seemed friendly, and that was that. I was glad to have met him and thought that made me one up.

The two women in the travel office who made your travel arrangements regarded all young FSOs with suspicion. Our arrangements were complicated. At the end of the course the entire class was to go to New York for a week during which they went to the United Nations, met the department's dispatch agent, and watched the shipping commissioners who regulated maritime trade and disputes, shipping and seamen being something we were likely to be involved with if were stationed at seaports. We would go to our new posts directly from New York.

Jeanne went to New York with me for part of the week, hoping to take in some plays. We left Alison with a babysitter in Virginia. Jeanne was to go back early, pick her up and return to Manhattan by train, where I would meet her. We would then take the train to San Francisco and a ship from there to Yokohama. I forget how we were to get from there to Seoul. We had all our tickets, rail and ship, and all arrangements were set in concrete. Then, as I was about to walk out the door on the morning Jeanne was to leave for Washington, the telephone rang and one of the dragons in the travel office was on the line asking me, "What arrangements have you made for going to Sydney?"

I then learned that my assignment had been changed some weeks earlier because Muccio had returned to Seoul and sent a telegram asking that no more officers with young children be assigned to that post. My orders had been changed immediately and sent to me in the mail in care of the Foreign Service Lounge (which ran a locator service) instead of the Foreign Service Institute next door. They reached me some six weeks after we arrived in Sydney, having first been routed to Seoul. Meanwhile, no one in personnel, where I had called and checked with a senior officer before going to New York, had the wit to tell me of the change. This was my introduction to a phenomenon that seemed almost permanent. All of my early assignments featured some sort of serious confusion regarding travel arrangements.

Jeanne proceeded to pick up Alison as planned and left for Manhattan. I met her there and we went on to San Francisco in accordance with our original schedule. There we stayed with Bud and Betty in Berkeley. Bud was earning a Masters in Engineering at the University of California. We saw Betsy Goode, who worked for an airline, and then departed by DC-6 on BCPA, the Australian airline, for an interminable flight (actually 39 hours) via Honolulu, Canton Island, Wake, and Fiji. I had been too shy to talk to the crew about taking better care of Alison's needs for warm milk, etc., and we arrived out of sorts. Our heads did not stop buzzing for days.

It was early winter in Sydney, of course, and all our winter clothes were in footlockers and boxes en route to Seoul. Intercepted at New Orleans, thanks to the dispatch agent, they did not reach us until winter was almost over. Shortly after arrival we moved into a furnished house with a semidetached landlord on Bellevue Hill (No.9 Warren Road). The landlady, Ms. Smythe, could enter our part of the house through the kitchen whether we liked it or not, and did so on occasion when she felt a need to interfere in our domestic arrangements.

Sydney, which had been an oasis of comfort during the war years, had outgrown its infrastructure and suffered some severe shortages while we were there. The most important was a shortage of gas brought on by a coalminers' strike. There was no gas for cooking or heating, and there were frequent blackouts because there was not enough gas for power generation. We were able to cope with the lack of gas for cooking because I had had the fore-sight to buy a couple of primus stoves, which used kerosene. But we had no heat.

At the end of a year we moved to a much larger place at Waver-ton, the first stop on the North Shore rail line. We had a beautiful view of the harbor, a heating stove in which we could burn coke, and a much pleasanter environment. I was the junior officer in the Consulate General, which occupied a whole floor in the Bank of New South Wales building in downtown Sydney. There were some ten other officers, including Consul General Orsen Nielsen, whose first post had been St. Petersburg in 1917. A desiccated man with a limp handshake, his attitude did not encourage familiarity. I re-marked once to his Australian secretary that he had a way of mak-ing you feel inferior. She said, "No, he has a way of pointing out to you that you are inferior."

The consulate general had the classic organization of such of-fices. There was a consular section that issued visas and passports, performed welfare and whereabouts services for American citizens, prepared consular invoices on goods being shipped to the United States, handled shipping and seamen, and took care of veterans, of whom there were a few—men who had served in Australia dur-ing the war and come back looking for business opportunities. Or perhaps for a girl who had been left behind. An economic and com-mercial section looked into trade opportunities and complaints. An agricultural office dealt with the considerable volume of trade in agricultural commodities. An administrative office paid people, managed the office space, and took care of the mail and transporta-tion.

I was what was later called the General Services Officer, the lowest man on the totem pole, in charge of miscellaneous jobs. I ordered the liquor, managed the diplomatic pouches, gave admin-istrative support to the embassy in Canberra, and was the security officer. Not very exciting, but sometimes fun, and interesting. Any routine job takes on a different coloration when it is performed in a new environment.

It was not the road to glory, however. That road led through po-litical reporting, of which there was very little at Sydney. Economic and consular work held more promise, but those jobs were already occupied. Then the consular officer, a maiden lady of firm views, went on leave, and I took her place for several months. It was valuable experience. I also managed to get in some time in the economic section when someone went on leave.

Officers were allowed two months of home leave every two years. If the post was in Australia and you opted to travel by ship, that could mean an absence of several months, and more if you performed any duties, such as attending the midcareer course at the Foreign Service Institute while in Washington.

There were four other consulates in Australia at the time—Melbourne, Brisbane, Adelaide, and Perth. Adelaide and Perth were "special purpose" posts and had only one officer and a couple of local clerical personnel each. In late 1949, we learned that John O'Grady, the vice consul in charge of the post at Adelaide, was going on home leave in January. He would be gone for about five months, and I was chosen to replace him and run the office during his absence. I was elated.

We left Sydney in mid-January, driving a brand new Canadian Ford sedan with right-hand drive and leather seats. Alison was in the back seat in her basket. Travel across Australia was something like travel across Texas, similar scenery but very different birds and animals. Parrots, kookaburras, and kangaroos. Adelaide was about a thousand miles by road west of Sydney. Much smaller than Sydney, it was much more comfortable, and we found it a very pleasant place. I had a three-room office with two helpful and friendly Australian assistants, and my workload was light. Indeed, I am not sure why we maintained a post there. It has been closed twice and reopened only once since we left in 1950.

This was a first step on the road to Glory. As the only career consul (there was an honorary Portuguese consul), I was the third-ranking officer in protocol terms in South Australia and the Northern Territories, an area one-third the size of the United States. I was also an extraordinary member of the Adelaide Club, which meant that I did not pay dues but could invite guests, which mere honorary members could not do. The club was the meeting place of the elite, most of them older men. The only man my age was Johnnie Althorp—Viscount Althorp—whose eventual daughter (he was not yet married at the time) was Princess Diana. He was the aide de camp to Sir Willoughby Norrie, the governor of South Australia. (Under the Commonwealth system each of the Australian states had a British governor sent out from England, and there was a governor general in Canberra.). They had a certain constitutional function—the law wasn't law unless they signed it—but the job was largely ceremonial.

Shortly after the O'Gradys left for the United States, we had the task of moving their furniture and effects into a new residence purchased by the Department of State on a slight rise south of town. The new house was delightful, with a wonderful garden, and we greatly enjoyed it. (The Foreign Service was mostly downhill for quite a while after that.) We also had an enjoyable social life, which included playing sardines at the governor's residence with Johnnie Althorp and other members of the *jeunesse dorée*. We made friends with a noted Australian author, Paul McGuire, and his wife and went with them on a tour of the Flinders range north of town, spending one night at Oodnadatta, which must have had the worst pub in Australia, which is saying quite a bit.

The O'Grady's returned in May, and we flew to Alice Springs. We planned to fly with a local air service (Canellan) to a variety of remote cattle stations for which the air service was the principal contact with civilization. Unfortunately unseasonal rains made flying impossible, and we spent most of a week in Underdown's Pub, with Alison sleeping in what was called a "meat-safe cot" to protect her from the flies. We did manage a trip to Ayer's Rock with a local prospector, however, and that was a memorable experience.

Still following a long-thought-out plan, we took the narrow-gauge train back to Adelaide. It moved very slowly at the best of times, with its passage marked by the clink of beer bottles being thrown out the window by thirsty Australians. It was raining when we left and we were stopped for several days about midway at the Hamilton River, where the track was laid on the usually dry river bottom. When we eventually crossed it, the water was up to the floor of the vestibule between cars. We were glad to get moving, because being confined to a small compartment with an eighteen-month-old whose diapers needed constant changing (and which we had to wash out in the toilet, which soon ran out of water) was getting old.

We were exhausted by the time we reached Adelaide. We bedded Alison down in a hotel, had two quick brandies, and went out and bought the Harley Griffith still life that hangs in the dining room today. We then took Alison to the dining room for family dinner, but she cried so loudly we were told to leave. The next day we said some quick goodbyes, got in the car, and took off for Melbourne and Sydney. We took the coastal route, which had many interesting stopping places en route—such as Mt. Gambier, where the bath water is blue, and the Dame Nelly Melba Tearoom in the Ottways Forest, where we spent the night after contemplating the kangaroos along the roadway.

In Melbourne we stayed with the defense attaché, Col. Rufus Ramey, and his wife and daughter. They had been with us at Ft. Leavenworth and their son Wheeler, who died during the war, had been a high school friend of mine. Our next stop was Lake's Entrance, where Jeff was conceived, and then up the coast to Sydney. Stopping at a gas station on the outskirts, I asked if they had had much rain. The attendant said, "About six feet." It was a wet year.

Soon after we returned home Jeanne realized that she was pregnant, and we began planning our strategy for getting her to the hospital when the day came. In particular, we worried about getting across the Harbor Bridge in time to get her to the Crown Street Women's Hospital. When the day did come, there was no problem. Jeff arrived handily in March, near the end of our two-year tour.

The last twelve months or so at Sydney I was the consular officer. I had five young Australian women working for me, and we ran the full gamut of consular services. My biggest problem concerned visas. A steady stream of European refugees was leaving China, which was being taken over by the Communists, and coming to Australia. Many of them wanted to go to the United States. The problem was that most of them could not prove their nonimmigrant status. That is, they could not prove that they were going on a visit and would surely return to Australia or some other place outside the United States at the end of their visit. They were, as Mr. Alexander of the Visa Office had told us, considered quota immigrants unless they could prove otherwise and were assigned to a quota according to their place of birth. With rare exceptions it would turn out that their quota was oversubscribed and a wait of years was required before their number would come up and they would be eligible to emigrate to the United States. This meant I had to tell many people they could not have a visa.

The stress of this constant negativism on my part generated steady headaches. When my successor, Art Wortzel, arrived, he was much impressed by the casual way I opened my desk drawer, took out a large bottle of aspirin, popped one into my mouth, and chewed it without bothering to have a drink of water.

At some point in 1950 I decided that I was going nowhere unless I had some language and area specialty. We looked at the post reports from the hard-language areas and decided that the Middle East looked the most interesting and most comfortable. I therefore wrote to the department and said I would like to specialize in Turkish or Arabic but would like a post in the area first. We were pleasantly surprised when the department came back with an assignment to Jerusalem. We were elated and sang "Jerusalem the Golden," not realizing what impact the Palestine problem would have on our lives.

We were scheduled to go to San Francisco by ship (the *Aorangi*), but there was a shipping strike and we had to fly to Honolulu and take a ship from there to San Diego. We left Sydney on a Pan American Stratoliner, which had berths. I made the sacrifice of taking Jeff with me, while Jeanne took Alison into her berth. Alison stayed up all night while Jeff slept like a lamb. We spent several nights in Honolulu and then boarded a Matson liner (the *Lurline*) for San Diego. Screen actor Alan Ladd and his family occupied the cabin across from ours.

We went first to San Francisco by train and from there to Manhattan, Kansas, where I dropped off Jeanne and the kids and continued to Washington for consultation. My departure coincided with the greatest flood in Manhattan's history, and Jeanne and her parents had a miserable time.

I forget most of what transpired during my consultation. Two weeks were normally allotted for that, and I left as soon as I could, went to Manhattan, picked up Jeanne and the kids and took the train to San Antonio. It was a good deal more complicated than it sounds, and the kids added an element of difficulty that I marvel at our accepting. After two or three weeks with Mother in San Antonio, we got back on the train and went to West Point, where we spent a week or two with Bud and Betty before boarding the *La Guardia* in New York. A passenger freighter, most of whose passengers were Jewish, took us to Haifa via Barcelona, Palermo, Naples, and Alexandria.

Arriving in Haifa on September 25, we were met on arrival by FSI classmate John Root, a bachelor, who was given Alison's toilet seat to carry down the gangplank. We had twenty-five pieces of baggage. John drove us up to Jerusalem in a consulate general station wagon, and we marveled at the aridity and severity of the landscape. We had arrived in the Promised Land!

7

Jerusalem

Jerusalem did not disappoint. The light and the air were marvelous. The politics were absorbing, the history fascinating, and the people unforgettable. But we had some difficult days.

The city had been divided into Jordanian and Israeli sectors by the 1948 fighting. The Consulate General's main office was in an attractive old Arab house on the Israeli side, but there was a branch office in another Arab house on the Arab side. The American government did not recognize the sovereignty of either Israel or Jordan over their respective sectors and still honored, at least formally, the UN resolution of 1947 that called for Jerusalem to be a *corpus separatum*, an international city run by the United Nations. Neither Israel nor Jordan accepted this, however, and while both governments permitted foreign states to maintain consuls in Jerusalem and to pass from one sector to the other with little hindrance, they did not recognize the extraterritorial status of the consuls.

Passage between the sectors was at a crossing point called the Mandelbaum Gate, named for a Jewish grocer whose establishment had been on a little plaza that had become a piece of the no-man's land between the two sectors.

The consulate general was a small office that reported directly to the Department of State and was quite independent of our embassies in Tel Aviv and Amman. I was one of two commissioned officers, plus the consul general, S. Roger Tyler. A handsome man with a handsome, strong-willed Swiss wife, Tyler was not what one would call an inspiring leader, and I fear I was not as accommodating as I should have been.

The big issue between us was housing. Initially, Tyler installed us in a large mansion that belonged to an Arab refugee on Balfour Street on the Israeli side of the line. There was plenty of room, but filling the tank of the oil-fired furnace took a month of my pay, and the water supply was unreliable. Not only was the supply from the municipality erratic, but also the storage tank on the roof was full of bullet holes and the pump in the cistern was broken. For some reason we could get neither repaired. The Tylers seemed unable to comprehend just how difficult it was to raise two small children, both still in diapers, without water.

In addition, the Israeli economy was unbelievably austere, and what little was available in the way of consumer goods, including food, was rationed. At the neighborhood grocery store, the only two things we could buy without a ration card were scouring powder and an unidentified canned vegetable. On the other hand, plenty of food and drink was available at moderate prices at a free market on the Jordan side of the line. The Israelis and Jordanians allowed us one grocery run a week, and we were dependent on that supply.

Meanwhile, the department had remodeled and furnished a very nice three- or four-bedroom apartment above the office on the Jordanian side. The water supply was good, servants were available, and grocery shopping was readily accessible. I thought we should be allowed to move into the apartment, but Tyler and his wife wanted it, in addition to the very comfortable quarters they had on the Israeli side, arguing that they needed it for late-night engagements and entertaining those on the Arab side.

Finally, after an exchange of stiff letters, Tyler ceded the Arab-side apartment to us. We moved in as soon as we could and spent a happy fifteen months there. For the first time in our career we had real servants, including a cook, a waiter, and a maid, and the government was paying for the utilities.

Arab Jerusalem was an exciting place in those days. The United Nations Truce Supervisory Organization (UNTSO) was headquartered at Government House. Under UNTSO came the Israel-Jordan Mixed Armistice Commission (MAC), a body staffed by Americans, Belgians, and other international civil servants and to whose meetings the Israelis and Jordanians sent their own representatives. It had the task of investigating border incidents, most of which were caused by Arabs infiltrating in search of lost cattle—or on some less legitimate errand—and Israeli armed retaliation against the village from which they thought the infiltrators had come. Those seeking details can find some of them in General E. L. M. Burns's *Between Arab and Israeli* (London: George Harrap, 1962). Burns was chief of staff of UNTSO from August 1954 until November 1956. The MAC's deliberations reported to us by the UN personnel were often exciting and full of portents of further fighting.

Perhaps the most exciting for us was when our van full of household effects arrived from Haifa at Mandelbaum Gate. In the shade cast by our truck full of belongings, there was a confrontation between the Israelis and the UNTSO officials over a barrel of oil the Israelis were trying to send up to the Hebrew University on Mt. Scopus, well within the Jordan line. The Scopus enclave was supposed to be demilitarized, but the Israelis had armed soldiers there; and upon an initial inspection the barrel appeared to contain either a machine gun or a mortar. We never knew, because the Israelis whisked it away rather than let UNTSO inspect it thoroughly. The altercation over the barrel did not include an exchange of fire but came very close, and our goods were held up for about ten days— although this was partly caused by my failure to call on the chief of police for the Jordanian sector. The barrel incident seems almost comical in retrospect, but it was deadly serious at the time.

The consulate's branch office was perhaps fifty yards from the Mandelbaum Gate, and one of my duties was to arrange for American travelers, mostly tourists, to receive passes permitting them to cross through the Jordanian side on a one-way trip. Except for government officials or other VIPs, the passes were issued for travel in one direction only. The branch office would secure permission from the Jordanians, and the main office across the line would take care of the Israeli permit. Border crossings were usually a fairly routine operation but were a continuing concern. Occasionally, we would confront a crisis involving a nonofficial traveler who was determined to cross in both directions, or whose credentials looked suspect to the Jordanians or Israelis. On one occasion I smuggled an elderly American woman being sued by her husband, an unscrupulous Arab souvenir dealer, across the line in the trunk of our car with the agreement of the attorney general of the West Bank, Sama'an Daoud, who could find no legal way to let her go but very much wanted her gone.

A more common problem was someone wandering across the armistice line into no-man's land and being arrested—or shot—by a sentry. One afternoon I was called to police headquarters, where two Israeli teenagers, a boy and a girl claiming American citizenship, were being held. They maintained their innocence, but neither had a passport, and their claims were dubious. The police lieutenant, whom I knew, said they were both phonies, because they admitted they were Jews but said they were not Israelis. How could a Jew not be an Israeli? I explained that that was quite possible and persuaded him to let me take the kids away. I drove them home, dropped them off, and never heard from them again. I often wondered if they realized how lucky they had been.

Arab Jerusalem was a small town where everyone knew everyone else. It was the sort of place where the telephone operator would tell you that the party you were trying to call had left his office and gone down to the suq (market). If you wanted to find him urgently, you could ask one of the basket boys who hung out at the Damascus Gate to go into the suq and find him. I had it happen to me. The basket boys knew all of us by name.

There was a small Western community: a couple of archeologists, two Western consuls and their staffs, the Anglican bishop and his staff, and officers of UNTSO and the MAC. The social arbiter was Bertha Spafford Vester of the American Colony Hotel, almost the last descendant of the original Americans that had come for the second coming of Christ back in the late nineteenth century. She was joined by an attractive daughter, Anna Grace Lind, a divorcee, who was being pursued by our ambassador to Jordan, the same Joseph Coy Green who told me I had passed the oral exam in 1948. Bertha's competition was Katie Antonious, the widow of George Antonious, author of *The Arab Awakening*, a much-appreciated work on the origins of modern Arab nationalism. One of the daughters of Nimr Pasha, a wealthy Egyptian of Lebanese origin, Katie was a woman of great charm and energy. She arrived on the scene shortly after we did, and her house quickly became the center of social life for Westerners and the English-speaking Palestinian elite.

Alison, at the age of three, was enrolled in the English-run Garden Tomb School. Westerners, Protestants in particular, have often been skeptical of the location of Christ's tomb in the Church of the

Holy Sepulchre. It does not look at all like what one imagines the grave in the garden of Joseph of Arimathea to have been. While staying in the old city of Jerusalem in the late nineteenth century, Charles "Chinese" Gordon, who subsequently died in Khartoum, saw outside the city wall what he thought must have been the true site of Calvary and the tomb, and one Protestant group has long maintained the site as an attractive alternative to the gloomy and metropolitan setting of the Sepulchre. There is a tomb cut into the rock of a low cliff, with a groove in front in which a large round stone, like a millstone, could be rolled back and forth to open and close the aperture. One can easily visualize the Marys coming here on the morning of the third day amongst the olive trees and flowers. The established archeologists have been skeptical of the Garden Tomb's claim, but amateurs of evangelical persuasion are still trying to dig in the nearby mound that Gordon thought was Golgotha, hoping to find the Ark of the Covenant.

Several other Western children Alison's age also attended the school. I don't think they learned a great deal, but one could wish for such a pleasant and possibly sacred school everywhere one moved.

A new Chevrolet Belair, the nicest car we ever had, arrived in Jerusalem a month or so after our own arrival, paid for by the tidy profit of selling our Canadian Ford in Sydney. We traveled a good deal in it. Our first trip was to Beirut to buy baby food, unavailable on either side of the line in Jerusalem. We stopped en route in Damascus and visited a couple from our FSI course on their first tour. They introduced us to another young officer and his wife, who were planning to study Arabic at FSI but were very critical of that facility's ability to teach, arguing it could not even teach people how to say "good morning" in a way that was understandable to Arabs.

Beirut was everything Jerusalem was not. Everything imaginable was for sale. There were good restaurants and nice hotels, and the place was humming with life. On another occasion we left the children in the care of their nursemaid, a young Palestinian woman named Huda, and used a three-day weekend to drive to Baghdad.

Baghdad was the opposite of Beirut. We drove straight through, arriving in the middle of a morning sandstorm that wiped my front license plate clean. I took one look at our hotel room's view and said to myself that if ever assigned there I would resign. Baghdad was a dull-and-grimy-looking place, but our embassy personnel seemed to be enjoying it. They were not bothered by the sandstorm, which had been only a one on a scale of ten, and they did not seem to realize just how depressing the main drag, Rashid Street, looked. We returned to Jerusalem and its bright air, glad to be able to breathe again and persuaded that we were most fortunate. Of all the places Bush could have chosen to liberate, it is unfortunate that he picked one as unappealing as Baghdad.

Our grandest expedition, taken in the fall of 1952, was to Palmyra and Aleppo. We also did a good deal of local exploring around Jerusalem. We visited holy sites with the Franciscan monks of the Pontifical Mission to Palestine and the keeper of the Garden of Gethsemane, learning a good deal about the Bible and Biblical sites.

When we were assigned to Jerusalem, I knew nothing about the Arab-Israeli problem and the merits of the Arab case. Because of my wartime experience I had a good deal of sympathy for the Jews, and I assumed the Israelis were the virtuous ones. It was not until I witnessed the misery of the Palestinian refugees that I began to wonder. I had been able to read two relevant books before arriving in Jerusalem, one by an economist and the other Arthur Koestler's *Promise and Fulfillment*. Although Koestler opened my eyes to the inherent contradictions of the unfortunate Balfour Declaration, neither book had anything good to say about the Arabs, and I had no idea what they were like. It took years before I realized that their claims of injustice were more than justified. Nearly sixty years later, I was more convinced than ever that there would be no peace in the Holy Land until the Palestinian Arabs are adequately compensated for what they lost in 1948 and until they have a viable state of their own.

My education began with the Arabs I met on the Jordan side of the line, largely through meeting educated Arabs at Katie Antonious's house. I found them vastly more civilized than I had imagined, and a good deal more polite and hospitable than the Israelis. I also began to study Arabic, paying from my own pocket for a high school teacher named Hafez Kemal to come by for an hour several mornings a week and begin teaching me at an elementary level. He was patient and good-humored, and by the time I left Jerusalem I could carry on a simple conversation, ask directions, and bargain in the suq.

In the fall of 1952, I applied for Arabic language and area training at the Foreign Service Institute. I understood that I might be considered for a course starting a year later. This would mean a two-year tour in Jerusalem, which was fine with us. Then, without warning, a telegram in March 1953 advised that a new course would be starting immediately and asked if I wanted to join it. I did, and Tyler, in one of his rare gracious moves toward me, agreed to let me go. Perhaps he thought he was doing himself a favor. It took several weeks to make arrangements for departure and to wind up office matters, and the class had been in session for almost a month by the time I arrived in Washington. Because of my studies in Jerusalem, I was still ahead of the others.

There were five of us in the Arabic class. We all took Arabic names that we used in conversation, and I was Abu Jeff. Four stayed on for the nearly two years of intensive instruction, including ten months in Washington followed by a year in Beirut. Our initial instruction was in Syrian colloquial, but before leaving Washington we started learning the written language, which is quite different from the spoken. Its grammar is wondrously complicated and I never did learn it well. The FSI method, developed by the same linguists who developed the Army's intensive language program during the war, consisted of intensive drilling in phrases and sentences of the spoken language by our three native Damascene instructors until the phrases came automatically, as they do in normal speech. This went on for the entire day, with occasional breaks. It was learning by rote, which did not work for everyone, but did for me. We all worked hard, however, and attained a reasonable level of competence by the time the course was complete.

Halfway through the Washington portion of the class, I received a letter from the department informing me that I had placed in the bottom 10 percent of the FSO Class 5. Two more years of the same and I would be out. This was catastrophic. Being singled out like this was hard to overcome. Someone had to be at the bottom, and the board was inevitably influenced by past records. I had not realized how unfavorable Tyler's report on me would look to others, but when I met a senior officer who reviewed such cases, it transpired that Tyler had a history of writing unfavorable reports and I was not in such bad shape after all. I still suffered a good deal of anxiety, however. Establishing a good rating was difficult when being graded by the non-FSO supervising linguists at FSI, and I was greatly relieved when I was finally promoted to Class 4 two years later.

In February 1954 we all went to Beirut for the last year of our course on one of the *Four Aces*, passenger-freighters that used to make the run from New York to Beirut and back with stops at other Mediterranean ports. They were not luxurious but comfortable, and the three-week trip was a nice vacation for everyone.

The Beirut embassy had grown enormously since we had last seen it in 1952. An AID mission had arrived, and there had been a population explosion. We took the ground floor of a brand-new modernistic duplex out in the country at Tell al-Za'atar (Hill of Wild Thyme). Our address was listed as "between the soap factory and the gas station in Sin al-Fil (The Elephant's Tooth)." We were surrounded by fields and had a lovely view, but—our apparent nemesis—we had a water problem. We had to haul water in buckets from a well fifty yards away after a storm washed out the water main, making the supply irregular. It took seven buckets to fill a washing machine, and we had two small children.

A scientific linguist ran the FSI School in Beirut, while an anthropologist ran the area studies program. Our language instructors were Lebanese and Palestinians, and we ended up speaking a dialect that we called Levantine, which sounded like Lebanese to other Arabs. We were encouraged to audit courses at the American University, and I audited an archeology course and one on the Ottoman Empire. The atmosphere was congenially academic. We had no diplomatic privileges and had to buy our cigarettes and liquor on the open market. This was no great hardship. Jeanne stopped smoking, which was good because she became pregnant with our third child.

Our family was growing quite nicely. We put Alison, now five, in an English-language school in Ras Beirut at first. We were so appalled at what happened to her English, however, that we moved her to College Protestant, the premier French language school in

West Beirut. The first day was traumatic for Alison when I dropped her off. It broke my heart to leave her crying, but she survived. Three-year-old Jeff, meanwhile, was left behind to play in the sandbox underneath the kitchen window at Tell al-Za'atar. This was an unhappy arrangement for Jeff, who was teased by the daughter of the couple upstairs.

Well before our year in Beirut drew to a close, we began to negotiate our next assignment, and I opted for Amman to take advantage of my language skills.

8

Amman

I liked the idea of going to Amman because it would enable us to complete our visits to archeological sites on the East bank of the Jordan and in particular to visit Machaerus, Herod's palace, where Salome danced. In addition, it was more comfortable than some places I had heard about, like Khartoum or Basra, and the job was a good one.

When it came time for me to leave for Amman, Jeanne was about a month short of delivering our third child, who turned out to be Jill. Jeanne remained with Alison and Jeff in Beirut, where the medical facilities were better, until she delivered. I drove to Amman and lodged temporarily with two AID officers who were renting a three-bedroom house. Azmi, the cook, waited until I had finished breakfast on the morning of February 4, 1955, to inform me that my wife had delivered a girl. I hopped into the car and took off for Beirut, stopping to receive the condolences of the Syrian border guards that it was only a girl and finding Jeanne unhappy that I had taken so long to get there.

To make room for Jill, I paid to have someone enclose with glass the porch of a two-bedroom stone house with a small garden. That work was still in progress when I brought Jeanne and the kids to Amman later in February. Jeanne was horrified at the workmen, who tramped though our bedroom before we got up in order to get at the porch and who cooed over Jill, sleeping in her basket, just as her siblings had. This basket was one made to order in Sydney, equipped with a movable frame for a mosquito net. There was room for it and a bassinette on the unheated porch. Indeed, the whole house was unheated except for a fireplace and several smelly kerosene heaters, and Amman could be quite cold at night. For the house I paid a year's rent in advance—a thousand dinar, as I recall, which I borrowed from the Arab Bank. We remained in this house for over a year before moving into a much larger house when the departure of the British made more desirable places available.

The American Embassy was located in a small house that had first been rented, I believe, by Wells Stabler, who was sent up from Jerusalem to become chargé d'affaires and open the first U.S. legation in Amman in 1948. There were four offices on the ground floor—for the ambassador, the deputy chief of mission, the economic officer, and the political officer. Our telephone operator and receptionist occupied what must have been the living room, and our secretaries and code clerks used a couple of rooms at the rear of the building. My own office was tiny, with room for a desk, a filing cabinet, and a chair for visitors. I had two local employees working for me who served as translators and interpreters of the news and who were with our administrative offices in an adjoining house. Fifty yards off to the left was the consular section and, eventually, two CIA men and a military attaché in another small house. The AID mission occupied a larger building across the street. The U.S. Information Service library was in town and was unsafe during times of stress and violence.

The ambassador, Lester Mallory, was a rough-hewn man who had been an agricultural attaché and whose principal area of expertise was agriculture. He was intelligent, direct, and honest, and I liked him very much. His wife Eleanor, a handsome Mexican woman, insisted on strict observance of social protocols, but she was a generous and lively person whose talents were, I fear, wasted on Amman.

The embassy routine started with a staff meeting every morning at which I, after having conferred with my two employees, would report the local news, and we would discuss what action was required. We did not have a great deal to work with. Our aid program was called Point Four, from President Truman's inaugural speech in 1949, where he mentioned his intention to start a program of technical and economic aid to the less developed countries. The aid director had a good deal of wisdom and a keen understanding of human nature, but the program was modest, with no money for major projects of the sort the Jordanians expected from us.

Jordan was created by the British in the wake of World War I and remained under substantial British influence until 1956, when King Hussein took everyone by surprise. The symbol of British authority over and protection for Jordan was Brigadier John Bagot Glubb. Known as Glubb Pasha, he ran the army, the senior officers of which were largely British and whose loyalty to the throne was never in doubt, at least in the minds of the Americans. The British commanded because they always had and because they gave an annual subvention of £10 million, or roughly $30 million, for the force's upkeep. It was into the house of Colonel Leslie Toogood, the army's adjutant, that we moved when the British left. Toogood's lovely blonde wife Thelma had been injured in the King David Hotel in Jerusalem when the militant Zionist underground organization, the Irgun, blew it up in 1946. It later transpired that Toogood, who had been in charge of personnel, was the only one of the British officers fully covered by the pension system he had designed. The Jordanian army was called the Arab Legion, a romantic name that reflected the exotic uniforms of some units and the exclusive nature of its recruitment. It was not very large, but it was the most effective of the Arab armies.

Amman, as befits the capital of a quasi-colony, was remarkably clean and well ordered. The traffic police were obeyed and there was little crime. Although it occupied an ancient site, its population was relatively new, composed of Palestinian refugees, the descendants of Circassian and Chechen settlers, and townspeople from other communities east of the Jordan, mostly very poor. Unemployment was high, and wages were very low. The kingdom's official name, "The Happy Hashemite Kingdom of the Jordan," was a bit of a travesty.

As political officer I was in the thick of the collapse of the British position in Jordan from the beginning, with the ill-fated British effort in the fall of 1955 to persuade King Hussein to join the Baghdad Pact, which inspired a rash of violent demonstrations. For the first ones, my office was the embassy's nerve center. I did what I thought was a masterful job of collating the various bits of information that kept flying in by one means or another. The world press descended on Amman in a small way, and we felt we were in the middle of historic changes. The second series of demonstrations was more serious and more dangerous. I was unable to keep up with what was happening, and my self-esteem underwent a sobering adjustment.

Then Hussein kicked out Glubb Pasha, catching everyone flat-footed. The British officer in charge of intelligence, a frequent contact of ours on matters of internal security, was basking in the sun down at Jericho when it happened. He was out of the country within a matter of days, and his British colleagues followed soon after, none too happy to find out about their pension situations. Glubb was not a popular figure with the Palestinians, who blamed him for the poor performance of the Arabs in the 1948 war. A rather saintly man with no malice in him, Glubb and his British colleagues had in fact created the only Arab army that could fight its way out of a paper bag. His thanks for this was summary dismissal. He was called to the prime minister's office and given twenty-four hours to pack his belongings.

When Glubb got to the airplane waiting to whisk him away, the royal chamberlain drove up hurriedly with a signed photo of the king in a silver frame. Everyone thought that pretty gross of Hussein, but Glubb seemed to appreciate the gesture and never spoke of Hussein's ingratitude. The causes of Glubb's dismissal were many, but in particular he was the victim of a plot by Ali Abu Nuwwar, a perennial cad on the Jordanian scene, who was military attaché in Paris and who convinced the king, after the disaster of the Baghdad Pact riots, that he should get rid of Glubb.

All of the knowledgeable diplomats in Amman were saying that Hussein could not last six months. People in Washington didn't have the time of day for him. Poor Hussein, who was always so grave and polite, perhaps too polite for his own good, must have been bored out of his skull at low-level Washington meetings. The Arab nationalists were going to get rid of him. In Egypt, Nasser was delighted, and disclaimed, correctly I think, all responsibility. Our prediction regarding Hussein was off by about a year, however. He rode the nationalist tiger rather well until the late winter of 1956–1957, when it became apparent that the Baathists, with the help of Ali Abu Nuwwar, were going to get him. Egypt, Syria, and Saudi

Arabia had promised to make up the British subsidy but had not in fact done so, and Prime Minister Suleiman Nabulsi had proven a weak leader who was letting the king down badly.

At this point he turned to the United States for help, naturally using the CIA man on the spot. The tide of decision to help what Secretary Foster Dulles called the Brave Young King, or BYK, was turned in part by an excellent memorandum prepared by Charlotte Morehouse in the Bureau of Intelligence and Research (INR), who demonstrated that if we did not do something to save Jordan, it would not disappear peacefully but would have its carcass contested by Israelis and Arabs. Dulles decided to send the first $10 million on a Saturday morning, when all the AID bottleneckers were home. Thus began what was known briefly as Operation BOGH-AKYPU (Be of Good Heart and Keep Your Pecker Up). By the end of the fiscal year we had sent him another $20 million, $10 million of which Eisenhower agreed to while on the golf course, and we embarked on a military assistance program. At one point we even got the president to declare that the independence and territorial integrity of Jordan were of vital interest to the United States. Those were the days. We also began the program of economic stabilization which looked well on its way to making Jordan economically viable until the 1967 war reversed all that.

The period of uncertainty about King Hussein and the future of the British in Jordan was a time of much tension. The kids had to spend a good deal of time at home because of the periodic curfews invoked to cope with the episodic violence. During curfews, nonofficials, meaning families and servants, could not leave the house for shopping or school or visits to doctors or for any other purpose, making life quite difficult. If one was out on the street, personal safety was a major concern, particularly when one had to transit downtown Amman as I did every day going to and from the office. On one occasion two of us had to thread our way through a mob at the center of town to rescue some Americans stranded in the Philadelphia Hotel, much sobered by the awareness that if something snapped we would be at the mob's mercy with no one to rescue us.

Enoch Duncan, the economic officer, and I relieved the tension somewhat by composing songs for the occasion. One, to the tune of "Hopping Down the Bunny Trail" went:

I'm a hap-hap-happy Hashemite,
Throwing rocks with all my might
Hippity hoppity, Glubb has gone away.

Another, to "Molly Malone," went:

In Amman's fair city, and sure 'tis no pity,
'Twas there that I threw my first stone as a boy.
Through streets wide and narrow, the British we'd harrow,
Shouting Yallah! and Imshi! Glubb Pasha must go!

We did not perform these songs in public. The atmosphere was much too tense for that. For entertainment, however, we could listen to Richard Sanger, our deputy chief of mission (DCM), who liked to reduce complicated events to simple formulas that he would then go around repeating portentously to anyone who would listen. First, with the second series of demonstrations he proclaimed, "They're attacking targets of the West." When Glubb left, he announced, "Hussein has packed his crown jewels with Glubb's baggage." I do not know whether Hussein had any crown jewels to pack. In fact, I don't think he had a crown.

With passage of time Jordan became much more a front-page country than it had been in my day. There was a remarkable effusion of sentiment over King Hussein's death in 1999. Yitzhak Rabin's widow said Rabin had "adored" Hussein. Armin Meyer, JFK's ambassador to Lebanon, described how he and the king were radio amateurs together. Jim Baker talked about the Plucky Little King. Tom Oliphant from Public Television told us the Congress "loved" him. President Clinton thought of him as a friend and mentor and said their contacts were among the high points of his presidency. Wise, skillful, charismatic, giant, heroic, courageous, you name it, the accolade was used. The Israelis sent a mammoth funeral delegation that included such nonfriends of Jordan as Ariel Sharon and Yitzhak Shamir, bringing to mind the Arab saying "The murderer marches in the funeral procession." Everyone agreed that he was a great friend of the United States and that he was universally admired in this country, but it had not always been that way.

But what did being a good boy get him? The Israelis were forever saying that if the Arabs would just sit down and talk, everything was negotiable, except territory and Jerusalem and the refugees, of course. What was the payoff when Hussein began talking to the Israelis? A shotgun, a peace treaty, and a big funeral delegation. All this American love did not get him an inch of his territory back. Our failure to solve the Palestine problem has remained our major Near East policy failure of the past fifty years, and the quality of our hypocrisy in that regard has not changed much. The comments about reducing our presence were a reaction to our overstuffed AID mission, which became the object of mob violence before the year was out.

Things in Amman settled down a bit after Glubb left. As spring wore on followed quickly by the summer of 1957, I began to have trouble getting going in the morning. I followed the advice of some colleague and began starting the day with a shot of brandy, which was the worst thing I could have done. I tried to carry on as normal, but after a few weeks it became clear that I was actually quite sick. The Jordanian doctor who came to look at me could find nothing specific and speculated that I had sand fly fever. Meanwhile I had a series of dreams that made me fear I was losing my mind. I was quite relieved one morning to look in the mirror and see that the whites of my eyes had turned yellow. I had hepatitis. Eventually a new doctor, an American-trained Jordanian, came to see me and ordered my evacuation to the AUB Hospital in Beirut. I left Amman by air with a thoroughly jaundiced view of the place that has never been fully supplanted. Jeanne had to "pack, pay, and follow" with the children, reaching Beirut several weeks after I did. I was due for home leave, and we all embarked for New York on one of the Four Aces of the American Export Line. We had a pleasant trip home, went out to California to spend Christmas with Mother, and then returned to Washington. I was not sent back to Amman but was assigned to the Office of Near East Affairs (NEA) as assistant to Donald Bergus on the Israel-Jordan desk.

9

Washington 1957–1961: NEA and AFN

On returning to Washington, our first priority was to find a place to live. Jeanne's father was on a temporary assignment at the Department of Agriculture, so we stayed briefly with the Jaccards in the Falls Church area before settling in a modern, four-bedroom house made of plywood and glass in a nearby development named Raymondale. We were surrounded by dozens of other young families with limited incomes and government jobs, paid $21,000 for the house, and financed it with a 2.5 percent loan guaranteed by the Veterans Administration. The house was well designed and pleasant, and we enjoyed it.

Alison and Jeff went to the Walnut Hill School next door. In time, Jill went to a nursery school down the hill on the edge of the development. All of them had friends their own age and plenty of possibilities for play and socializing.

Getting to work was less pleasant, however. There was no suitable public transportation to the Department of State. I joined a car pool, but it took about forty-five minutes each way, some days longer. Originally there were two other officers, neither of whom had any connection with NEA. Eventually three or four other Arabists joined us in the neighborhood, and we held monthly meetings, with our wives, in which we practiced Arabic on each other.

Our office hours were long and often prolonged by emergencies of one kind or another. I usually arrived home after dark. Jill in her pajamas would be waiting for me by the glass door, jumping with excitement when the car pulled in the driveway. Our evenings were pretty quiet. We had no TV until late in our stay, and we were too tired to do much beyond the dishes and bed.

Jeanne mostly stayed at home, taking care first of Jill and then of Richard, who was born on May 5, 1958. Well along in our stay she entered a cooking class that changed our lives forever. Never a bad cook, Jeanne became very good. We have long praised Mme. Petro Colonna for the enlightenment she brought.

In 1957, the coverage of the Bureau of Near East and African Affairs (NEA) stretched from India to Egypt and included Greece and Turkey as well. It did not include North Africa and the colonial possessions of our NATO allies, France, Britain, and Belgium. The Bureau of African Affairs, which eventually embraced all of Africa except Egypt, was not established until about 1958. Greece and Turkey were eventually put in the Bureau of European Affairs (EUR).

The Office of Near East Affairs (NE) was composed of the director and his deputy, an economic section, and four country desks. Each desk had an officer-in-charge (OIC) and one or more assistants known as desk officers. The four desks were Arabian Peninsula, including Iraq; Egypt and Sudan; Syria and Lebanon; and Israel and Jordan, where I was desk officer under Donald Bergus.

An accomplished bureaucrat, Bergus was born in 1920 and had served in a variety of Arab posts, including Baghdad, Jeddah, and Beirut, and had completed two sessions of Arabic training. But I did not have the impression he thought of himself as an Arabist. His command of the language was limited. He was a jovial fellow, but our relationship was not always happy. I found myself occupied almost exclusively with Jordan, while he enjoyed dealing with the Israelis. We stayed out of each other's way. The Suez crisis was not yet resolved, and it was a fascinating time. I was very busy.

In the spring of 1957, King Hussein decided to throw in his lot with us, and I was once again deeply involved in Operation BOGH-AKYPU. My function was to do the bureaucratic legwork needed to give substance to the policy decisions our superiors took with regard to supporting Jordan, including drafting papers and getting them cleared regarding budgetary support, military assistance, technical assistance with transportation, and public information. (A more detailed description of what we did can be found in chapter 7 of *The Middle East and the United States*, David Lesch, editor [Westview Press, 1999]).

My most notable accomplishment was to do the complicated paperwork and consultation that led to the decision to fund the East Ghor irrigation project in the Jordan Valley. This involved diversion of water from the Yarmouk River and was all that came out of the Eric Johnston plan for unified development of the Jordan River waters.

Early in 1957 King Saud of Saudi Arabia paid a state visit to Washington, and I was one of the interpreters. I was temporarily assigned to the Arabian Peninsula desk, and my first task was to write a speech for President Eisenhower to give on King Saud's arrival at National Airport. I was told not to worry too much over what I wrote, because the wording would be changed up the line. The important thing to do was to prepare a piece of paper for consideration. I was much surprised then, to hear all of my words uttered verbatim by the president on greeting the king.

The Saudi party was lodged at Blair House, and I was assigned as interpreter to ride there from the airport with General Maxwell Taylor, Army chief of staff, and two Saudi princes, Fahd and Sultan, both handsome young men ready to go out on the town if allowed to do so. Fahd later became king and Sultan Minister of Defense. The princes commented on how impressive the airport was, and General Taylor responded that we were running out of air space above it. The princes could not understand this, since the sky was limitless. We had similar exchanges as we went up the George Washington Parkway and across Memorial Bridge, passing the monument of "Ibrahim" Lincoln, passing a high school band with well-proportioned black drum majorettes who caught Sultan's eye, and then up past the Treasury, where General Taylor commented that we did not like the secretary of the Treasury because he took our money. This was hard to explain, and the princes looked uneasy and seemed to fear that Taylor was being mutinous.

During the weeklong visit I was assigned as interpreter to Prince Musa'id bin Abd al-Rahman, a diminutive fellow who was head of the *diwan* of complaints, or ombudsman. I interpreted for him and Vice President Nixon, Senator Alexander Wiley, Secretary of Commerce Sinclair Weeks, and Secretary of State Dulles. Prince Musa'id suffered patiently through my efforts at translation and did not seem to mind, but he gave me no present when he left.

I never had much luck with that sort of thing. Neither did the other FSO interpreters. The only one of us who received a present was Bob Sherwood, who was not even an Arabist and was not assigned to anyone. He received a gold watch, perhaps on the recommendation of the Saudi embassy, with which he had worked on arrangements for the visit. On his departure for Casablanca some months later, he was disappointed because he had wanted to go to black Africa but was to be rewarded with the title of consul instead. I wrote the following lines, my first effort as poet laureate of NE.

> Sherwood, Sherwood, must you go
> Far to the north of Fernando Po
> To Dar al-Bayda and Muhammad Cinque?
> With Saudi watch and consul's rank?

When Syria and Egypt united in 1958 and called themselves the United Arab Republic, or UAR, Jordan and Iraq responded by forming the Arab Union, with its capital in Baghdad. This necessitated a number of organizational changes. Our embassy in Amman was downgraded, as our embassy in Damascus had been when the UAR made Cairo its capital. The Syria-Lebanon desk was abolished. Syrian Affairs were amalgamated with Egypt, and Lebanon was twinned with Israel, while Jordan and Iraq formed a new desk. I went over to the Jordan-Iraq desk, where Bill Lakeland, who had been in the economic office, was made officer-in-charge. We both had a good deal of learning to do, but things went along pretty well until July 14, 1958, when there was a violent coup in Baghdad. The royal family and the prime minister were murdered, and an unknown army colonel assumed power.

It happened that Lakeland was on leave in Vermont at the time, but he cut his leave short and returned a couple of days later. I had the busiest days of my life until he returned. Late on the 14th, the decision was taken to land troops in Lebanon to forestall potential repercussions there, and a new era began. Our reaction reflected our initial assumption that the Baghdad coup had been the work of the UAR, which was not the case. This was the overleaf of our general lack of insight into what was going on in Iraq at the time.

I stayed on the Jordan-Iraq desk until late in 1958, when I moved to the Libyan desk in the office of North African Affairs (AFN), part of the new Bureau of African Affairs (AF). Working for the office director, Bill Porter, was an education. He was a master of bureaucratic skills and knew better than anyone how to get things that seemed impossible done.

A few weeks before I came onboard with Libya, generous quantities of oil were discovered there, and our view of Libya changed dramatically. Heretofore, it had no marketable resources to speak of. Esparto grass, cuttlefish bone, and World War II scrap were its only exports. It had been dependent on some modest budgetary support from the British and the Americans to pay the cost of government, something like $6,500 a year from the United States and less from the British. Our principal—in fact our only—interest in Libya prior to the discovery of oil was Wheelus Air Base at Tripoli and a number of bombing ranges nearby. These, we were told by the Pentagon, were vital to the maintenance of a functioning air force in Europe, where the weather was so poor that our Air Force pilots could not do the training and practice needed to keep themselves in fighting trim. These were performed instead at Wheelus, and planes landed and took off there every few minutes throughout the day and into the night.

Wheelus was a major nuisance to the Tripolitanians, and it marred their Arab image, leading other Arabs to think that Libya was too closely allied with the West. To compensate for the nuisance and the image problem, the Libyans wanted us to pay additional rent for Wheelus. But the Pentagon assumed a lofty demeanor and said that Wheelus was Libya's contribution to the defense of the free world, which included Libya, and the Libyans should be grateful. The Air Force had an elaborate community relations program of the Rotary Club sort but would not pay any rent. This was a matter of principle. My major accomplishment in two years on the desk was to get that changed. By pushing the paperwork up the ladder of different offices, with Bill Porter's initial guidance, to the National Security Council, we got a presidential decision to pay a modest yearly rental. This guaranteed our tenure at Wheelus until the Qadhafi coup in 1969.

An important question in our policy deliberations became how much money Libya would earn from oil. It soon became clear that its reserves were very large and, based on what I was told by people in the oil industry, I estimated in one paper in 1960 that the Libyan government would have an annual income of $600 million from oil in a few years. The CIA representative at the Planning Committee meeting where the paper was discussed scoffed at this, but it turned out that I had grossly underestimated. This did not become apparent until much later, however, and the decision to pay rent was based on the assumption that a modest sum would be important to the Libyans. It was for awhile, thanks to the importance King Idris attached to his relationship with the British and the Americans.

Soon after taking the job I was allowed an orientation trip to Libya. It was timed to coincide with the first public appearance of the newly designated crown prince, Hasan al-Rida. King Idris had been concerned, along with the rest of us, that he had no heir. His wife had had a hysterectomy, at Wheelus in fact, and a new wife recruited by the Egyptians did not appeal to him. Hasan al-Rida was a distant relative who had some claim to royal status. A very passive-looking young man, he radiated no personality whatever, and his presentation caused almost audible disappointment by the crowd. It was just as well that he never succeeded to the throne.

Our position in Libya rested very much on our relationship with King Idris who, in spite of his advanced age and mild looks, could rule with an iron fist when needed and who saw his relationship with the Americans and British as an important guarantee of his own security. He wanted nothing to disrupt that relationship. Thanks to him Libya was one Arab country that, in spite of public demonstrations against the United States, did not break relations with us over the Egyptian accusation that we had participated in the Israeli attack of June 5, 1967.

The Libyan desk was not a position of great importance in the foreign affairs agencies, but it was fun to be the only person who knew anything about the country and to work for people who were friendly and content to let me watch what was happening and tell them what to do about it. Libya was just emerging from its long colonial tutelage, and it would be a long time before it assumed any importance on the world stage. That happened only when Qadhafi the troublemaker came along ten years after I left the desk. Though eccentric, he seemed not to have been a lunatic, in spite of Egyptian claims to the contrary.

Among the unforgettable events during this period was the death of Pop Goode, the senior American officer at Oflag 64. He had retired from the army and for a number of years run the Soldiers' Home in Washington, where Jeanne and I had visited him and his wife. We attended his funeral at Arlington, where he had been one of the officers at my father's funeral some twenty years earlier.

This was an exciting time to be in Washington. The Kennedys were a great change from the Eisenhowers, and Kennedy swept out or altered many of the fixtures of his predecessor's administration. The most important of these was the system for coordinating policy decisions among the various agencies through a set of committees and boards that led to presentation of coordinated recommendations to the National Security Council for final approval. One of these organs was the Operations Coordinating Board, or OCB, which was constantly taking our time for meetings to discuss policy recommendations going up to the White House. Early in his administration Kennedy abolished the OCB. We all rejoiced, but policy coordination has been a problem ever since.

By late 1960, it was time for me to move on. After a few false starts, including abortive assignments to Khartoum and Libya, I was assigned as political officer at Beirut under Ambassador Robert McClintock. I spent the first three months of 1961 taking a refresher in Arabic at the FSI. I worked with a couple of tutors and spent a lot of time reading and memorizing. At the conclusion I received an S-4 R-4 rating, meaning that I was fluent in both speaking and reading. I was told that I was the first non-native speaker to do this at the FSI. A colleague disputes this, but I am certain that my recollection is correct. After the Arabic refresher, I took the three-month French course, which Jeanne also joined for a while. I emerged with a lower grade than I had obtained in Arabic, although I could read French better than Arabic. A precise rating system for language competence remains to be developed.

In the spring of 1961, we sold our house for a tidy profit and took off with the children on one of the big liners, with a new Ford Falcon station wagon in the hold. We spent a few days in France, then it was on to Rome and eventually Naples, where, after a day on Capri, we boarded one of the Four Aces for Beirut, arriving there some four or five days later. I have recorded a more precise itinerary, not because it is of general interest, but so that our children will be able to tell their children what giant journeys they took in the olden days and maybe take a sentimental journey themselves some day, although none of them is likely to remember any of this early trip.

10

Beirut

Our second tour in Beirut, though not without problems, was the most fun of any of our assignments. The Lebanese economy was booming, Americans were popular, the Lebanese were hospitable, and the social life was frenetic. The Arab-Israel issue was in the icebox, and internal tensions were minimal. We met and came to know a good many people whose company we enjoyed and who remained friends. We lived in an apartment off Rue Verdun with a view of the sea and which in retrospect was one of the nicer places we lived in. It belonged to a merchant named Zaki Soubra, who lived on one of the upper floors along with a couple of other American families.

Alison and Jill were enrolled in the Collège Protestant, a French school, where Richard eventually followed. Jeff went first to the Italian boys' school and later to the International College, an American-run boys' primary and secondary school. The Italian school had a Boy Scout troop to which Jeff belonged, but other than that we were spared much in the way of extracurricular activities. We shared a small cabin at the beach, where we went often, and we did good deal of picnicking. We made expeditions to sites of historic interest, of which there were many in Lebanon: Crusader castles at Sidon, Beaufort, Crac des Chevaliers, and Qulayla; Roman temples at Baalbek; and the sights at Damascus and Aleppo. I fear those trips did not make much impression on the kids, who seemed immune to history.

I never met Ambassador McClintock, who left Beirut just before we arrived and went on to be ambassador to Argentina and then Venezuela. He was succeeded by Armin Meyer, who presented credentials in January 1962. I had known him as deputy director of NE. Although he was someone who could talk only about work and was not very exciting, I learned a good deal from him. His deputy, Evan Wilson, was a bit of a stuffed shirt but a very decent person with a great deal of useful knowledge about the Foreign Service and the conduct of foreign relations. The Wilsons and the Meyers did not get along, but we, on the other hand, found the Wilsons very congenial and became great friends.

The political section in Beirut was larger than Amman's. There was a chief and a deputy plus two or three secretaries, a geographic attaché, and an UNRWA affairs officer. UNRWA, the United Nations Relief and Works Agency for Palestinian refugees, was headquartered in Beirut, and the director was an American who would talk at great length on any occasion. Across the hall was the CIA station, which was included in what we called the greater political section. The station chief was Edgar Applewhite, an urbane man with a busy intellect. A number of these men have written interesting books since then.

When I was assigned to Beirut, I understood that I was to be chief of the political section, but arrived to find that I was working under the genial direction of a Turkish specialist who knew very little about the Arab world. We got along well. When he left after six months or so, I assumed full charge. My deputy was David Korn. The ambassador, who spoke no foreign language, brought him on as a French translator. The result was a most uncomfortable relationship for me, in which Korn would go with Ambassador Meyer to see the president of the republic, General Fuad Chehab, and was party to their deliberations, while I was not. Korn thus took a condescending attitude toward my contacts, which were of lesser importance than his, and it was hard to be civil toward him.

I would like to mention something significant I did in Beirut, but nothing comes to mind. Political work in Lebanon involved calling on many people and receiving many calls in return. There were many notables to be cultivated, many memorial services to attend, many cups of coffee to be drunk and meals to be consumed.

Roughly, my area of responsibility was the lesser Muslim notables and Christians who were on the outs with the regime. I was much aided in my task by Halim Maamari, our chief local employee, who had been an official of the Ministry of Interior and who knew everybody when they were something else. He could be difficult, and many of the junior local employees disliked him; but I found him indispensable.

One of the last calls I made in 1961 before taking Jeanne to Amman and Jerusalem for New Year's was on Abdallah Saadeh, the intellectual leader of the SSNP or PPS, the Syrian Socialist Nationalist Party, which staged an abortive coup on New Year's Eve while we were in Amman. I was always surprised that the Lebanese authorities made no connection between my visit to him and the coup attempt, although it had been a simple courtesy call in which we had a very interesting conversation about the unreliability of pigeon fanciers, among other things, and I had no inkling of what he was planning. Many years later I learned from one of Halim's friends that Saadeh had been planning to put Jawad Boulos of Zghorta-Ehden in the presidency in place of General Chehab. Boulos had spent the night of the coup attempt waiting to be summoned. He was an intelligent, handsome historian, but he would have made a lousy president.

Beirut was experiencing what seems in retrospect to have been a golden age. It was a thriving center of international finance, thanks to the permissive Lebanese banking laws. You could not swing a cat without hitting a foreign businessman, often accompanied by his family, come to live in comfort, or even luxury, while Daddy made money selling trucks to Arabs in the desert. There were extremes of wealth and poverty, but even the poor were better off than their contemporaries in most of the Arab world. The quality of life as measured by such things as literacy and death rates was the highest in the region. Lebanon was also a favorite summer resort of wealthy Arabs, who could leave their families in mountain villages, reasonably sure that they would be protected and comfortable, while Daddy lived it up in the nightclub suq in Beirut.

Hanging over this paradise, however, was the shadow of the Palestinian refugee problem created in 1948 by Israel's refusal to let the 750,000 refugees, who had either been expelled by the Israeli army or had fled the fighting voluntarily, return to their homes in areas under its control. My colleagues and I thought at the time that if this problem were not somehow solved there would eventually be an explosion. It still has not been solved, and the violence to date is only a sample of what may eventually come. It was during the early sixties that the United States made its first, and so far only, serious attempt to solve the problem. Dr. Joseph Johnson of the Carnegie Endowment was selected by President Kennedy to find a solution. His proposal, in brief, was to give the refugees what amounted to an unlimited choice of locations to resettle, including letting a limited number, controlled by Israel, return to their homes. We estimated that only 20 percent would opt to go to Israel, which would have been about 200,000 at the time, but the Israelis were unwilling to even consider the proposal and the White House was unwilling to confront them.

I took Jeanne on a tour of Lebanon from north to south, including a drive along the border with Israel in the south. We later tried to do the same thing from the Israeli side of the line, but were stopped by the border police. There were almost no troops visible on the Lebanese side, and the area was very peaceful, with Lebanese villagers shrugging about the unavoidable presence of their unwelcome Jewish cousins next door. We can thank the Palestinians and the Israelis for the subsequent deterioration of security in the area, but those events were ten or fifteen years off.

The chickens came home to roost in Lebanon following the expulsion of the Palestinian "commandos" from Jordan in 1970 and their subsequent establishment of a Palestinian enclave in south Lebanon. The fragile Lebanese political system collapsed under the weight of this armed presence, and in due course a civil war erupted. This war was eventually terminated officially, but the internal situation subsequently deteriorated, with a new set of actors unfamiliar to me. Hezbollah, for instance, was not a factor in the period before 1983, when it blew up our Embassy and the Marine encampment near the airport. Lebanon has yet to recreate the atmosphere and assurance of its golden years. As of this writing, it was still unable to resolve the problem of some 350,000 Palestinians not allowed to resettle officially in Lebanon, and the balance of power between Lebanese factions looked worse than at any time since the Civil War.

It is hard to realize how distant from all this the Lebanon of the 1960s was. I had no inkling in 1961 that the South would come back to haunt me sixteen years later. We thought that a war was coming sooner or later but that it would be much later, after the Arabs had fully absorbed the military equipment they were receiving from the Soviets. Lebanon's involvement would be peripheral in any event. In the meantime, our concerns were rather superficial and largely centered on enjoying the present.

The length of a normal tour in those days was three years at post, and I was to be moved on in the summer of 1964. Now at forty years of age, I was due for assignment to one of the war colleges for a year, but I applied instead for appointment as a midcareer fellow at Princeton's Woodrow Wilson School of Public and International Affairs. I felt that I already knew about military life and thought some Ivy League exposure would do me more good by broadening my educational background.

To my pleasant surprise, I was picked for the Princeton fellowship, and we immediately began thinking about departure plans. What a glorious trip it was! We decided to follow, in reverse order, the crusader invasion route. We flew to Istanbul and then took the Orient Express to Belgrade and the Warsaw Express from there to Budapest. Budapest in the summer was very pleasant, although the Cold War was on and it was evident that we were the objects of intelligence surveillance. We stayed at a nice hotel, rode on Budapest's first subway route, and did some sightseeing. We then took a Soviet-made hydrofoil up the Danube to Vienna. The Hungarian police were suspicious of us and made us wait to be the last passengers on the boat.

From Vienna we took the train up north and then a ferry to England to spend the better part of a week in London. While there, we all went out to Fairford, the Cotswold village where I had been billeted in 1944. The Quonset huts our men had been in had disappeared, of course, but so had the manor house in which the officers had been quartered. Finally, we sailed from Southampton to New York on a large American liner.

Six months later, while in bed with the flu, I received a notice from the State Department addressed to "Parker, R." informing me that our steamship travel had not been authorized because we had taken an indirect route to get to London rather than flying direct from Beirut, and we therefore owed $1,500, the cost of our ship tickets. I appealed, pointing out that our travel from Beirut to London had cost less than air fare, that our route was in fact the most direct land route between the two points, and that I was following the secretary of state's recommendation that we get out and see the country. Miraculously, I eventually found someone sympathetic in the upper ranks of the administration and did not have to pay the $1,500. The lesson was clear: one should fight against injustice.

On arrival in New York, we rented a car, drove down the Jersey Turnpike to Princeton, and then on to Washington for consultation. Returning to Princeton after a week, we decided not to take the tiny apartment reserved for us in university housing and instead rented the upper floors of a large yellow frame house on Nassau Street. We settled in for a comfortable year at Princeton.

Princeton

Our year at Princeton passed quickly, and we would gladly have spent another year or two in the same place. The house on Nassau Street was comfortable, and there was a lot going on in Princeton to keep us all busy and entertained. We were free to audit any course on the campus. Judging by subsequent use made of them, I benefited most from courses on ancient art, one on demography, and one on diplomatic history. I also found the library very useful as a place to read up on our next post, which was to be Cairo. I discovered the *Description de l'Egypte* and could have usefully spent all my time in poking through it.

Jeanne was also allowed to audit and enjoyed the Ancient Art class and a number of art history classes. Alison was the star of the French Club at the high school. She and I visited Vassar, Wellesley, and Middlebury in the spring. She eventually applied to all three and was accepted by Vassar and Wellesley. Jeff seemed to have a good enough time, but broke no records at Witherspoon Junior High. Jill was the star of her school's production of *Pippi Longstocking*. Richard managed to survive the Nassau Street School pretty well. During the year my mother and then Jeanne's parents and her brother Bob and his family all visited. We went to Manhattan for Christmas, and I went to San Francisco to see Mother.

The Woodrow Wilson School at Princeton had recently come into a large endowment and was one of the leading schools of government and international affairs in the country. It suffered from not having a recognized discipline to teach, borrowing here from the political science department and there from sociology and economics. Political science and sociology were in the early stages of their ruination by excess theorizing, and were hurtling toward complete obscurity.

There were nineteen of us Mid-Career Fellows. Only two were Foreign Service officers. The others were from government departments across the spectrum, from the Veterans Administration and Defense to CIA and Agriculture. They were a congenial group, but we did not have many interests in common and I have seen very little of them since. Although the midcareer program was highly praised by the participants, who generally found that their careers were enhanced by this year away, it was abandoned some five or ten years ago.

By the middle of the spring we had to start making preparations for our move to Cairo. I had been promoted to Class II and was assigned as political counselor, the third-ranking job in a sizeable embassy. At 42, I was firmly on the road to glory. With luck I would eventually have an embassy of my own. My luck held, but there were a number of twists and turns, and it would take ten more years.

We all left Princeton with a feeling of having been privileged to have had a glimpse of an exceptional side of life. Among the notable people at Princeton in 1964 were Philip Hitti, the dean of Near Eastern studies in the United States, and George Kennan, the former diplomat and author of our policy of containment of the Soviet Union. Both were historic figures. There is a satisfaction one takes from knowing people like that. Most memorably, we were invited to the Kennans for dinner one night and met the 83-year-old Alexander Kerensky, the moderate Russian revolutionist. It was an unexpected brush with history I will never forget.

Thanks to my appointment to the Advisory Council on Near East Studies, I was able to maintain a Princeton connection from the early 1980s that meant a trip there every couple of years. I have valued those trips as occasions to see what was going on in the academic world. The Advisory Council has not been very effective, however, and Near Eastern Studies at Princeton has declined from the proud summit it dominated at the end of World War II.

Photo Gallery I

Marguerite Blossom Parker and Roscoe Parker with baby David, Fort Huachuca, Arizona, circa 1920

(L to R:) David S. Parker, Roscoe Parker, Richard B. "Dick" Parker, Northfield, Vermont, 1931

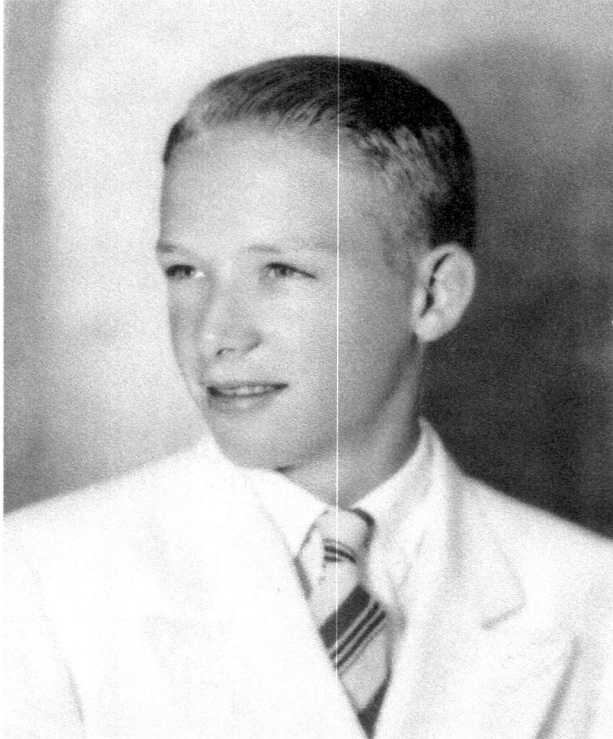

Dick, age 15, San Antonio, 1938

Wedding of Richard B. Parker to Jeanne Jaccard, June 23, 1944.
(L to R:) Jack Kilkenny, Gabe Sellers, the groom, the bride, Marilyn Mason, and Helen Gromer.

Dick, Alison, Jeanne, and Jeff in Jerusalem, 1952.

Consular Officer Dick Parker and Consul General Roger Tyler at Mandel-baum Gate, meeting with Jordanian officials in 1952.

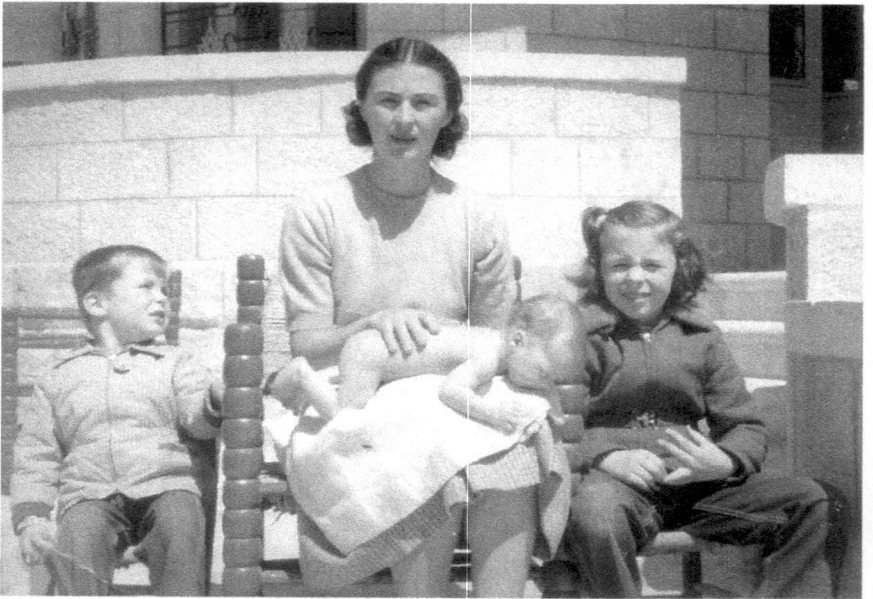

Jeff, Jeanne with infant Jill sunning on her lap, and Alison, Amman, 1955.

Dick Parker in Baalbeck, drawing attention to the scale of the place, circa 1954–55

11

Cairo

I left for Cairo by air in early July 1965, just in time for the July 14 reception at the French Embassy. I arrived as our relations with Egypt, which was then called the United Arab Republic, or UAR, were taking a serious turn for the worse. The honeymoon that had begun with John F. Kennedy in the White House was ending. Kennedy and Walt Rostow, the national security advisor, had urged that we motivate Egyptian president Gamal Abd al-Nasser to focus on domestic reform rather than foreign adventure by giving him a great deal of aid in the form of surplus agricultural products. By 1965, the United States was supplying 86 percent of Egypt's grain requirements, but our friends in the area—the Jordanians, Saudis, and Libyans in particular—continued to see Nasser as a menace and kept urging us to "turn down the faucet" of grain in order to discipline him.

This was the period of the Arab Cold War, so well described by Malcolm Kerr in his book by that name. It was a struggle for influence, even survival, between the radicals led by Egypt and the moderates, with Saudi Arabia as the main contender. Morocco, Tunisia, and Jordan were on the moderate sidelines, while Algeria and Syria were becoming progressively more radical. Iraq was experiencing a series of rough changes that led eventually to the installation of Saddam Hussein at the top of the heap. The hottest arena was Yemen, where the Saudis were supporting an insurgency by royalists opposed to the "republican" government that Egypt had helped install in 1962 and which the Egyptian army was supporting with men and equipment.

Politically, Egypt was the most important of the Arab states. Nasser was unquestionably the leading political figure in the Arab world, and his words and actions could shake the foundations of other Arab governments. No other modern Arab leader has had his influence. As the champion of Arab nationalism, he led the struggle against Israel. We all assumed this struggle would lead to another war sooner or later, once the Arabs had absorbed and become proficient with the weapons they were receiving from the Soviet bloc. Although we continued to profess our hopes for a 'just and lasting peace," we in fact were doing nothing to promote one beyond uttering pious phrases. The year 1965 was not a very propitious time for Arab-Israel peacemaking in any event. There was no serious interest on either side, and tensions had been rising since 1964 because of Israel's plans to divert water from the Jordan River. The Arabs reacted by creating the Palestine Liberation Organization, or PLO, which immediately added another radical note to the chorus. (I described the deterioration of U.S.-Egyptian relations in the 1960s in some detail in chapter 5 of *The Politics of Miscalculation in the Middle East* [Indiana University Press, 1993] and refer the inquisitive reader to that book.)

U.S. relations with Egypt ratcheted down another notch immediately after my arrival, when the Egyptians arrested a CIA officer, Bruce Odell, in the act of paying an Egyptian journalist, Mustafa Amin, his regular stipend for inside information on the doings of upper-level Egyptians. This liaison arrangement had been made with Nasser's approval some time earlier, and we thought it was still approved; but for reasons that were never clear to us, the Egyptians decided to declare that Amin had not been authorized to talk to us. Odell enjoyed diplomatic immunity but was declared persona non grata.

Our ambassador, a southerner of intense charm and credibility, was Lucius D. Battle. He had developed remarkably friendly relations with the Egyptian leadership, including Nasser and Muhammad Haikal, the publisher of the Arab world weekly *al-Ahram* and insider par excellence. Haikal, a faithful proponent and explainer of Nasser's policies, seemed to know everything. Whenever Ambassador Battle had an appointment with Nasser, Haikal would call him soon after he returned to the office to let him know that he had heard the tape of the conversation. One of Battle's first actions when Odell was caught was to go see Haikal, who promised that he would not publicize the event. He kept his promise for about a week. Then, the day after Battle left town on leave, he published the story, with photos, on the front page of *al-Ahram.*

Don Bergus, the political counselor I was to succeed, had also developed friendly relations with Haikal. He persuaded himself that Haikal, who reportedly hated the journalist Amin, had managed to delay action on Odell until Bergus was on his way out so that his goodbyes in Cairo would not be soured by the incident. I disagreed with Bergus, but in any event the responsibility for picking up the personnel pieces fell to me. That was probably why Haikal later thought I was CIA. Whatever the reason, I was never able to develop a personal relationship with him.

The first problem I faced in Cairo was that our CIA personnel were afraid to escort Odell to the airport for his departure. They feared that they would compromise themselves and that Egyptian intelligence agents would seize him or whoever was with him. They were not sure that they had enough diplomatic immunity to protect him or themselves if that were to happen. The chief of station, Eugene Milligan, asked me to accompany Odell instead. He left on a scheduled airline flight without incident.

Next on the schedule were Mrs. Odell and her children. They were in a house in Maadi and had been visited by one or more CIA wives, but the men of the CIA station were afraid of being compromised by seeing her. I went instead to assure her that all would be taken care of and eventually escorted her and her children to the airport for their plane to parts west. It was indicative of the atmosphere in Cairo that people felt the need to tiptoe around. The police and Mukhabarat, or Intelligence, were everywhere. They were not very efficient, but we assumed they bugged all of the telephones and were able to track who was visiting whom. They would summon and interrogate Egyptians who had no valid official excuse for consorting with foreigners and who happened to visit an American house. Did this mean that any Egyptian who came to your house for dinner was allowed to do so because he would report what his host and the other guests said? We thought so.

Initially I stayed at the Hilton, where I incautiously ate a shrimp cocktail and became terribly sick. I was grateful when the Berguses departed and I could move into their house out in Maadi. It had five bedrooms, one for each kid, and a very large garden with a gardener. I also inherited several household servants, plus a *mikwaggi*, or ironer, an irritable fellow who came once a week to iron the laundry. The house was not air-conditioned but we had window units that were fairly effective. Jeanne and the children arrived in Alexandria by ship about a month after I did. I went up to meet them and drove them back to Cairo in our Ford Falcon station wagon, which made it across the Atlantic three times before I sold it for a small profit in 1967.

Maadi was a modern, twentieth-century suburb south of Cairo. The streets were laid out on a numbered rectangular grid. It was a golden ghetto for foreigners, with very few Egyptians living among them. The Maadi Club had a swimming pool and a chip-and-putt golf course. There was a poor shopping area and a train that ran north along the Nile into town. I eventually became a partner in the *Bluebird*, a day sailer, with Eugene Bird and Kenneth Levick, an AID official, at a boat club on the Nile. Our children rather enjoyed the living space they had and the pool. All four of them went to the Cairo American College, within walking distance of our house. They seemed to fit into the school well and developed friends among the other Americans. In time we acquired a wire-haired fox terrier we named Freddie, who bit the ankles of our children's friends but was otherwise a lovable addition to the family.

Between personnel of our embassy and the AID mission, faculty at the American University in Cairo, a U.S. Navy medical research facility on the outskirts of town, and the American oil company Pan American there was a substantial American community in Cairo at the time, maybe a thousand souls. It was enough to support a community school with all the programs of the usual American high school. Because Jeanne and I had the largest garden, we hosted the annual Fourth of July party for the community, with some 600 guests.

Counting nondiplomatic personnel such as our secretaries, the Marine guards, and local employees, we had something like five hundred people working in our large compound in Garden City, making our embassy certainly the largest diplomatic establishment in town. Forty-five were on the diplomatic list, enjoying duty-free imports and diplomatic immunity. I had three FSOs helping me— Clifford J. (Pat) Quinlan, Wilbur I. Wright, and Pierce K. Bullen— and we had three secretaries among us. We occupied the second floor of the rather graceful older building that served as our chancery. The ambassador, the DCM, and our conference room were on the ground floor.

Although I was junior in personal rank to the economic counselor and Aid Mission director, as political counselor I was functionally the third-ranking officer in the embassy, taking the deputy chief of mission's place whenever he was absent. The DCM was David D. Nes, a career officer with long experience. He was direct and quick on the draw. He, Battle, and I got along well enough together, and I think we made an effective team. I was responsible for all the political communications going out of the embassy, including our reports on the internal political situation and diplomatic issues such as the Yemen dispute and the Arab-Israel question, our communications with the UAR government and other embassies, and our communications with other American offices in the region, such as our consulates at Port Said and Alexandria and our embassies and consulates in other Arab states and Israel.

Our political reporting from Cairo was not very inspiring. We had no information sources of much value. Government officials would not talk about "personalities" and were coy about giving out information of possible political significance, in part because they didn't have any. It was unhealthy for private individuals to have meaningful contact with us, and they did not know much anyway. The press was not to be believed. Egyptian journalists could repeat the party line and that was about all. Mustafa Amin had been an exception, and he had been disowned. There was one journalist who evidently was allowed to talk to us, a man named Mursi Saad el-Din, who was quite cultivated and pleasant but professed not to know much himself. He never told us anything of much value. Our diplomatic colleagues were no better off than we were. Like most diplomats in the third world, we were all reduced to exchanging rumors and misinformation at cocktail parties and had no idea what was really going on in the inner circles of the government.

The American, British, and French embassies were unique in

having Arabists doing their political work, not that it did much good. At one point the Italians brought in a man that they described as an Arabist, although I was not sure about his level of competence. He came to see me one day and said there was no food in the market, then looked surprised when I told him he should go down to the suq. The Soviets had no one who spoke Arabic, although they had one man who claimed some experience in the Arab world. I had a pleasant conversation with him about Soviet plans to supply wheat to Egypt and then got him in trouble by telling an Egyptian official about it. The Egyptians evidently were disturbed that the Soviets and Americans would compare notes.

We had a substantial military attaché office with eight officers and an airplane, but they had no meaningful contact with the Egyptian military, the most important organization in the country. They saw occasional parades and exhibitions, but had no clue as to the inner workings of the Egyptian military establishment. It is illustrative of our isolation from the political dynamics among Egyptian senior officers that neither we nor any other embassy in town was aware of the Nasser-Amer rivalry that was to be such a factor in the 1967 June War crisis.

I had two regular and unique contacts in the UAR presidency: Hassan Sabry al-Khouly and Mustafa Abd al-Aziz. Khouly was Nasser's special adviser on Arab affairs, and on Yemen in particular. We had become involved in efforts to mediate that conflict, thanks to the singular efforts of Ellsworth Bunker, who talked to all sides and seemed to have brought the Saudis and Egyptians close to an understanding in 1965. It fell apart, unfortunately, because of Saudi unwillingness to grant Egypt a role in Yemen and Egypt's unwillingness to pull out its troops without some assurance that the Yemeni royal family would not be allowed back in power. I was detailed as the Yemen *wallah* and met regularly with al-Khouly to discuss developments there. Khouly was an amiable fellow, but no fool. While he offered to be helpful, he was very careful about what he agreed to do.

Mustafa Abd al-Aziz was special assistant to Zakaria Muhieddin, the vice president. He was friendly and helpful, within the limits imposed by Egyptian sensibilities, and I liked him. He had an attractive wife and a couple of children, and we entertained each other's families several times. Mustafa was no fount of information and gave me no inside information about anything, but he was well informed and would correct my misapprehensions from time to time. Our liaison was specifically approved by Vice President Muhieddin and proved very useful when our air attaché and his assistant were caught trying to take photos of a secluded air base. It was unfortunate that I had been introduced to Mustafa by a former CIA agent, because this was probably one of the elements in the Egyptian portrait of me as a CIA man.

Keeping up with what was going on in Egypt was not a full-time job, because the country's politics were in a state of stasis. Nevertheless, the routine problems that had to be dealt with at the Foreign Ministry or elsewhere were enough to keep me busy. There were plenty of other diversions, so we never lacked for something to do. Shortly after Jeanne and the kids arrived, she and I took a boat trip up the Nile to Aswan, stopping at the historic sites en route. That is the only way to see Egypt if you can possibly manage it. We also shared a large pyramidal tent out near the Pyramids and made frequent weekend excursions there with the kids. It was one of the few places you could go in Egypt and be out of sight of other humans. Ten years earlier, Ambassador Henry Byroade had allegedly been surprised one night in the arms of a belly dancer there, or maybe in Alexandria, but nothing that exciting happened during our stay.

At Christmastime in 1965, Evan and Leila Wilson, whom we had served with in Beirut, came down to visit us from Jerusalem, where Evan was now consul general. One day they suggested that we go out for a picnic to Barquq, the funeral complex of the Mamluk Sultan of that name, located in the great Northern Cemetery, a complex of domes and minarets along the road to the airport. I had often noticed these structures when passing them to or from the airport but knew nothing about them. The guidebooks were uninformative about Islamic, as opposed to Pharaonic, Cairo. A book by Dorothea Russell, who had been the wife of Russell Pasha, the British police commissioner before the war, described many of the monuments; but she gave no directions on how to get to them. The visit with the Wilsons inspired me to write my own guidebook with my own maps, and I began using weekends to visit and photograph Islamic monuments all over Cairo. The result almost ten years later was my first book, *A Practical Guide to the Islamic Monuments of Cairo,* published by the American University in Cairo Press. This was the beginning of a long interest in the subject that has enabled me to keep my sanity from time to time. Many people have come up to me from time to time to say that my book was their introduction to Islamic art.

In the summer of 1966, we spent three weeks in Cyprus, renting a house on Apollo Street in Kyrenia and trading cars with Uberto and Barbara Bozzini of the Italian embassy. Cyprus was lovely, and we briefly toyed with getting a vacation home there. This was the summer that Alison flew the nest. She had graduated from Cairo American College and was going off to Wellesley. We put her on the plane in Nicosia and off she went to a new life and new friends. The night before she left, Richard cried at the prospect, and we were all very touched. At Christmas we made a tape of the kids and ourselves that we sent to Alison, who spent the holiday with the Jaccards in Manhattan, Kansas.

The Parker Team

In April 1967 we made a trip with John and Nene Dorman to the Greek Orthodox monastery of St. Catherine at the foot of Mt. Sinai, or Jabal Musa, where Moses saw the burning bush and the Israelites worshipped the golden calf. John was a retired FSO who had been the deputy director of Near East Affairs when I left there in 1959. In retirement, he had been appointed director of the American Research Center in Cairo, an office supported by a consortium of U.S. colleges and universities, which facilitated the efforts of American researchers in Egypt who needed help with government permits, housing, and other administrative problems. We planned the trip for the last week in the month, which was the Orthodox Easter.

We drove to Suez on April 29 and rented two taxis to take us to the monastery, as the road was too rough for our cars. When I stepped out of the taxi on arriving at St. Catherine's, I noticed on the ground a violet-colored soft drink cap with Hebrew lettering on it, a harbinger of things to come.

We lodged at the monastery, where a team of technicians from Greece was restoring icons. On the morning of the 30th we started the trek up Jabal Musa on camels. As we ambled along, an Egyptian came by on his camel with a portable radio playing. I asked him what the news was. He said there was a crisis in U.S.-Yemeni relations. The Americans had attacked a Yemeni army post with a rocket launcher, and President Sallal had summoned the American chargé, broken relations, and expelled the American AID mission. This sounded pretty fantastic, and we wondered what the real story was. We continued up the mountain, past the grotto of Elijah to the summit. It was easy to imagine Moses up there, even if he were a fictional character. When we made it back to the monastery, we found the Greek restorers much agitated by news of the colonels' coup in Athens. Much was happening, but we had no inkling of the war that would break out over the Sinai in six weeks.

When we arrived back in Cairo the following night, we learned more about the Yemeni affair. Someone had fired two bazooka rounds at a Yemeni army post at Ta'izz. We learned much later that this was an operation sponsored by our British friends in Aden, but at the time we had no idea who it was. The Yemenis, however, perhaps inspired by the Egyptians who were really running the country, had arrested two Americans from the AID mission in Ta'izz. Steve Liapis was a mild-mannered Alexandrian Greek who spoke Arabic and was therefore automatically a suspect, and Harold Hartman was a hunter from Montana or one of the Dakotas. He had a rifle concealed, he thought, in his bathroom. That would have been enough to convict him, whatever else he might have done to excite suspicion.

Around the time of their arrest, a mob had sacked the AID mission's headquarters in Ta'izz, and President Sallal had ordered the mission to leave on twenty-four-hours' notice. When the AID mission director, Robert Hamer, arrived in Asmara with the other expellees, he reported that the safe behind his desk contained some compromising papers he had been unable to destroy before leaving. There might also be some classified material in the file room, which had a sturdy combination lock door but was full of file cabinets left open by the file clerk who had been at lunch when the mob struck and had been unable get back in and lock the drawers. Not that it would have made much difference to a determined burglar if she had.

The Yemenis would not permit the staff of our branch office at Ta'izz to enter the building to assess the damage, and they and their Egyptian advisers were meanwhile taking a leisurely look at the building's contents. The glow of an acetylene torch one evening indicated that they were trying to cut their way into something, perhaps Hamer's safe or the file room.

Suddenly, rescue of the papers became a major preoccupation in Washington. Efforts to get third parties to help, the Indians and Yugoslavs in particular, proved useless. An unprecedented exchange of communications between Secretary of State Rusk and Marshal Abdul Hakim Amer, the de facto commander of the Egyptian military establishment, was set in motion and the Egyptians agreed to allow a small team to go from Cairo to Ta'izz and evacuate the building's contents. The Egyptians would provide transport and an escort. There was no mention of Yemeni approval.

I was chosen to lead the team, which consisted of Nathaniel Howell and Gordon Brown, two young FSOs from the Cairo embassy; Don Hackl, a security technician from the Beirut embassy; and me. We left Cairo the night of May 8 on a DC-6 that had once belonged to Northwest Airways and that the Egyptians were using as a troop transport. We were segregated from the troops at the front of the aircraft. On arrival in Sana'a the next morning we were met by Lee Dinsmore, the American chargé, and a Captain Ahmad, who said he was our escort officer and would be at our service. We were flown to Ta'izz in the Egyptian commanding general's Antonov and taken to the branch office, where we found an understandably tense crew waiting to see what, if anything, we could do.

We learned that Liapis and Hartman were being held at the security headquarters up the hill from the branch office. They were in a room, not a cell, and the Americans were carrying meals up to them. We all hoped that the presence of us outsiders under official sanction would somehow open up the possibility of getting them out of their predicament. There were five Americans in the branch office, including two who had been sent down from the embassy in Sana'a to help. There were no wives, but servants provided a reasonable cuisine.

Our first priority was to retrieve the documents, and after some discussion Captain Ahmad allowed our team and one officer from

the branch office to enter the AID office, a two- or three-story building down the hill from the branch office. We first located Hamer's
office. His safe was missing. There was blood on the wall and a trail
of asbestos—indicating that the Egyptians had used a sledge ham-
mer—leading from room to room and finally out of the building.
They had taken the safe elsewhere to open it.

We went to the file room, which had a large safe door with
a Sergeant and Greenleaf combination lock; Don Hackl quickly
opened it and declared that it had not been forced. We found the
room's contents as the file clerk had left them, with perhaps half a
dozen four-door file cabinets full of paper, which we were allowed
to remove and take to the branch office. It took us two days to burn
the contents in the incinerator. The documents included many
that were highly classified, up to and including Top Secret. They
should never have been in the AID office in the first place, and it
was one of the most egregious security violations I have ever seen.
The Egyptians and Yemenis did not see these documents, but judging by subsequent remarks of the Egyptian foreign minister, Mahmoud Riad, they found some interesting things in Hamer's safe,
probably related to personnel, but I don't know that it made much
difference. As Ambassador Raymond Hare once remarked, were it
not for the need to maintain cryptographic security, there was little
reason why most of our classified messages could not have been
shown to other governments.

After destroying the documents, we did what we could to clean
up the mess in the building, including removing the rotting meat
from the basement freezers that had been without electricity for
some time. After several days we had done as much as we could,
and I sensed that the Egyptians were getting tired of us. I sent a
message to the department saying that I was running low on *baraka*
and suggested that it was time for my team and I to go back to
Cairo. I received an immediate response that I was to stay until the
Liapis and Hartman affair was settled. I suspected that Bill Brewer,
the officer in charge of Arabian Peninsula affairs, had drafted that
message and swore at him.

Visiting the prisoners that afternoon, we arrived just in time
to witness the arrival of a senior Yemeni official who read out a
decree. The two prisoners were to be taken to Sana'a for trial on

charges of crimes against the state. This was very ominous. There was a notorious tribunal in Sana'a where travesty trials were held in which defendants were routinely condemned to death and led out to be shot without further ado. It sounded as though Liapis and Hartman were headed in that direction, and there was no authority in Ta'izz to whom we could appeal.

Around that time, I accompanied Captain Ahmad and another Egyptian officer to a hotel for tea on a terrace overlooking the town. I told the Egyptians that I had commanded an antitank platoon in the war and could not visualize Liapis and Hartman carrying out an attack of the type we understood had taken place. Neither man had any military training, nor did they know how to operate a bazooka. It might be a simple weapon, but it took some knowledge to operate it. I told them the story of Sorenson and Peterson, my sadly untrained battlefield soldiers who couldn't operate a bazooka. They enjoyed the story.

Somehow it was arranged that the next morning Captain Ahmad and I accompanied the two prisoners up to Sana'a in another Antonov. With us on the plane was the minister of the interior, who was thought to be the evil force behind the detention and planned trial of the two men. On arrival in Sana'a we parted ways with Captain Ahmad and were taken to chargé Lee Dinsmore's residence, where we learned that the foreign minister had agreed to release the two men to Dinsmore's custody pending trial, in return for a bail bond of $10,000 that Dinsmore had paid in cash from the embassy's emergency evacuation funds. I understood that this arrangement was tenuous and might be overturned at any time.

Early the next morning, Liapis, Hartman, and I were taken to the airport and put on the Yemen Airways flight for Hodeida and Asmara. The plane took off on schedule, landed at Hodeida for refueling while the Yugoslav pilot drank a beer in the shade of the wing, and arrived in Asmara on schedule. Liapis and Hartman rejoined some of their former AID associates there, while Sam Gammon, the consul general, arranged for me to fly back to Cairo the next day. It all seemed very uneventful, but, unbeknownst to us, officials of the Yemeni ministry of the interior had arrived at the airport after we left, set to stop us from leaving Sana'a. For some reason our arrival in Asmara was not reported promptly and for a

good while there was concern in both Sana'a and Cairo that we had
been taken off the plane at Hodeida.

On the presentation of a superior service award to Howell,
Brown, Hackl, and me by the department, Gordon Brown penned
the following tribute:

Oh, me name is Captain Parker,
I'm the leader of the Team
That went to Yemen (Occupied)
For business near obscene.
Well, Ahnumi roared
Captain Ahmad snored
While Liapis and Hartman groaned.
But the mission done,
It's Fame we won.
That glorious Parker Team.

Howell and Brown had remained in Ta'izz for another week clean-
ing up. They packed up and shipped personal effects from the AID
housing compound during the day and destroyed cryptographic
and other sensitive equipment at the branch office during the night.
They arrived back in Cairo just in time to see their families depart
on May 26 in the midst of the growing crisis. I arrived in Cairo on
May 15 to find that Egyptian troops were pouring into the Sinai
Peninsula. One of my first acts was to send a detailed report of the
paper rescue operation to Washington. My next action was to warn
the various members of the country team about the importance of
destroying unnecessary papers as soon as possible. Everyone co-
operated except for the defense attaché's office. We still had much
paper to burn when the war began.

The June War

I have already written at length about the origins of the June War
of 1967 and will spare repetition of all the details. The following are
some atmospheric and personal observations, some of which I have
not set down on paper before.

U.S.-Egyptian relations began to deteriorate as soon as Lyndon

Johnson assumed office. The Arabs naturally suspected that he was involved in Kennedy's assassination, and they recalled that as senator he had opposed Eisenhower's plans to impose economic sanctions on Israel if it did not withdraw its troops from Sinai in 1957. Johnson tried to continue the "personal" correspondence that Kennedy had with Nasser, but the Egyptians immediately declared that this language did not have the grace of Kennedy, even though the same scriveners had written both. LBJ could not win, but it might have helped had some of his senior subordinates been more sympathetic toward Egypt. As it was, he and Nasser both showed a deplorable lack of tact in dealing with each other.

It is my view, not shared by my colleagues, that Yemen was the straw that broke the camel's back. Had we not sided with the Saudis in early 1967 on one of the contentious issues regarding the conditions for Egyptian withdrawal, Nasser might not have concluded that we were conspiring with the conservative Arabs to get him. The Cairo and Jidda embassies were each urging different actions on our part, and Hermann Eilts, our ambassador to Saudi Arabia, was rather smug during a stopover in Cairo about the decision having gone his way.

That Nasser thought we were out to get him was clear from, among other things, his May Day speech in 1967. Nevertheless, had Luke Battle remained in Cairo as ambassador, the war might have been averted. Battle had access to and was liked by Nasser and might have been able to talk him out of committing the blunders that led to the Israeli sneak attack of June 5. On the other hand, if Nasser really believed his army was ready to take on Israel, which seemed to be the case, perhaps nothing could have stopped him from rushing to confrontation when he did.

As it was, Battle had left in early March to take up the position of assistant secretary of state for NEA, and his successor, Richard Nolte, showed no sense of urgency about arriving on the scene. He did not do so for over two months, despite the pleas of David Nes, the chargé d'affaires, who sensed that trouble was coming. The department seemed to think Nes was overreacting, but the truth is that Washington was asleep at the switch, including Battle and Bergus, officer in charge of the UAR at State, who should have known better.

Whatever the cause, when the crisis began in mid-May we had no ambassador in Cairo. Nasser did not normally receive the chargé d'affaires, so we had no access to him and no credibility with the Egyptians. Had we had someone on the spot with Nasser's confidence, things might have gone differently.

Nes was experienced, courageous, and intelligent, but he was very quick to arrive at conclusions, which sometimes got him into trouble and, in this instance, affected his credibility in Washington. He had managed to take a number of prudent steps to prepare for a break in relations, which he saw coming. He had obtained agreement that Spain would be our protecting power if it came to a break, and he had laid in a supply of flashlights and batteries. Both steps proved very useful.

When Ambassador Nolte finally arrived in Cairo on May 21, 1967, the die was all but cast. The Egyptians had sent large numbers of troops into the Sinai and demanded the withdrawal of the United Nations Emergency Force (UNEF) that had been stationed along the armistice line with Israel since 1957 to prevent conflict. Closure of the Strait of Tiran, which the Israelis said would be a *casus belli*, would be announced two days later. The world press was already there, and Nolte held a brief press conference at the airport. When a reporter asked for his views on the crisis, Nolte replied, "What crisis?" He meant to say that crises were endemic in the Middle East and we should take this one in our stride. That was not how the comment registered with the press, however, which understood it to mean Nolte was out to lunch.

Nolte was an accomplished grants man, an academic, who was intelligent, outgoing, and knowledgeable about Egypt and the Middle East. He had no previous exposure to the culture of government and to that of the Department of State in particular and was ignorant of the basic mechanics of our operations. Sending him to Cairo at that point was like sending Hanson W. Baldwin to command a division in the midst of a firefight in Vietnam. Nolte knew a lot about the subject but had no experience grappling with the real-life details. His unfamiliarity with the culture extended to how to deal with the press.

Nes and I knew better than to let him loose with a group of journalists again, but our public affairs officer, Robert Bauer, persuaded him to hold a press conference at the Embassy on May 22 or 23. On that morning Nolte and Nes had called on Foreign Minister Mahmoud Riad and given him an aide-mémoire that said we could not rule out the use of force to keep the Strait of Tiran open to shipping. There was a good deal of tension in the air.

Nolte began by saying that he assumed all the journalists were gentlemen and he could rely on them to respect his confidences; where he got that strange idea I do not know. He made some innocuous opening remarks and then called for questions, the first of which was whether he had told Riad that we would use force to keep the Strait open. He replied, "I would say that the implication that we would not use force was not there." The journalists, of course, immediately reported that we had threatened to use force, which upset the department a good deal. I can still picture two of the journalists standing in the lobby of the Chancery and asking each other cynically what Nolte meant by "gentlemen." They did not see themselves in that category.

It happened that as part of my anticipated four-year tour in Cairo, Jeanne and I had opted to take home leave in the summer of 1967. We had agreed to rent the economic counselor's Lake Champlain cabin for June and July. Jeanne and the two youngest children had reservations to leave on May 26, and Jeff was to leave somewhat later for Vermont via Paris, where he was to spend a couple of weeks with a family to improve his French. I was to follow later. All of this had been laid out since April.

When the Egyptians announced closure of the Strait of Tiran to Israeli shipping on May 23, I concluded that war was inevitable. We had a staff meeting that day or the next at which Nolte asked for thoughts on whether we should evacuate dependents. The question went around the room, with our service attachés and section heads all declaring that it would be premature to do so. I was the last to respond and said that the others might not be scared but I was. War was coming, and we should get started on evacuating dependents right away. I could see a look of relief on everyone's face. The first dependents left for Rome with Jeanne, Jill, and Richard on May 26 to the tune of "Smile Though Your Heart Is Breaking." Jeanne and company stayed briefly with an old Jerusalem friend in Rome and then boarded the SS *America* in Naples and sailed for New York.

CBS did a feature on the evacuation that included a sequence of Jill deciding which valued possessions to take with her.

I assumed that when the break in relations came, we would all be interned on very short notice, so I brought a suitcase full of spare clothes and toiletries to the office for when that happened. Smartest thing I ever did. I also sent Jeff off to Paris earlier than originally planned.

Those were hectic days, and so much happened so quickly that I can remember only a few of the details. There was a great proliferation of messages to and fro. The bureaucracy excretes paper in times of crisis like a nervous white rat excretes pellets. On one occasion, Nolte and Nes were meeting with Mahmoud Riad when an urgent message containing the text of an aide-mémoire came through. Unfortunately a vital page was left out, and I was so harried that I did not notice. I rushed the text we had over to the Foreign Ministry and carried it to Riad's office. The text without the missing page seemed to indicate that we did not accept Egyptian authority over Gaza. Riad hit the ceiling, and I don't know that we ever corrected the misunderstanding.

Officials at the Foreign Ministry let us know early in the process that they had no voice in what was happening. It was all in the hands of the military. Of those officials, the only one who would give us a straight answer about anything was Ismail Fahmy, who was in charge of United Nations Affairs.

What was most striking to us was the apparent confidence of the Egyptians that they were ready for whatever the Israelis could deliver. Soraya Antonious, the daughter of Jerusalem friends, was working as a correspondent for a Lebanese paper and came to see me shortly after Nasser's speech of May 28, in which he said that if the Israelis wanted war they were welcome to it. Soraya reeled off how many tanks, aircraft, and men the Egyptians had. For her, the only question was at what point we would intervene to stop the march on Tel Aviv. This was the common perception in Cairo. Egyptian perceptions were heightened by a front-page spread in *al-Ahram* of lean young Egyptian pilots in their pressure suits. The idea that Egypt had such advanced technology was exhilarating to the man in the street and to others outside the military establishment, whose judgment in such matters was usually quite uninformed.

We knew that the intelligence people in Washington were unanimous in their belief that Israel's war potential was greater than that of all the Arabs put together, but we on the ground thought the Egyptians, who looked impressive on parade, would give a good account of themselves and that the war could last some time. Our expectations were also skewed by the fact that we knew nothing of the fateful rivalry between Nasser and Marshall Abdul Hakim Amer. We had no inkling of the degree to which Nasser had to keep himself out of operational military matters. Our ignorance in this regard is surprising, even incredible, to students of Middle East affairs, who cherish the illusion that the CIA knew everything that was going on.

I do not recall being in contact with Hassan Sabry al-Khouly at the Presidency during the crisis, but was in regular touch with Mustafa Abd al-Aziz, special assistant to the vice president. One night before the evacuation began, I went out to tell him that Egypt was headed for a war it was going to lose. He and his family were welcome to come and stay with us in Maadi, where we had a bomb shelter of sorts. He thanked me but said he did not think that would be necessary. The Israelis were about to learn that they could no longer be the bully on the block. On a visit to Cairo in 1989, I saw Vice President Zakaria Muhieddin at a dinner party, and he agreed that I had been right.

The week of May 28 to June 3 was relatively quiet. The departure of dependents was followed by that of "nonessential" personnel, a term much resented by the latter, most of whom were AID employees sent to the Palestine Hotel in Alexandria. This reduced the number of problems we had to deal with, and I turned to the problem of destroying classified papers.

For normal destruction we had an effective incinerator, but we also had a chemical process that could be used for emergency burning. You put the papers in a 50-gallon drum, poured the chemical on top and whoosh! We had such a drum on the roof of the Chancery, and I went up there with a couple of Marines to supervise our first attempt at use of the chemical to burn the last holdings of the political section. We put the papers in the drum, added the chemical, and hastily popped the lid on. That was a mistake. There was a loud noise, and a column of smoke and fire shot up. The fire trucks and police came immediately. There was considerable embarrassment, and I withdrew from further burning.

On June 4, it looked as though we were moving toward a political solution. Zakaria Muhieddin was scheduled to fly to Washington on the 7th to talk about peace, and the Israelis had promised not to attack for a week or two. Nolte, Eugene Bird, and I went out for a sail. I was still living at home, where, during the previous week, I had given a rather nice dinner in the garden for Charles Yost, who had been sent out to hold our hands. The dinner was the last of its kind for a long time.

On June 5, Nolte was scheduled to present his credentials to Nasser. I dressed in my blue tropical worsted suit from Kort, the tailor in Arab Jerusalem, and drove in to the Embassy. I called al-Aziz at about 8:00 a.m. to see if the credentials ceremony was still on. His wife answered the telephone and said Mustafa had gone to the office and that the Jews were attacking. Hadn't I heard? This was our first word that the war had begun. There was some confusion in Washington as to who had started the fighting, the Israelis having lied to us in that regard, but there was no doubt in Cairo.

I waited a few minutes and called Mustafa at his office. He confirmed that the Israelis had attacked and said something like, "Thank God! Now you'll see." The credentials ceremony was cancelled, of course, and I was stuck in my blue suit. I never did get back to our house and thanked God more than once for the packed suitcase I had brought in earlier. I lived out of it for the next three or four months. Nolte never did get to present his credentials, living in a diplomatic limbo in Cairo until he departed with the rest of us.

That evening, I moved into the dark and gloomy ambassadorial residence with Nolte. After dinner we watched TV footage of marching and exercising soldiers accompanied by martial music. Throughout the day the government had issued communiqués detailing the Israeli aircraft that had been shot down. We had no idea that the Egyptian air force had been destroyed on the ground in the early minutes of the Israeli attack and that the Egyptian army was about to attempt a hasty withdrawal that turned into a rout.

The next morning we awoke early to newscasts blaming the Americans and the British for the damage done by Israeli aircraft. As soon as I could, I called Mustafa to tell him this was nonsense.

He replied, "For your information, the Israelis could not possibly have done what they did yesterday without help. And that means you and possibly the British, the only people who have the ability to provide it." I told him there was no American aircraft carrier within 300 miles of Egypt, but that did not impress him. We pleaded with the department to have Voice of America come on the air with a rebuttal, but it was the middle of the night in Washington and rousing that agency seemed to be impossible. It continued to broadcast its prerecorded programs on farming in Arkansas, or something like that. It was terribly frustrating for us.

As the day of June 6 wore on, the accusations grew louder until at 6:00 p.m. the radio announced that diplomatic relations with the United States had been broken. Shortly thereafter three colonels from the Ministry of the Interior came to the Embassy and informed us that all American citizens were to be assembled prior to deportation. They asked to see our consular files, although they said they knew where everybody was. We saw no alternative to cooperating with them, so our consular and economic personnel met with them to compare notes on where Americans were. It was soon evident that the Egyptian records were long out of date and inaccurate. Working through the night, however, most of the Americans in Cairo were rounded up and taken to the Hilton Hotel. Journalists were sent to the Nile Hotel, not far from the Embassy. Americans imbedded elsewhere in Egypt were also rounded up in the following three days. These included a retired engineering professor from Kansas State whom I had known and who was teaching at the university in Assiut, plus his wife, and an elderly woman known as Umm Seti, who had been in Aswan since World War I. Her passport, issued in 1916, was a single page, not a booklet.

As soon as the Egyptians announced that they were breaking relations, Nes had called the Spanish ambassador, Angel Sagaz, and the next morning Sagaz came to the Embassy for a brief ceremony. He and one or two of his officers and Nolte, Nes, Nat Howell, and I plus a couple of Marines, went up to the roof, took down the American flag and raised the Spanish flag Sagaz had brought with him. I remarked that the Spanish-American War was now over. The Spanish flag continued to fly there until 1974, when the Egyptians finally agreed to restore relations.

Sagaz was a very congenial colleague with a lovely wife. We could not have asked for a better protector. A year later, when I was in charge of UAR affairs in the department, I returned to Cairo with a signed photo of LBJ in a silver frame, which I presented to him. A collector of such photos for display on his piano, he was quite pleased, but Egyptian friends thought it was hilarious, as LBJ was the most hated man in Egypt. At the same time, I presented a military medal to the Spanish military attaché in appreciation for his help with our evacuation and a certificate of appreciation to the Spanish first secretary for his help with representational issues.

Traditionally, a break in relations meant the departure of all embassy personnel except possibly a person or two to handle consular and financial problems, and all representation to the host government would be performed by the protecting power, which assumed control of the departing embassy's property. By the time of the break with Egypt, however, there had developed the concept of an "interests section," which amounted to a mini embassy technically inside the protecting power's embassy. This permits the maintenance of the substance of relations, up to a point, without acknowledging that fact. All communications with the host government are nominally to or from the embassy of the protecting power, and the personnel of the interests section are shown in the diplomatic list as officers of that embassy.

Nes worked out an agreement with the Foreign Ministry that we would be allowed to have a six-person interests section in the Spanish embassy in Cairo while the Egyptians would be allowed a mission of the same size within the Indian embassy in Washington. I was proposed and accepted as chief of the U.S. interests section and discussion began immediately on who the other five would be. The Foreign Ministry informed us that certain people would be persona non grata. Their list seemed to be directed at suspected intelligence officers—everyone who belonged to the famous Gezira Club, for instance –although why that would be seen as an indication of intelligence function was not clear to us. On the other hand, they did not bat an eye at the inclusion of William Bromell, the CIA station chief who had been declared as such to them. The final list, aside from Bromell and me, included the ambassador's secretary, our general services officer, and two CIA communicators. All the other Americans from the mission were to leave for Alexandria by train at 10:00 p.m. on Friday, June 10. They would proceed from there to Athens by boat.

Meanwhile, Egypt accepted a cease-fire on the evening of June 8. The Israelis had reached the Suez Canal and the Egyptian armed forces were in tatters, although we did not yet know the extent of their disarray. The mood in the country was ugly, anti-American sentiment was high, and we did not know what to expect. The members of the interests section were to move into one of my FSO's apartments in a Nile-side building a block from the Embassy and remain there until things calmed down.

The next day, Friday, it was announced that Nasser would be giving a major speech in the evening. David Nes, Bob Bauer, Bill Bromell, and I met at Nolte's residence to finish off the steaks in his freezer and to hear the speech. Nasser came on the air shortly after seven and announced that he was resigning and Vice President Zakaria Muhieddin would take his place. Almost immediately there was a prolonged burst of antiaircraft fire and, we later found, people began pouring into Midan al-Tahrir (Liberation Square) two or three blocks from the Embassy. A crowd eventually arrived at Nasser's house on the far side of town and demanded that he retract his resignation, which he refused to do. There was immediate suspicion that the demonstration had been organized in advance.

Just then, Angel Sagaz called to tell me that the Egyptians insisted that I could not stay and must leave the next day with the others. I protested that this was impossible. I had not been to my house since Monday. Something had to be done about our dog and our possessions. Sagaz repeated that he was told I would have to leave. Bromell, in an act of considerable courage for which we later gave him a State Department decoration, drove across town in the blackout to meet Salah Nasir, the director of general intelligence, to see if this decision could be reversed. He returned to say that it had been a decision by Nasser himself. No reason was given, but I was later told that the Egyptians had thought I was CIA because I "did not act like a diplomat." Mustafa Abd al-Aziz told me that my Yemen adventure was one of the reasons I was suspected. I wondered if my command of Arabic was also a factor. Ironically, it was Bromell who assumed charge of the interests section on my departure. I have always thought that he was so low-key the Egyptians could not believe he was really CIA (though at least one colleague thought the Egyptians chose Bromell because as station chief he had back channels of communication to Washington and the ability to continue "secret" payments to select members of the state apparatus).

Meanwhile, on arriving at the embassy compound to continue the evacuation, we found pandemonium. The place was surrounded by policemen crowded elbow to elbow, while the crowd roared in the Midan. Our personnel were gathered inside the Chancery wondering what was going to happen next. Our press officer foolishly wandered over to the Midan to see what was going on and reported back that people were happy; but he did not understand Arabic. Inside the Embassy, Katie de Angelis, the wife of the Pan American Airways office manager, manned the switchboard in the lobby and seemed to be the only sane person there, as various Americans who had not been rounded up called to ask what they should do. She told them to come to the Embassy. A group of oilmen from Standard of Indiana, which had been prospecting in Egypt and was about ready to start production, called from a house in Maadi to ask what they should do. Their Egyptian contacts had told them that if they chose to stay they would be taken care of, but if they left they need not bother to come back. I told them it was their decision, and we had no idea what was going to happen next. They opted to stay, except for a couple of executives from the home office who chose to leave with the rest of us.

Eventually, we got everyone together and set off for the train station. There were two detectives at the station to make sure I was on board, and on the train was the Spanish military attaché, Colonel Aguilar, who was keeping an eye on us and watching for signs that we were being harassed. The train left at about midnight. We numbered perhaps two hundred, including some of the American University in Cairo faculty who had initially responded to our evacuation announcement by saying that they, in contrast to diplomats, were friends of the Egyptian people and planned to stay. The train moved slowly and we did not reach Alexandria until about seven in the morning. The governor of Alexandria had warned Cairo that he could not be responsible for the safety of Americans, and as we made our way to the port, spectators held up their shoes with the soles toward us, a maximum gesture of contempt.

At the port, we were hustled from the train and directed up a long flight of stairs leading to a large shed, where we were to be subject to customs inspection. The Egyptians were quite inhospitable. No porterage was provided, which was very hard on the elderly, like Umm Seti, who were carrying heavy suitcases. I told the guards they should be ashamed, and they replied that the younger ones among us could do the carrying. Inside the shed the inspectors confiscated the currency carried by nondiplomats, but Colonel Aguilar retrieved and redistributed most of it. There was no water and no food. Our consul general from Alexandria, David Fritzlan, and his staff were in a lower area at the customs shed, but as far as we could tell did nothing to help us. He made one appearance to tell us we must understand how upset the Egyptians were and then disappeared.

Late in the morning Nasser announced that he had withdrawn his resignation and the atmosphere improved slightly. Meanwhile, one American had died from violence in Alexandria, which had been more unruly than Cairo from the beginning of the war. A mob had sacked the USIS library and tried to burn down the Consulate General on day one. A mob had also attacked our Consulate in Port Said but had been repelled by a group of American oilfield workers, who threw them down the stairs as our consul and his wife escaped by ship.

The ferry that our embassy in Athens had chartered to pick us up had gotten no further than Crete, where it burst a boiler trying to hurry to Alexandria. It did not arrive until late in the afternoon. Nolte and Nes were both slumped in exhaustion, and I was left as the sole functioning member of the troika. The only other functioning senior officer I could find was our agricultural attaché, Jim Hutchins. He and I, with help from Nat Howell and Gordon Brown, supervised the boarding when the ship finally arrived. Fritzlan reappeared as the boat pulled in and was the first person on board, with his secretary, not to be seen again. His number two, Jack Bowie, had found something to drink and was so unsteady when he got on board that he fell and hurt himself badly. We left Alexandria at about six Saturday evening, and I sent a radiogram to the Department of State informing it that we were underway. Shortly thereafter an American destroyer showed up to escort us, a very welcome sight.

Nes and I shared a tiny cabin, and the next day he asked me to absent myself for a couple of hours while he talked to Franklin Fenton, a newspaperman from Nes's home town of Baltimore. I agreed and heard nothing more about it until we arrived in Athens on the second day. Washington was in an uproar because Nes had given Fenton a full and frank account of his frustrations with, and lack of support from, the comatose Department of State, particularly with regard to the delay in Nolte's arrival. It had all been printed in the *Baltimore Sun* and elsewhere. Nes disappeared as soon as we arrived in Athens and took the first plane out. He said he had an important sailing date in Annapolis. In spite of Senator Fulbright's intervention on his behalf, his punishment when he eventually returned to Washington was to be given a nonjob in an office lined with faux walnut on the top floor of the old New State building. He had no secretary, received no papers or instructions, and had no function. He retired after a while.

After saying goodbye to the other voyagers, including my secretary, Elaine Petrie (who was eventually sent to Amman, married one of the Marines, and wrote her own semifictional account of these events), I took a plane to Washington, thinking that the department would probably want to talk to me about Nes and that I could explain his anger, which was well-justified in my view. My brother Bud, who was then stationed at the Pentagon, was waiting for me at National. I spent the night with him and Betty and went to the department the next day. No one seemed interested in what I had to say about Nes. After attending the NEA staff meeting and giving an account of the events in Cairo, I flew up to Burlington, where Jeanne and the kids met me and we began two months of pleasant leave at Charlotte, on the shore of Lake Champlain. So ended our Cairo adventure.

12

Washington 1967–1970

In due course, Freddie the wire-haired terrier arrived at Burlington by air, apparently no worse for what must have been a torturous trip from Egypt. Indeed, all of our possessions from the house at Maadi eventually arrived safely and with minimum damage. The credit for this feat goes to Martin Armstrong, our general services officer, and to Nadia Rizk, our principal Egyptian employee and a tower of wisdom and practicality.

We settled down to Lake Champlain living and were visited serially by Jeanne's parents, her family, and my mother. In the evenings Alison regaled us with tales of life at Wellesley and the Mamas and the Papas, and we listened to my portable radio, which I had brought from Cairo. Soon discussion began about where we would go next.

The first proposal was that I go to Rabat as deputy chief of mission. We would have liked that, but someone senior had promised the job to Dwight Dickinson and felt the promise had to be kept. Another possibility was a seat on the Policy Planning Council at State. That sounded interesting, but it would be off the NEA career track. The best option was that I replace Don Bergus as country director for Egypt in the Department of State. He was being sent to Cairo to replace Bill Bromell as chief of the interests section. We decided to take the Bergus job. He and I seemed doomed to follow each other forever.

Bergus enjoyed himself in the Cairo job. He was a chief of mission, with minimal administrative and managerial responsibility and a good deal of scope for freewheeling. He did not remain under the tutelary wing of the Spanish for long and was soon discussing policy issues with everyone but Nasser himself. The Egyptians remained formally hostile, but considerations of mutual interest in lessening the crisis created by the war often intervened. A certain amount of civilized discourse was necessary if the Egyptians were going to move the Americans to do what they wanted them to do. They had little success in this regard, however, since we refused to take them seriously after their humiliating defeat at the hands of Israel showed how shallow their pretensions were. They finally had to start another war in 1973 before we would take them seriously.

Jeanne and I were totally unprepared for a Washington assignment. We had no house and no money. All of our planning and expenditures had been based on the assumption that we would spend four years in Cairo. This was the third time an assignment had been terminated early because of unexpected events, and there would be three more before we were finished.

At the end of the summer of 1967 we moved to Washington. Jeanne started looking for a house while I went to work. She eventually found one previously owned by the Marine commandant at Quantico in an area of northwest Washington known as Barnaby Wood. It cost us $39,000, had three bedrooms and a finished basement, and was too small for us. Richard eventually slept in the attic, while Alison used the maid's room in the basement when she came to visit. Jeff was sent to Woodrow Wilson High School, graduated in 1969, and went off to Kenyon College that fall. Jill went to Alice Deal Junior High, which was deteriorating rapidly, then to National Cathedral School for Girls, while Richard went to Lafayette Elementary School. Jeanne took education courses at Catholic University and began working as an assistant in inner city schools, but we left again before she got very far with that.

The organization of the geographic bureaus in State had been reshuffled since I was last in Washington. The old geographic offices such as Near Eastern Affairs and North African Affairs had been scrapped. Now, below the assistant secretary was a group of deputy assistant secretaries whose areas of responsibility corresponded with those of the old office directors but without such an immediate grasp of the problems of management and control. Below them were country directors, who initially were supposed to have the as-similated rank and prestige of ambassadors; but that did not work out in practice because of the suffocating layer of deputy assistant secretaries looking over their shoulders. The office of Near Eastern Affairs (NE) became a group of four country directorates, which replaced the former country desks. The deputy assistant secretary was Rodger Davies, who had been the director of NE. There was one directorate for the Arabian Peninsula (ARP); one for the Arab North (ARN), including Syria, Lebanon, Iraq, and Jordan; one for Israel and Arab Israel affairs (AIA); and one for Egypt, still called the UAR, where I was to be director.

The UAR directorate consisted of three or four officers and two secretaries. My secretary, Catherine Fish, had been the ambassador's secretary in Cairo. Hard-working and competent, she was a jewel. We no longer call them secretaries—I guess they like to be called executive assistants—but this loss is like the disappearance of nurses' uniforms from hospitals, something I regret. My first deputy, Eugene Bovis, was an Arabist who also spoke Hebrew.

Our Soviet rivals had lost considerable influence because of their failure to come to Egypt's aid effectively during the June War, but they still managed to expand their military presence in Egypt significantly. We concentrated on holding what we had and hoping for the best, but the principal issue was what to do about making Israel withdraw from the Arab territories it had occupied in the war. We had long been committed formally under the Tripartite Declaration with Britain and France to oppose, with retaliatory force if necessary, forceful attempts to change the 1949 armistice lines in the Middle East. Britain and France had repudiated their commitment when they conspired in the Israeli attack on Egypt in 1956, but Lyndon Johnson had reaffirmed our own commitment on the eve of the June War, and our natural expectation was that he meant it. But there was no further mention of the Tripartite Declaration once the war began and it became clear that Israel was winning. One cannot imagine Johnson failing to force the Egyptians to withdraw if they had invaded Israel, but the latter benefited from the double standard we traditionally apply where Israel is concerned. In retrospect, it is clear that the Israelis got to Johnson and persuaded him not to take a serious step to effect a withdrawal; but no written record of that contact seems to exist. There have been allegations that the Israelis' instrument was Mathilde Krim, who was alleged to have had an affair with LBJ and who was once described to me as the Mossad resident in the White House. Some day we may know the truth, but I rather doubt it.

It only became clear that we were not going to do anything serious about forcing Israel to withdraw after the passage of Security Council Resolution 242 in November 1967. It called for "withdrawal from territories occupied," not "the" territories occupied. The Israelis had insisted on elimination of the definite article in order to make the resolution as vague as possible and we had supported them against the Arabs, who wanted the resolution to read "withdrawal from all the territories occupied." In order to get the Arabs to go along with the resolution, Arthur Goldberg, our UN representative, among others, assured them that once the resolution was passed we would move to bring about withdrawal from substantially all, or at least most, of the territories involved. I recall, for instance, Under Secretary of State Katzenbach assuring Don Bergus, who was home from Cairo on consultation, that once there was a credible Arab commitment to nonbelligerency—not even peace—we would start putting pressure on the Israelis to withdraw. We did nothing of the kind, of course.

In the first place, the Arabs were not ready to talk of a peace that would involve dealing directly with Israel. They would talk about peaceful coexistence or living at peace with Israel, and eventually about nonbelligerency, but they specifically rejected the concept of *sulh*, or reconciliation. They were not ready to negotiate directly with the Israelis or even to sign their names to the same piece of paper with them. They might have been willing to accept the same sort of indirect negotiations that had led to the 1949 armistice agreements, but they might not. A reported statement attributed to Mahmoud Riad, the Egyptian foreign minister, to the effect that Egypt would accept the "Rhodes formula" was repudiated immediately by the Egyptian government.

Gunnar Jarring, the Swedish ambassador to Moscow, was chosen as the UN mediator to bring the parties together in implementing the resolution. He never got to first base. An admirable diplomat with much experience, he knew nothing about the Middle East and did not receive the support he needed from the United States, which did nothing to move the Israelis from an increasingly hard line on territory. At first saying they did not want an inch of territory—except, it transpired, the West Bank and Jerusalem—they were soon unwilling to give up any of it.

In the fall of 1968, Luke Battle retired from the Department of State to go to work with COMSAT. He was succeeded as assistant secretary for Near Eastern and South Asian Affairs by Parker T. Hart, known as "Pete," who had been dragged home unwillingly from his post as ambassador to Turkey. Pete was an old NEA hand, closely associated with Saudi Arabia, about which he eventually wrote a book. He was a very straightforward man, disinterested, and too decent to engage in bureaucratic politics. I had helped prepare him for his abortive assignment as ambassador to Jordan in 1958 and liked him very much, but he was no match for the bureaucratic jackals who swarmed around the Arab-Israel issue in those days.

In late October we went to New York to meet with Mahmoud Riad, who was there for the UN General Assembly session. The Egyptians had begun a "forward" policy of heavy artillery bombardments and commando raids across the Suez Canal. Hart told Riad this was not helping the UN mediation. Riad replied that we had not seen anything yet. The Egyptians would no longer sit with arms folded while the Israelis continued arrogantly to occupy their land. This was the beginning of what came to be called the War of Attrition between Israel and Egypt. It led eventually to the Soviets' assuming responsibility for the air defense of Egypt. (The details may be found in pages 125–164 of my *Politics of Miscalculation in the Middle East.*)

A few days later Secretary Rusk met with Riad and gave him an eight-point proposal for an Egyptian-Israeli settlement (described on page 132 of *The Politics of Miscalculation*). I seem to be the only surviving American witness of that meeting. Two days later, the Democrats lost the election and the Egyptians concluded there was no need to take Rusk seriously. The Arabs had been hoping for a Republican victory because they thought Nixon would be more interested in the Arabs and less dependent on Jewish support than the Democrats. They did not anticipate Kissinger and Joe Sisco.

During the Christmas 1968 lull, Sisco, then assistant secretary for International Organizations, called me at home to make some suggestions about how we should respond to a message from the Egyptians. It was not a message about UN matters but about something bilateral that was not within his bailiwick at all. I expressed surprise at his call, and he said something vague to the effect that he was following the matter with interest. That was the end of the conversation. I reported it to Pete Hart the following day and neither of us knew what to make of it.

A week or so later Sisco called me to his office and asked what the Arabs thought of him. I said they associated him with Arthur Goldberg and what they considered misleading assurances about Israeli withdrawal given to them during the discussions about what became Resolution 242. They were in fact quite suspicious of him. I knew how they felt from conversations with Egyptian ambassador Ashraf Ghorbal and Abdul Hamid Sharaf, the Jordanian ambassador, both of whom expressed themselves quite freely as distrusting Sisco. As far as I could tell, none of the Arabs trusted Sisco, and he was never able to overcome their suspicions, whatever he and his acolytes may have felt to the contrary.

Sisco's motive in asking me all this became clear when the Nixon administration came in. Sisco was named assistant secretary of NEA and poor Pete Hart was exiled to the Foreign Service Institute as director. Although commissioned as a Foreign Service officer, Sisco never served abroad and was much resented for that and for his devious and bullying tactics. He proved to be the most effective assistant secretary NEA ever had, but the people who enjoyed working for him were rare, at least in my generation. I was not among them.

I had already crossed swords with Sisco before Luke Battle left NEA over a proposal by U Thant, the UN secretary general, to reopen the Suez Canal. The canal had been blocked since the June War, to the distress of a number of our European friends, including the Italians, among others, who relied on canal transit for much of their commerce. I had written a memorandum suggesting that we support the proposal, but Sisco came into Luke's office, waving my memo and saying, in his bullying way, that it was a bad idea and he would oppose it. Luke refused to quarrel with him or support me, and I lost. Sisco and George Ball subsequently toured Europe like the Gold Dust Twins, telling our friends that it was in the Western interest to keep the canal closed because this would make it more difficult for the Soviets to send ships to the Red Sea and the Indian Ocean. This was Israeli Minister of Defense Moshe Dayan's argument and was bought by a number of people in Washington who should have known better.

I was told Sisco speculated that I would be one of his biggest problems in NEA. Someone else said he considered me a foil and I should feel complimented. In any event, we had a confrontational relationship and a most difficult year ensued. I did my best to be a good soldier and provide him with what he needed; but I also felt it was my duty to tell him the truth as I saw it. My views were often at odds with his, and he did not welcome constructive dissent. In particular, I could not get his support for a presidential statement saying the Israelis must withdraw from the occupied territories. He kept rejecting my drafts and putting no ideas of his own forward. He was a trimmer, of course, and did not want to do anything that might raise questions about his loyalty to White House ideology or to Israel's interests. Years later Robert Kaplan wrote in his book *The Arabists* that Sisco told him I could not draft as well as Roy Atherton, country director of Arab Israel affairs. I cannot recall ever reading anything remarkable that Roy wrote, but he did not feel as strongly about things as I did.

In the fall of 1969, I discovered that Sisco and Atherton were drafting an Egyptian-Israeli peace proposal without consulting me. The peace plan they outlined was put forth by Secretary of State William Rogers in a speech on October 28, 1969. Subsequently dubbed "The Rogers Plan," it went nowhere because the White House, Kissinger in particular, did not support it. Meanwhile, the War of Attrition continued to heat up, and Israel began its "deep penetration" raids into the Nile Valley. When the Soviets warned us that if we did not do something to restrain Israel they would have to do something serious to help Egypt, I advised that the Soviets meant introducing either Soviet pilots or Soviet missile crews, both of which they did. They took over the air defense of Egypt, which set off alarm bells in Israel and Washington. My counsel had been dismissed by Sisco and the Soviet specialists, and we thumbed our noses at the Soviets. When Sisco met with Dayan in Israel in April 1970, Dayan, who always feared Soviet intervention, asked if we knew the Soviets would respond as they did. Sisco said, "That was our estimate." This was untrue, of course, but truth was not a big issue with Sisco when talking on policy.

I went on that trip with Sisco and Atherton as far as Cairo and then went to Brussels for a meeting of NATO "experts" on the Middle East. The British representative and I were the only ones who knew anything at all about the Middle East. That was my swan song in NEA. I had decided it was time to move on after Sisco and Atherton had not consulted me on their idea for a peace plan. I obviously did not have Sisco's confidence and could not continue working in such an atmosphere, so I had begun looking around for another job.

Sisco learned of this and told me to stick with him and he would take care of me. I put no faith in that promise, and when Stuart Rockwell walked into my office one day early in 1970 and asked if I would like to be his DCM in Rabat, where he had just been named as ambassador, I accepted without hesitation. In May, I went to the FSI for a French refresher, and we left for Morocco in July. Later, the *New York Times* carried a long article by Joseph Kraft on Arabists in the Department of State. In it he said Sisco had exiled me to Rabat. I assume he heard that from Sisco himself.

13

Rabat I

I had always wanted to go to Morocco, for no particular reason other than to see it. I had made a brief orientation visit there in 1966 when we were in Cairo, but I knew very little about the country. Jeanne was looking forward to a new place, and both of us were looking forward to a more comfortable life, with servants, a chauffeur, and government housing. Alison had just graduated from Wellesley but was still eligible for travel at government expense, so we all clambered on board the Italian liner *Raffaello*, including our terrier Freddie. We landed at Algeciras, spent the night there, and then took the ferry across the Strait to Tangier. It was our last boat ride at government expense, made possible by "counterpart funds" generated by the sale of surplus agricultural commodities to countries like Yugoslavia that were unable to feed their populations on their own. That door was closed soon after our trip, and all our subsequent travel across the ocean was by air.

Morocco is unique in its preservation of traditional dress and historic medinas, or towns. The French did their best to uproot and destroy Algerian culture but behaved in a much more humane and responsible manner in Morocco, thanks to Marshal Hubert Lyautey, the first French governor. Towns like Fes and Marrakesh consequently retained their antique culture and charm. Walking through them can be memorable, and the suqs are full of interesting things to buy.

Rabat was less interesting than Fes or Marrakech to the casual observer but had many impressive monuments of the Almohad and Merinid periods. These are described in my guide to the monuments, and I will spare the reader the details. By 1970 when we arrived in Rabat, I was seriously interested in Islamic architecture. My book on Cairo was nearing completion, and I was resolved to do a similar book on Morocco.

Rabat was blessed with a mild maritime climate, comfortable housing, good food, many recreational opportunities, and few challenges. Because of this lack of challenge, morale in the embassy was chronically poor. People quarreled about what they saw as favoritism in the allocation of housing and complained about the minor irritations of living in a foreign environment and missing the comforts of home. Our military assistance group, the Moroccan-U.S. Liaison Office, or MUSLO, even used to bring back Wonder Bread from the Navy commissary when they flew their DC-3 up to the base at Rota, Spain—this in a country where the quality of local bread was very high.

In truth, Rabat was dull. King Hassan II was an absolute monarch, in spite of some parliamentary trappings. He made all decisions of any importance, and many of none. His cabinet ministers had little authority and were generally afraid to say anything significant. Contact with foreigners was limited by the traditional inward orientation of Moroccan families and royal disapproval of ostentation by wealthy Moroccans. While there was a fair amount of official hospitality, private entertainment of foreigners was not encouraged, and there was almost no political gossip. The Throne was sacrosanct, and diplomats had almost no one to talk to except other members of the foreign community, not unlike Eastern Europe during the Cold War. (More detailed comments on Morocco can be found in my book *North Africa—Regional Tensions and Strategic Concerns* [Praeger, 1984]).

Ambassador Stuart Rockwell was the most competent drafter I ever encountered in the Foreign Service. Until he had gone over your draft and marked it up, you did not know what drafting was. A very handsome man, he often seemed cold to people who were put off by his body language. Beneath a rather austere exterior he was a warm and sympathetic person.

The DCM residence on Tariq Ibn Ziyad Street had been the residence of our first ambassador, Cavendish W. Cannon, who served in 1956–58. Perched on a high bluff overlooking the lush valley of the Bou Regreg (Sparkling) River, it had a small but very pleasant garden and though modest in size was a comfortable house, with one exception. In the morning swarms of commuters from Salé, across the river, roared up the hill at the bottom of the cliff on their motor bikes and in low-powered cars, shifting gears and making so much noise that it was impossible to sleep with the windows open.

As compensation, we had a good staff. Abdallah the butler, a Berber from the south, was somewhat officious with lesser people, but he was ever ready and solicitous with the family, and Richard loved to imitate him. Our cook, Fatima, also a Berber from the south, had worked for Americans since her youth. She was good-humored and conscientious, and we all liked her. Finally, there was Aisha, the maid, an Arab and the only one of the three with whom I could communicate in her native language. She was much younger than the others and recently married to a man of very modest means who claimed to be a *sharif*, or descendant of the Prophet.

We enrolled Jill in the French *lycée*, much to her disgust, and put Richard in the American community school. Jill did very well, eventually winning the Prix d'Excellence at the end of her first and second years. Richard did okay at the community school. In the meantime, Jeff continued at Kenyon and Alison began teaching art history at Rosemary Hall in Greenwich, Connecticut.

Our first year in Rabat passed smoothly. Nothing much happened. We toured the usual sites and visited the Peace Corps volunteers around the country with Dick Holbrooke, the director, and his wife. We swam in the ocean and joined the Yacht Club and bought a tiny sailboat, an Optimiste, for Richard. I worked to improve communication between the various sections of the mission and tried without much success to study Moroccan Arabic.

Then one day in May 1971, after swimming in the Yacht Club pool, I fainted in the dressing room. Shortly thereafter I took advantage of a trip to Germany for a conference to go to the Air Force hospital at Wiesbaden for an examination by a military cardiologist. He said I should have a heart valve replacement sooner rather than later. Although I had known that this point was likely to be reached sooner or later, it was still unsettling. On receipt of the cardiologist's report, the medical people in the department and my Washington cardiologist put in motion a process that led to scheduling an operation at the Mayo Clinic in Rochester for that December.

Meanwhile, things began to happen in Rabat. First, in early July our political officer, Earl Russell, set out for Dakar, his new post, with his wife Beatrice and son Scott in a Peugeot station wagon. An axle broke in the Mauritanian desert, and Earl died of heat exhaustion before help arrived. We were stunned. Earl was so strong and experienced in outback travel that we had not thought to question the wisdom of his travel plans.

Then, on July 15, officers of the royal armed forces staged a coup attempt during the king's birthday party at his seaside palace at Skhirat, south of Rabat. Those in attendance, including Ambassador Rockwell and most of the other chiefs of mission who made up the Rabat diplomatic corps, were spread-eagled on the grass under the hot sun. The Belgian ambassador was killed while trying to escape. In Rabat we had no way of knowing what was going on and were much relieved when Rockwell finally appeared, red as a lobster. Loyal officers had put down the coup after a few hours, and it was all over, for the moment.

The man behind the coup was General Medbuh, a Berber from the Rif whose name means "slaughtered." He was well known to the diplomatic corps because he was in charge of the golf course and the racetrack. As a nongolfer, I never met him. The king always harbored a suspicion that the Americans were somehow involved in the affair. He said as much to Rockwell, who replied that the Americans' chief representative in Morocco might have been killed. The king replied that for the CIA that would have been no obstacle.

Jeanne and I left for Washington and the Mayo Clinic in early December. After a week of tests the operation was performed on December 13. The doctor found a birth defect in my aortic valve; it was bicuspid instead of the normal tricuspid. They replaced it with a Starr-Edwards valve, a plastic ball in a birdcage. It has the virtue of rugged simplicity and has worked well; but it tends to produce clots, and I am on blood thinners for life. Whatever happens from now on, Uncle Sam has certainly gotten his money's worth out of that operation.

I was out of the hospital by Christmas, and Jeff came up from Kenyon to help us celebrate. Shortly after New Year's Day we took off on what seems in retrospect an incredible journey. We went first to Kenyon, where, at Jeff's request, Jeanne cooked a roast beef for him and his friends, who were living in conditions of considerable squalor. Then we went to Manhattan to visit Jeanne's parents and then to Phoenix, where we spent some time with Jeanne's college roommate, and finally to Washington.

Jeanne returned to Rabat toward the end of the month, and I was to begin working at the department while convalescing. I had barely sat down at my desk in the Bureau of African Affairs when the telephone rang. It was Jeanne's father, Roy Jaccard, telling me her mother, Ruth, was in the hospital and I had better get there quick. After calling her doctor to hear what her condition was, I flew to Manhattan. Ruth was unconscious and died a few days later. Jeanne arrived shortly thereafter, as did her brother Bob's widow, Babs. After the funeral we did what we could to assure that Roy would be able to continue living in the apartment, which he shared with Ruth's slightly dotty sister, Mary, and returned to Rabat. That summer, Jeanne had to return and install Roy in a nursing home, where he died two years later.

People in Rabat were glad to see us back, but the fact that I had been gone for some two months and had not really been missed at work, as far as I could tell, was an indication of how much was going on in Rabat. For the summer, we decided to swap houses with a couple from the embassy in Paris. In late July, after the king's birthday, which I attended as chargé since Stuart Rockwell was on leave, I left Francis De Tarr in charge in Rabat. We drove up to Tangier, took the ferry to Algeciras, and after a night in Ronda drove north. As we were approaching Madrid we heard a Spanish newscast saying that something untoward involving the king had happened in Morocco. I immediately detoured to the U.S. airbase at Torrejon, outside Madrid, and learned that Moroccan Air Force officers from the base at Kenitra, north of Rabat, had tried to shoot down the king's plane on its way back from Europe. The leader of the coup was General Oufkir, the senior officer in the army, who had been shot. I called Francis to see whether I should return to Rabat, but he seemed to be in pretty good control, so we decided to continue on our way to Paris.

Paris was a pleasant interlude, except that I experienced the first of many episodes of dizziness that continued to trouble me for the rest of my Foreign Service career. Suddenly, with no warning, my head would start spinning and I could not walk. This first attack occurred as I was walking along the street near our apartment. Jeanne took me to the American Hospital in Neuilly, where they found nothing but kept me for the night just in case. Subsequent examinations by various cardiologists and neurologists have never come up with a satisfactory explanation. The spasms diminished in frequency over the years and seemed related to tension. After years in retirement I have had only one, but the thought that one could occur at any minute is always with me.

The Moroccans of course suspected that we must have been involved in Oufkir's plot, since Americans ran the control tower at the Kenitra base from which the planes took off. Furthermore, the Moroccan pilots were American-trained and flying American aircraft (F-5s). One of them had an American wife. That Rockwell and I were both out of town would have been seen as deliberate, and there was no getting around that as far as the Moroccans were concerned. Nothing striking happened to our relations, but they cooled noticeably; and I suspect that the Moroccans complained in Washington and that this was a factor in Rockwell's departure from the post in 1973. He went back to Washington to become deputy chief of protocol, a job in which he was very good but which was well below the sort of post he should have had. It was an unfortunate waste of unusual talent but not the first or the last such in the department, which is notoriously ungrateful and forgetful, not to say stupid about personnel matters.

Rockwell was succeeded by Robert Neumann, a political appointee from California, who arrived in September 1973. Rockwell remarked that Neumann seemed to be his nemesis, having earlier done him out of the ambassadorship to Afghanistan. Neumann had had an academic career but had connections with the Republican political machine in California, and that explained his appointment. He had no experience in or knowledge of North Africa and the Arab World. Very Mittel European in outlook, he made a good match with Hassan II, taking him seriously and catering to his pretensions.

In spite of our differences of perspective, I liked working for Neumann. Rockwell was so competent that I had little to do. As Neumann was not well organized, I found myself fully employed as the voice of reason.

In 1973 I turned fifty. I had promised myself earlier that if by reaching that age I had not had an ambassadorship I would retire and go into academia. Had I stayed with Sisco he might have rewarded me with a post by this time, but I could not have picked a better post than Rabat from which to be absent for a major operation. I decided to wait one more year and to make a decision at fifty-one.

That same year, 1973, Jeff graduated from Kenyon and Jill from National Cathedral. We had promised to let her spend her last year of high school there if she would stick with the lycée for two years. We decided not to attend either graduation because of the expense involved, a decision I have regretted ever since. Jill was accepted at Yale and Jeff at the University of Wisconsin graduate school, and both came to spend the summer in Rabat.

Early in 1974 I was offered and accepted the post of DCM in Athens. The ambassador, Henry Tasca, had asked for me; and while it was not a chief of mission job, it was important and could lead to bigger things. I would give it a try. Tasca's wife was famously difficult, but I thought we could deal with her. We followed the usual steps: enrolling Richard in the Athens community high school, arranging to buy my predecessor's stock of liquor and canned goods, doing an interview with an Athens paper, and informing everyone where we were going. My successor at Rabat was to be Carleton Coon.

We took various preparatory steps, but by June our movement orders had not arrived. The Coons would soon be on our doorstep. Our telegrams to the department asking for my orders went unanswered. Finally, Roy Atherton, by then assistant secretary for NEA, called to say that he was trying to arrange for me to be assigned as Bill Eagleton's successor as chief of the interests section at Algiers, with the understanding that when the Algerians renewed relations, which they had broken in 1967, I would be the first ambassador. He did not yet have Kissinger's agreement to this. I would be issued travel orders allowing us to go to Paris or elsewhere and hang out there or come home on leave if we wanted, until such time as the deal was sealed. Given Kissinger's sometimes petty and spiteful attitude toward the Foreign Service, this was a risky business. I had briefly been his control officer on his first visit to the Arab world in 1973 but doubted that he had any recollection of me or would feel any need to be helpful to me even if he did.

I decided, however, that the prospect of a summer in Europe at government expense was an opportunity not to be missed. We flew to Paris—with Freddie—in mid-June, stayed initially at one of the modest hotels where embassies lodged visitors, and then went to Brittany by train. At Les Invalides terminal we managed to intercept Richard, who had been at a Boy Scout camp in Spain and was due to transit Paris en route to Athens. He went with us to Brittany, surprised to learn that he would not be going to school in Athens. In Brittany, we stayed with our friends Bill and Marie-Ange Underwood, who were renting a surprisingly large gardener's cottage on a French estate near Dinan. Freddie, however, we left in Paris with a woman who boarded dogs.

Taking home leave would have been the sensible alternative, but we had no home to go to. Our only house, in Barnaby Woods, had tenants living in it. Jeanne's parents were both gone, and there was no place to stay in Manhattan. My mother did not have space for us in San Francisco. We decided that we needed to find a house somewhere in Europe that we could use as a refuge at such times and began planning with the Underwoods a car trip to a variety of places in France to see houses that were advertised in the Paris *Herald Tribune*. We had begun making reservations and other arrangements when the Paris embassy called and said that Kissinger wanted to see me right away.

I took the train to Paris and flew to Washington to discover that there were three ambassadorial posts to be filled: Algiers, Nicosia, and Damascus. There were three candidates for the jobs: Richard Murphy, ambassador to Mauritania; Bill Crawford, ambassador to Yemen; and me. Kissinger wanted to see each of us before deciding who should go where. I was asked my preference and said Damascus, but Dick Murphy got that assignment, and I was to chosen for Algiers. I was told to hang out somewhere until the Algerians agreed to my coming, at which point I would receive further instructions. In light of this development, we decided that it would be unrealistic to make a trip of any length in France and so went to Rome to look into schooling for Richard and to try looking for a house in Italy. We had $39,000 from Jeanne's father's estate. That would buy almost nothing in France and, we discovered, not much more in Tuscany than a ruin with no roof, no water, no road, and no land around it.

On arrival in Rome we rented a small Fiat and took off for the North. We spent the first night in Orvieto, which we found very attractive. Our next stop was a Tuscan village that we did not find attractive. We saw some of the ruins that were for sale and soon concluded that with our limited means Tuscany was not for us. We shopped around near Assisi and were tempted to buy a ruin with a view of Lake Trasimeno near Cortona but decided that first we should look into a place near the village of Monterubbiano in the Marche that had been advertised for sale in the *Herald Tribune* a year earlier, a complete house on the side of a hill for $25,000. Our friends Grant and Pauli McClanahan, who had a house in Italy, had reconnoitered the place for us the previous fall and had reported that the price was reasonable. But the house was on a well-traveled road, and the village did not look very appealing to them. From Assisi we sent a telegram to the agent, Filippo Baraschi, asking if the place was still for sale, but he didn't read English, and neither did anyone else, and we received no answer. We decided to take a look anyway and went over the mountains to the Adriatic coast at Fano and down to Monterubbiano.

We found the house from the McClanahan's sketch map without difficulty and were looking at the downhill side of it when the new owner appeared and regarded us with suspicion, not to say hostility, and said the house had been sold. We proceeded to the village and found the agent Baraschi without difficulty. He produced a young American girl, Ann Engel, whose parents had a house near the village, to interpret. Why she wasn't recruited to translate our telegram was not clear.

Her father, Sidney Engel, was with the Joint Distribution Committee, a Jewish charity that helped Jews in Arab countries and facilitated their migration to Israel. He had been involved in that operation in Morocco and we had known him and his wife, Jean, there. She was actively pursuing what became a business of exporting Berber textiles to England for sale there.

Baraschi said that if we really wanted to buy a house he had some to show us. The first two did not look very inviting. The third was on a hillside about a mile from the other side of the village. It was a solidly built farmhouse with a roof, a road, its own well, and city water. There was no bathroom or outhouse, though, and people had relieved themselves on the ground floor of the stable where the cattle and pigs were kept. The house came with 5 hectares, 12.5 acres, of land. The price was $15,000. We decided we could not afford not to buy it.

The house belonged to the remaining members of the Pazzi family, which operated the town's biggest hotel and had moved out of the farmhouse a generation earlier. Giovanni Pazzi and I agreed on terms and conditions to be finalized when I returned for the settlement ceremony at the office of a notary in a matter of months. Meanwhile, Baraschi found a *muratore*, or mason, who would install two bathrooms and a kitchen and clean out the stables to make a dining room. Baraschi and I ordered the bathroom fixtures and a kitchen sink from the hardware store in Fermo. A cousin of Giovanni's got the contract for the electrical work, installing a meter and wiring outlets throughout the house.

After seeing that the house was taken care of, we headed back to Rome, and lodged near the Embassy. We heard the depressing news of Rodger Davies's assassination in Nicosia and waited for word about our own fate. Tired of hanging out on the Via Veneto, we went south for a brief stay and came back to learn that Kissinger wanted to see me one more time. I hurried to Washington to meet with him for about twenty minutes to be told that if the Algerians, who had broken relations over the 1967 June war, did not renew relations within a reasonable time, he would withdraw me. That was the sort of language they would understand. I asked what a "reasonable" period was, and he said six months. I was afraid to tell Jeanne, who was worn out from wandering, and did not do so until it was clear the Algerians would renew relations within the fateful period.

I returned to Rome, and we immediately began making arrangements to go to Algiers. We placed Richard in St. Stephens

School in Rome, where he changed his name to Jack. For some reason we had to ship Freddie by air in advance of our departure, and he was met and cared for by Bob Pelletreau, the political officer. I had just turned fifty-one, and Jeanne and I were finally heading off to my first post as ambassador.

14

Algiers

We arrived in Algiers on September 17, 1974, the first day of Ramadan. It was very hot. We were met at the airport by two men from the Foreign Ministry, Political Officer Bob Pelletreau, and our chauffeur, Mustafa, who took us to our Residence in an upscale residential area next to the Embassy. The town seemed very quiet, with little traffic and few signs of commercial activity.

The Residence, Villa Montfeld, was a nineteenth-century palazzo built in the style of the corsair country houses sprinkled around the suburbs of the city. It had been built by two English ladies who had come to Algiers for their health, and the U.S. government had purchased it from its French owner, the publisher of a right-wing newspaper, *The Echo* of Oran, on the eve of Algerian independence. Richly decorated with old Turkish tiles, it was one of the most attractive residences the U.S. government owned abroad and certainly the most attractive we ever lived in.

Surrounded by a large park, with fruit-bearing olive and persimmon trees and meandering shaded paths, it had a small swimming pool and a splendid terrace with a sweeping view of the Bay of Algiers. Although the electrical system had to be replaced by a team of Navy Seabees while we were in residence, and the plumbing needed it too, it was very spacious and comfortable. We had a competent staff, including a French cook and a Moroccan Berber couple, Tayyib and Fatima, who served as butler and maid. We had to fire the Eagleton's nursemaid-laundress because she was receiving male guests in her room at odd hours. I should explain at this point that the Algerians did not make good servants. They were too independent and did not readily accept the servant-master relationship, which is why we had Moroccan servants

While we were well situated, other diplomats were less fortunate. Housing was in acutely short supply. There was also a shortage of almost every consumer good, from vegetables to automobiles, and skilled craftsmen—like plumbers and electricians—were hard to find. It was ironic that a country that should have been the market garden of Europe was importing fruit, vegetables, poultry, and meat. At one point it was the world's largest importer of eggs, thanks to the dead hand of socialism. People on state farms were paid whether they produced or not, and their rewards were chits to be exchanged in company stores that had little on their shelves of interest to consumers. Finding something to buy in the suq was a challenge, made more difficult by the churlish attitude of the shopkeepers, who seemed to have no interest in pleasing customers. We were lucky to have a kitchen garden where we grew cherry tomatoes, lettuce, and other crops, but our Algerian gardeners knew very little about farming.

The Swiss had been our protecting power in Algeria. The Swiss ambassador, Etienne Vallotton, had been a colleague in Beirut and was very friendly. He and his lovely wife Monique were a great help to us. When relations were resumed and we became an embassy again, we held a flag-raising ceremony at the Residence, and I presented Vallotton and his deputy honorary commissions as first and second secretaries of embassy.

Our interests section was about three times the size of the Swiss embassy, of which we were nominally a small part. A chief, a political officer, an economic officer, three CIA officers, two CIA communicators, two American secretaries, one State communicator, and a records clerk made up the eleven Americans in all (we had no Marine guards), and we had perhaps twenty-five local nationals as drivers, maintenance staff, clerks, and secretaries.

Algeria was at that point one of the leading powers of the Third World. Its president, Houari Boumediene (or Bumadyan), was secretary general of the Non-Aligned Movement, in which role he had launched an ambitious plan to establish a New International Economic Order (NIEO) to redress the imbalance between the nations of the wealthy North and the impoverished South. He had received an enthusiastic response from the lesser-developed countries, but it was giving some of the industrialized states, including the United States, fits. Algeria itself had plenty of money from its oil and gas deposits and was launched on an overly ambitious industrialization program that produced a number of white elephants and very little social progress. The United States initially took a negative stand toward the NIEO but adopted a more relaxed and utilitarian policy when Thomas Enders was replaced as under secretary for economic affairs by Charles Robinson, a successful businessman who came to Algiers and quickly established a rapport with the Algerians.

Algeria's political and economic importance attracted diplomatic representatives from all over. Countries around the world thought it was important to have an embassy there, but the shortage of housing and consumer goods and the inaccessibility of government officials meant that diplomats in Algiers were an unhappy bunch. Here is a report I wrote in 1976:

DIPLOMATIC LIFE IN ALGIERS

"The Minister does not receive Ambassadors. One Ambassador, after two years without seeing the Minister, finally asked if we would just print in the papers that he had been received by him. We refused, of course." (Foreign Ministry official Mohamed Aberkane)

The following is a brief survey of the status of the foreign diplomatic community in Algiers. It is submitted as of interest to AFN and of possible utility to officers assigned here in the future.

Description

By Third World standards Algiers has a sizeable diplomatic community. At latest count, there are 73 resident missions here. Most of these have resident ambassadors, although there are a few ambassadors resident elsewhere. In the past two years a number of countries have moved their regionally accredited ambassadors here from places such as Tunis in the belief that this is the more important capital. The Algerians actively encourage such moves and make promises of help with housing and administrative support. Unfortunately, they are unable to make good on such promises because the housing situation here is unbelievably tight. Many ambassadors from smaller countries spend months, and even years, in hotels. The Omani ambassador, for instance, finally left in disgust after a year at the St. George, and the United Arab Emirates and Qatari ambassadors are still without residences after a year. They have moved to the new Aurassi hotel, where the cheapest single room costs $65 a day and where they are paying upwards of $300 a day for suites. Reflecting the housing shortage, rents are astronomical. The latest middle grade officer's residence rented by us is costing DA11,000, or roughly $2,850, a month. (See our A-65, Dec. 13, 1974 for more details.)

The office space situation is fully as bad as the housing. In the first place, there is almost nothing available. In the second, buildings have been largely unmaintained since 1962. Their elevators have not worked for years and services are appalling. Only those embassies that were open at the time of, or soon after, independence and had the foresight to buy properties beforehand have anything decent to work from today.

The Algerian response to this problem is twofold. On the one hand, the Foreign Ministry continues to invite unwary Third World countries to send ambassadors here and thus compound the problem (a type of diplomatic homeopathy?). On the other, plans are proceeding for the construction of a diplomatic enclave on an insalubrious piece of coastal plain just beyond the airport. The Algerians have in mind requiring all missions to move to the enclave, which is to be adjacent to the new seat of government, but are meeting with resistance and the diplomatic corps fervently hopes they will reconsider. No one, except those with no quarters at all, wants to move to the new location.

Working Conditions

There are undoubtedly capitals where it is more difficult to do business with the host government, e.g. Kampala, Tripoli or Saigon, but there can be few diplomats more frustrated than those working in Algiers. Were the Algerians not so active in world affairs, and were this capital not considered important, their frustrations would be much milder. As it is, all of their governments expect them to conduct diplomacy with the Algerians, and none of them has much luck. Except occasionally on the technical level where the Algerians want help, none of them has much reliable, meaningful local contact. They have no access to the Foreign Minister (neither do the representatives of major powers), and the Ministry below him is a wasteland pockmarked with oubliettes where diplomatic demarches are consigned. Direct contact with other ministries is closely controlled, and all requests for meetings are supposed to be sent through the Foreign Ministry. This can be avoided sometimes and sometimes not. It is a very time-consuming process, further complicated by the fact that officials having contact with foreigners are supposed to report their conversations in writing. This is a severe inhibition on contacts and conversation.

As a matter of practice, most Algerian officials do not return telephone calls. In their defense one must admit that they are overworked and understaffed and that their secretaries often do not record or transmit messages left with them. As a result, one must call repeatedly. This annoys everyone. The official when you finally reach him is likely to be forthcoming and friendly as long as you are in the room with him or have him on the telephone, but his solemn promise to give you an answer in half an hour is rarely kept. Your request ends up somewhere in the maw, perhaps to be answered a week later, perhaps never.

In addition to the simple frustrations of establishing any useful contact, there is the frustration of there being little hard economic or political information to be had, even if contact is established. The Algerians start from the assumption that any foreign diplomat seeking information, and particularly statistics, is up to no good, and they are chary about giving out information which could in any way be construed as of possible utility to an enemy. It should be kept in mind, however, that particularly with regard to statistics, there is very little hard information to provide. The Algerians do not really know themselves how many people they are or how much wheat they are growing.

When it is a case of the Algerians wanting something, the telephone works and a quick reply is expected of you. The diplomat with a positive outlook sends an immediate telegram and tries to meet an Algerian request, no matter how trivial it might be. The more tired and cynical send a night letter. It does not seem to make all that much difference. There is a certain amount of whimsy operating on the other end of the line too. In any event, the diplomat who has done his best to get a favorable answer and succeeds bears it triumphantly to the Algerian concerned, hoping it will gain him kudos and preferment next time he makes a request. It does nothing of the kind, of course. His favorable reply is received matter-of-factly by the man's aide (the man himself is in a meeting). The favorable response is no big deal, he learns, and then it too disappears into the maw. The man for whom he has done the favor will not even accept his invitation for dinner for fear he might be compromised.

Everyone takes consolation from the fact that everyone else gets the same treatment. The communist and Arab countries are treated no better than the Western capitalists. The complaint is universal, and it leads to a particular pattern of diplomatic behavior. Firstly, since all the diplomats are in the same boat, they tend to be rather "matey" and except for the darkest antagonisms, as between Cuba and the United States, the lack of relations or conflicting ideologies is no bar to social and official contacts. Secondly, everyone gets away from Algiers as often and for as long as he can. Thirdly, one goes to national days and social events in the hope, however faint, of seeing a government minister there and getting some work done. The Algerians seem to be aware of this and therefore normally designate one minister to represent the entire government at national day celebrations (thereby minimizing the possibilities for contact).

The most frequent attendee is the Minister of Information and Culture, Dr. Taleb Ibrahimi. He must receive the complaints and requests, and the other ministers are spared. From the Foreign Ministry the turnout is also very sparse. One division head, apparently picked by turns, and someone from Protocol, but never the chief of protocol (a shy cat lover), will turn up. As a result, the diplomats are forced to spend most of their time talking to each other. Since most of the substantive subjects have already been exhausted, and those that have not are too delicate to be discussed, the level of such conversations tends to be low. It was therefore with something akin to gratitude that the corps received the dramatic news of the Indian ambassador's shooting scrape, which provided a very satisfying subject of conversation for almost two weeks. (In his car, with his wife and children in search of a picnic spot, he had blundered into a compound where either Boumediene or Ahmad Ben Bella lived and had been shot and lightly wounded by a sentry.) It is indicative of the climate of secrecy in Algiers that no one in the diplomatic corps knows who lives in the compound or where the president of the republic sleeps. As John Robinson, the British ambassador, remarked, the Algerians could not have picked a less deserving target. The Indian is a *New Statesman* liberal, fully sympathetic with Algerian socialism. The excuse offered by one Algerian official was that the guard mistook him for an Algerian. The corps found that hilarious, but it is probably exactly what did happen.

Privileges and Immunities

The Algerians are signatories to the Vienna convention on diplomatic privileges and immunities, but they are not overly scrupulous about observing it. The most constant complaint of diplomatic missions is the behavior of the customs authorities, who recognize no authority except the customs regulations, which they always interpret in the most unfavorable possible way. It is slight comfort to know

202 Memoirs of a Foreign Service Arabist

that the Algerian government has the same problem with items it imports, and that millions of dollars worth of valuable commodities have been ruined by the delays imposed by recalcitrant customs officials.

Each chief of mission is issued with a red ID card which is supposed to get him through customs and passport controls at the airport and other ports of entry and which should protect him against molestation by the police or military. It did not work in the case of the Indian ambassador, but it usually does and the corps has little to complain about in this respect.

Other diplomats are issued brown ID cards, which are less effective at the airport but usually suffice for most purposes.

Surveillance

As indicated above, local officials having contact with foreigners are required to submit written reports of their conversations. It is assumed that all telephones are tapped, and that bugging of diplomatic premises is a common occurrence. The Algerians are alleged to be fairly expert in this regard, and to be importing modern material from Europe for the purpose.

Routine police surveillance and shadowing of diplomats is much less in evidence. On occasion we have noted that the policeman in front of the Embassy records the license plates of cars entering the premises, but this does not seem to be a routine practice, or at least he is discreet about it if it is. All diplomats (but not nondiplomatic staff) are required to get a deplacement or travel permit each time they make a trip in Algeria beyond the limits of the Algiers Wilaya province. These permits are issued in a matter of three or four days. They are rarely requested by local authorities, but in some localities such as Cherchell, where there is a military academy, one is likely to be stopped and asked to produce it. According to diplomatic colleagues, on at least some occasions the local police take note of diplomatic license tags and report them to Algiers, where they are checked against deplacement requests. We do not doubt it, but cannot prove it.

There does not seem to be the concerted effort to compromise our staff which is common in some other Arab countries. If the Algerians are making serious efforts to spy on the Embassy, they are very discreet about it. That does not mean, however, that we are not regarded with particular suspicion, because we are. One recently arrived officer, for instance, was told by a wife from the German embassy that whenever they invited Algerians to a function they were asked if Americans were to be present. The Algerians would not come if they were, according to her.

[Note: This report is undated and seems to be in a memorandum rather than an Airgram format. I recall writing it in 1976, and must have sent it by pouch as an unclassified official informal communication to the Algerian desk in the department.]

We are taught to avoid stereotypes, but there is a certain thread of wariness or resistance that seems to characterize Algerian attitudes toward others over the centuries. The center of the Circumcellion phenomenon of the Donatist heresy of the fourth century was Constantine, for instance. Consuls (there were no ambassadors) resident in Algiers in the eighteenth century would not find my description of diplomatic life in Algiers in 1976 all that strange, and an instruction from our consul, Richard O'Brien, in 1803 or 1804 rings true today:

January 1804[?]
Rules for government. U.S. Ships of War entering Algiers
OBSERVATIONS for the Commander of an American Ship of War coming to the Port of Algiers

1st   On a Ship of war of the United States coming in sight of Algiers, the Consul must obtain the Dey's permission to go off her; without which no Consul can go off. Said Vessel is to hoist her pendant & Ensign and fire a Gun to Leeward and then hoist the American Jack at the Fore top

Gallant Mast head. She is not to approach nearer Algiers than 5 or 6 miles, until the Algerine Boat, with the Consular flag, is coming off.

2d   If there be no contagious disorder in Algiers, the Boat, with the Consul, will go along side; but if any contagious disorder prevails, she will drop astern and confer at a distance.

3d   The Consul will have a detail of affairs, or news ready written to give to the Commander; and the Commander will also give, in writing, all requisite information to the Consul. By this means nothing will be forgotten.

4th   The Ship should take care to anchor before that, by light winds, calms, or currents, she would be set within cannon shot of the Algerine batteries. But must never anchor until visited by the Consul and is informed by him on the state of affairs between the U. States and the Regency.

5th   Should the business of the Ship require her anchoring, the best place will be to the SE of the Lighthouse on the Marine, a little to the east of the second Castle on the Southern shore; which is the second Battery from the Cape North of the Metafour River.

OBSERVE . . . When you anchor in the Bay of Algiers, be always ready for action; and always ready for getting under way. Here are always sudden Gales; and I may add, you are never secure in your affairs.

The whole crew of the Algerine boat which comes out with the Consul should not be permitted to go on board the Ship. By their enquiries false news is often circulated, and representations made prejudicial to our national affairs. Communicate nothing to the people who come on board, but treat them with civility and attentions.

. . . . .

After the Commander has landed, and has seen the General of Marine or Admiral, he then proceeds to the Consular house; and if requisite, visits the Dey at his Palace. The Consul must first obtain permission on this point through his Drogerman.

The oars are always taken out of the Ship's boat by the Algerines, when they land. This is to prevent Slaves from making an escape with the boat. When the boat is ready to return, the oars will be delivered up.

The next day after the Ship anchors, it is customary for the Regency to send a present to the Ship of Bullocks, Sheep, Poultry, &s, on receiving, which the Ship fires three Guns, and the Consul pays for it 15 or 20 dollars.

. . . . .

Any Captives, or Turks, or Moors, or Jews, of Algiers, who should illegally get on board the Ship, the Commander must report them to the Consul, and he will endeavor to obtain pardon for them. At all events they must be given up.

. . . . .

When the Ship is ready to depart the Consul gives the intimation thereof to the Dey, through the Drogerman. It is customary for the Dey (if he be in the City) to see the Commander before his Departure. On this visit he will say, "Has Your Highness any Commands? I am destined for Sea".

. . . .

OBSERVE, only the Port of Algiers, Bona, and Oran, are public ports. The others should never be entered but by necessity, as the Inhabitants are very savage, and often commit outrages & arrests on Officers and Crews of Boats.

. . . . .

Unless the U. States Vessels of War have some very particular business, I would not recommend their Anchoring. They had better lay off & on two or three days, to avoid the danger of Gales & bad weather in the Winter Season, as well as the Caprice of the Government.

[LC. EPP, Vol. 9, Jan.–Feb. 1804]
Wars with the Barbary Powers Vol. III, Part 3[?] pp. 305–6

I sent a copy of O'Brien's instructions to our ambassador in Algiers several years ago and received the following response: "Thank you so much for the copy of the orders for our Navy—in 1802. You will be pleased to learn that things have not changed that much. Many of those strictures are still in place and Algerian bureaucracy lives. I am laughing about it through tears, because we are having a major property dispute with the government."

In 1974, American companies had a stake of some $1 billion in Algeria, primarily in the oil and gas sectors. They were exploring and drilling for oil, building gas liquefaction plants, opening a home electronics plant and training its workers, constructing an irrigation project in a remote desert area of western Algeria, planning a two thousand–bed hospital for Algiers, erecting a satellite communication network, and so forth. Because of the American economic role and the role Henry Kissinger was playing in the Arab-Israeli conflict, the Americans in Algiers enjoyed considerably more access and influence than their diplomatic colleagues. Even while relations were broken, we had a contact in the presidency, Ismail Hamdani, who was helpful and effective to a degree unheard of from the Algerian bureaucracy.

In November 1974, the Algerians agreed to restore relations, and I presented my credentials in January 1975. I made my remarks in Arabic at the presentation ceremony televised around the country, and all my subsequent conversations with President Boumediene were carried out in that language. This became a point of honor with both of us, and Boumediene, who had a good command of the language and was pushing Arabization, reportedly told his cabinet that if I could conduct my business in Arabic so could they.

In the colonial period, education of Algerians was minimal and higher education was in French. Colloquial Algerian Arabic in 1975 was full of French borrowings and quite inelegant. Polite conversation was likely to be in French. Literacy in Arabic was limited; none of our local employees could read it. This has undoubtedly changed somewhat in the intervening years, but as late as 1989 when I had to lecture in Arabic at the University of Algiers, the students in the audience, when it came to question time, still had difficulty expressing themselves in Arabic.

In any event, not only the American economic role but also my speaking Arabic and dispensing with the need for an interpreter enabled me to develop a personal relationship with Boumediene that none of my colleagues enjoyed. Most of them never spoke to him except to present credentials and to say goodbye when they left. I could get in to see him on short notice whenever the need arose. He projected an austere and humorless image, but he had a quiet sense of humor, and our conversations were normally amiable and pleasant. The one exception was when I was summoned three nights running in 1975 to be scolded for our role in the Green March, Morocco's seizure of the Western Sahara.

To explain briefly, Juan Carlos of Spain had vowed publicly that the Spanish would repel with force Morocco's planned march of 300,000 civilians into the Spanish colony of Rio de Oro, or Western Sahara, that Spain was about to surrender. When the marchers approached, the Spanish withdrew and did nothing to stop them. Boumediene accused us of having pressured the Spanish not to resist. I denied it. But years later learned that he was right and I had been uninformed by the cretins in the Office of North African Affairs, if in fact they knew what was going on. Bill Eagleton, who had been the UN Secretary General's personal representative for the Sahara, told me that General Vernon Walters later said that he had been sent by Secretary Kissinger to dissuade Juan Carlos from using force against Moroccan civilians.

The Sahara problem remained a potential cloud over our relations, but its impact was lessened by the fact that the Polisario guerrillas supported by Algiers were faring well against the Moroccans. Our embassies in Algiers and Rabat had a substantial debate by telegram about the military aspects of the problem, with Ambassador Neumann and Carl Coon, my successor in Rabat, arguing that the Algerians had no chance against the Moroccans, while we argued to the contrary. We were right initially, but the Moroccans eventually changed the ground rules by building a long wall of sand and rock to cope with the Polisario's Land Rover raids.

Our biggest preoccupation was the American business community spread across the country. The engineers and construction people had little or no preparation for dealing with the Algerians, who tended to be suspicious, not to say paranoid, and to be uncooperative with people trying to help them. Their most bothersome regulation was a requirement that persons leaving the country obtain an exit permit from the Ministry of the Interior, which could take two or three weeks. An oil man forced to wait like that when he had a family emergency at home in Houston was unlikely to come back. The Algerians could also be quite uncooperative with regard to fulfillment of their side of a contract. Unwillingness to admit that this was often the result of incompetence by someone on their side was taken as a sign that it was deliberate.

The single worst problem we had concerned the failure of the American company Chemico to uphold its side of a contract to build a gas liquefaction plant. The company, discouraged by the Algerians' noncompliance with their side of the contract and persuaded that it was going to lose money on the deal, set out to and eventually did break the contract. I subsequently testified against the company at a tribunal in Geneva.

We also had problems with Americans getting arrested. Soon after my arrival in 1974, before the restoration of relations, the number two man at the Dutch embassy came to see me about two Americans working for Swindler under contract to the Dutch who had been imprisoned in Oran for insulting President Boumediene. The Dutch had no meaningful contact with anyone in authority and asked if I could help. I called Ismail Hamdani, and he got the men out of jail immediately. I never found out what it was they had done or said.

I had less luck with two young men from Wichita who tried to drive through Algeria and on to Europe in a new Chevrolet Corvette stuffed with Moroccan hashish. They were condemned to long prison terms and sent to the prison at Lambese, east of Constantine. I learned of them from Jim Hesse, my mucker from Oflag 64, then a practicing lawyer in Wichita. He called out of the blue one day—I had not heard from him since 1945 or 1946—to ask me to intervene on their behalf. Jeanne and I flew to Constantine and drove to Lambese, taking cigarettes and brownies for the two. We were allowed to meet with them in the presence of a prison official. I told them I would do what I could for them, but they had done something very stupid and would have to pay for it. They were well aware of that already. I subsequently raised the case with Boumediene, pointing out that the men had been sentenced under an ex post facto law, a point on which the minister of justice had agreed with me in an earlier meeting, and the U.S. Government hoped he would exercise clemency. He said it was a serious matter but would look into it. We left soon thereafter and I do not know what happened to the two men. I never heard further from Hesse.

The third case involved a young American who, for reasons that were never clear, was involved in a bomb attack against a government-owned newspaper in Algiers in the fall of 1976. This very serious offense would normally be punished severely. The man's mother retained the prominent Washington lawyer and fixer, Clark Clifford, who came to Algiers in the early fall. We gave him lunch, and he saw Boumediene. I also mentioned the case to him, but I was careful not to put myself in the position of defending terrorism. I do not know what happened to the young man.

Both Jeanne and I found that we liked the Algerians, who would give you a straight answer, although it was likely to be No; while it was often difficult to get one from the Moroccans, who were subtler and tried to avoid saying the n-word. Still, Algiers was a tough post. The general unresponsiveness of the bureaucracy, the housing problem, the lack of cultural and recreational facilities, and the ritual anti-Americanism of the press made the atmosphere, in Eagleton's word, "heavy." While Jeanne and I were comfortable and well off, some of our subordinates were not, and morale was a problem. Security, however, was not. Unlike most ambassadors to Arab states at the time, I had no bodyguard, and we walked unescorted all over the Algiers casbah without worrying about protection. That still seemed to be more or less the case when I last visited Algiers in 1989. Chris Ross, the ambassador, took me downtown in his SUV to eat dinner at a Chinese restaurant. He had no guard and no driver and seemed to feel no threat of any kind. Soon thereafter, however, the security situation deteriorated drastically, and Algiers was no longer safe for anyone.

Soon after Carter's 1976 election, Jeanne and I went home on consultation. We timed it to be there for our son Jeff's wedding in Annapolis the day after Christmas. Following that, I was going to California to visit Mother and begin a tour of American companies doing business in Algeria. While in Washington I called on Under Secretary for Political Affairs Phil Habib, Clark Clifford, and Charles Robinson, among others. Clifford was a great raconteur and told me he had been chosen to educate Jimmy Carter on the realities of Washington. He said Carter was full of Black Holes. Then he told me for the second time about playing poker with Winston Churchill on the train from Fulton, Missouri, to Washington. Then he asked me what I wanted, assuming I was looking for a job. I said I was not looking for anything and just wanted to inform him of my séance with Boumediene about his client, the teenage bomber. He didn't seem terribly interested.

As soon as I sat down with Habib and his assistant, Phyllis Oakley, he asked what I was doing in Washington and excoriated me for disobeying orders to all chiefs of mission not to come to Washington looking for jobs during the transition between the Ford and Carter administrations. I said I was unaware of such an order and had come in order to attend Jeff's wedding. He sniffed at that and proceeded to bully me for fifteen minutes. He was most disagreeable. I still regret not telling him to go to hell.

While waiting in Robinson's outer office I was surprised to see my old friend Ghassan Tueni, publisher of *An-Nahar*, the Beirut daily, emerging from the depths. I later learned that he was there to urge that the Americans send an ambassador to Lebanon to succeed Frank Meloy, who had been assassinated six months earlier. Given his conspiratorial view of the universe, he undoubtedly thought my presence was not coincidental.

Then I went to see Carol Laise, the director general of the Foreign Service, in effect, the head of personnel. She asked what my plans were and whether I had seen Roy Atherton, the assistant secretary for NEA. She suggested I see him right away, because he was planning to send me to Beirut. When I did, Atherton told me he did not feel happy about sending anyone to Lebanon, but 40,000 Syrian troops were maintaining order there and he thought it would be reasonably secure. Nothing had been decided yet. My name was one of three that would be forwarded to Carter, who would make the decision.

The day after Christmas, we went to Annapolis for Jeff's wedding to Nancy Belkov. It was our first Jewish wedding, following which the happy couple took off on a honeymoon armed with Nancy's mother's credit card. Jeff was at that point a graduate student at the University of Wisconsin, and they had no money. Neither did we, and we hoped Nancy's mother did.

After the wedding, Jeanne and I flew to San Francisco to visit Mother and Bud and Betty. Bud had retired from his post as governor of the Panama Canal Zone and from the army the year before and had gone to work for the International Engineering Company, a subsidiary of Morrison Knudsen, the well-known construction company. Bud and Betty had bought a cute little house on the lagoon in the Marin County suburb of Belvedere. Mother was appalled that they had paid $150,000 for it.

I had naively planned a business tour, hoping to persuade U.S. companies operating in Algeria to give their personnel some substantive briefing and orientation on the problems they would encounter there. I operated on the assumption that when people understood the background of actions they found unreasonable on first sight, they were better able to cope with them. As far as I could tell, none took my advice.

I made my first presentation on staff orientation to Bechtel, which had a major contract to complete work on the Chemico gas liquefaction plant at Arzew. I found complete incomprehension. Our next stop was Houston, where I spoke to a group of oilmen at the Cattleman's Club and visited executives of several companies with Algerian contracts. I was in the fancy suite of one of these executives when a call came through from Roy Atherton, who told me I had been promoted to Career Minister and President Carter had decided to send me to Beirut. We agreed that I should complete my scheduled consultations and talks in Chicago and Boston and then go to Washington to meet Cyrus Vance, the new secretary of state, who wanted to see me before agreeing to my assignment.

It was early January 1977, and time was running out. Vance wanted to go to the Middle East in February and wanted me to be there on the ground when he arrived. I reached Washington in mid-January, ready to roll. We visualized a stay of two or three days and were taken in by poor Dayton and Julie Mak in their one-bathroom house on P Street. But the Senate Foreign Relations Committee would not be hurried and did not schedule a confirmation hearing until the last week in January. The hearing itself was perfunctory, and we left for Algiers almost immediately thereafter, not even having time to be sworn in. That office was performed by Jim Ledesma, our consular officer, in Algiers, where I'd gone to pack and say goodbye. I was the first ambassador to a foreign country appointed by Carter, at least in part because I already had the necessary security clearances.

In Algiers, there was no time for farewell parties. I called on Boumediene, who made a nice remark about Carter picking the best man for a difficult job, and on the Czech ambassador, Vaclav Pleskot, dean of the diplomatic corps, who said the corps would give me the traditional silver tray in spite of the brevity of my stay. I paid hasty calls on a few colleagues with whom we had been close, the British, French, Italian, and Brazilians, I believe, and left for Rome, where we were met by my bodyguard, David Marshal, and went on to Beirut, arriving on the 13th of February. I presented my credentials on the 15th and Vance arrived on the 17th. We were off to the races.

Photo Gallery II

(L to R:) Egyptian Foreign Minister Mahmoud Riad, Political Counselor Richard B. Parker, and Economic Counselor Owen T. Jones, Cairo, ca. 1966

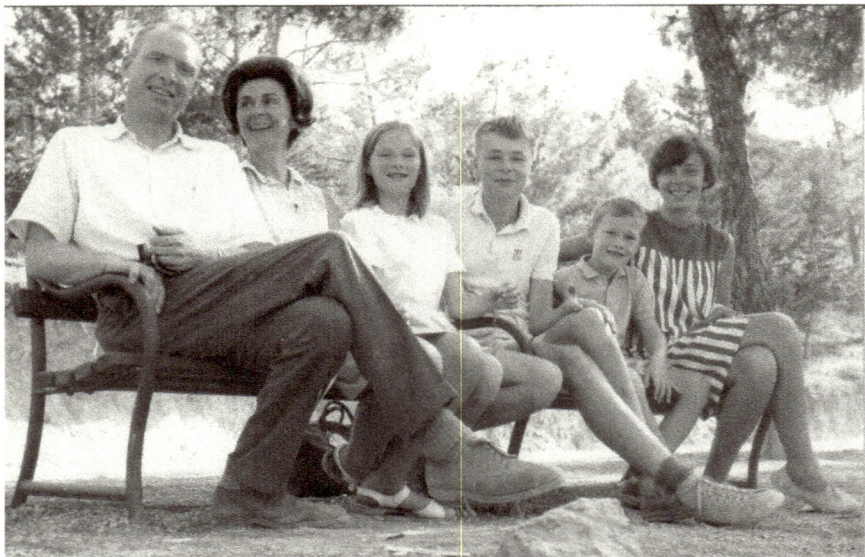

Picnic in Cyprus, August, 1966, Dick, Jeanne, Jill, Jeff, Jack, and Alison

Aboard the boat from Alexandria to Greece following the evacuation from Egypt, 1967

The Spanish flag being raised on the roof of the American Embassy, Cairo, June 7, 1967. (L to R:) Public Affairs Officer Bob Bauer, Political Counselor Richard Parker, Col. Aguilar, David Nes, Richard Nolte, Spanish Ambassador Angel Sagaz, and U.S. Marines

Exuberance at Ait Ben Haddou, Morocco, February 1971, while serving as deputy chief of mission in Rabat.

The Swiss had been the protecting power for the United States in Algeria following the break in June 1967. When relations were resumed in November 1974, the U.S. Interests Section at the Swiss Embassy was terminated and Ambassador Etienne Vallotton and Ambassador Richard Parker celebrated with a ceremony at the Residence.

Ambassador Richard Parker presents his credentials to President Elias Sarkis of Lebanon, with Foreign Minister Fuad Boutros in the background, Beirut, February 15, 1977.

Rabat, October 31, 1978 – Presentation of credentials to King Hassan II of Morocco. Seated at left is the new Lebanese ambassador

Buccaneers somewhere on the Mediterranean, circa 1987

15

Beirut Again

On February 7, 1985, I heard Professor Kainal Salibi, the American University of Beirut historian, speaking on the divergent views of Lebanon's recent history as seen from the two sides of Beirut. It was a fascinating comparison of the myths from both sides, often contradictory but strangely complementary in the sense that the conspiracy theories and accusations of bad faith both revolved around assertions of support for the concept of a free and independent Lebanon in which all Lebanese could live in peace. According to Salibi, the gap between them could be bridged by a rather small leap, which would have to be made by the Christians. The essential step in his view was small—reform of the army, so that the Druze and Muslims could trust it, which they still did not.

Reform of the army had, of course, been a major issue for some time. I had thought that progress in that regard had been registered with passage of the Army Law some years back, but the army's performance in bombarding Ras Beirut, including Salibi's house, apparently erased that forward movement. Druze suspicions of the army's intentions in south Lebanon were blocking deployment there, and the Druze position looked negative and destructive—understandable in the Lebanese context but suicidal in the long term. The Syrians reportedly tried to pressure the Druze and other groups having militias to relax their opposition to the army's entry into the area, but there was no indication whether their efforts were having any effect.

[Twenty years later, all of this had been overtaken and outdated by the move of the Syrian-Iranian-sponsored Hezbollah militia into the south, facing Israel on the border. The resulting complexities are beyond the scope of this book.]

Reform of the army, however, is only part of what has to be done. There are deep-seated socioeconomic and political problems that must also be dealt with, and the leadership of Lebanon has yet to show that it is up to the task. Nor was President Elias Sarkis and his team, or Suleiman Frangieh or Charles Helu. Indeed, the drama of Lebanon over the past twenty years has been one of incompetent leadership, whether those leaders have tried to continue the Chehabian system of minimal activity, as in the case of Helu and Sarkis, or the tribal politics of Frangieh and Amin Gemayel. It has reached the point that people look back on President Fuad Chehab's era with nostalgia as a golden age, and yet Chehab was not widely loved, at least by the Christians, as Salibi noted, and his disdain for political institutions, such as they were, was one reason these did not take on more substance. He at least had the merit of controlling the country effectively, however, and had the good sense to repair relations with Nasser and, to a lesser extent, the Syrians, who broke away from Nasser in 1961 and were therefore suspicious of Chehab because he stayed on good terms with him.

As I listened to Salibi talk, I thought back on the catalogue of errors that led us to the debacle of February 8, 1984. Taking 1958 and the Murphy mission as a clean break with the ill-conceived Eisenhower doctrine and CIA shenanigans in Lebanon, we had something of a tabula rasa in the early 1960s. All systems were go, and Lebanon was headed for an era of prosperity and economic expansion based on its banking system and genial anarchy.

Our first mistake was in giving the nod to Charles Helu as Chehab's successor. That is perhaps an overstatement of what we did, but that was how the Lebanese perceived it. All the presidential candidates were swarming around us in the summer of 1964—Fuad Ammoun, Charles Helu, Suleiman Frangieh, Yusuf Hitti, Raymond Edde, Jawad Boulos, Abdul Aziz Chehab, Manuel Yunis, and others whose names I forget. Raymond Edde was the most attractive of them all, but he was disliked by Chehab and not taken as seriously as he should have been by the Americans, including Armin Meyer, who was then our ambassador (I was political officer at the time). One night Armin had a big dinner party at Yarze to which he invited a number of the would-be candidates. I remember that everyone knew he was being looked over and that the air was electric with double entendres and jokes about foreign political interference of the sort so dear to the Lebanese.

The next morning Armin and I talked over the candidates, and Armin said he rather liked Charles Helu. So did I. He was intelligent, eloquent, and had a sense of humor. I left soon after to go to Princeton for a year, but understood that Armin, in a conversation with Chehab some days after my departure, gave him to understand that we would not support a bid by him for a second term (for which Chehab was angling) and that we had no objection to Charles Helu.

Helu was a weak man. He had no political base at all, and he was saved only by his native wit. He managed to govern from weakness with considerable skill, but he negotiated the Cairo agreement in 1969, which allowed the armed Palestinians to operate freely, or almost so, from Lebanon, and that was the principal seed that sprouted into the civil war. In Helu's defense, he had no support from the other Arabs, all of whom conspired to dump on Lebanon the refuse from their own camps. Had he made a spirited resistance, he might have won, but perhaps not. Muslim loyalties to Lebanon, as opposed to Arab nationalism, were questionable at that point. Helu himself openly said "mea culpa," but it is far from obvious to me that he had any real choice.

Suleiman Frangieh was elected in 1970 with the idea that, as a *qabaday*, or political thug, he would be tough on the Palestinians and other troublemakers, but he proved to be a disappointment. Thrown into prominence by the sudden incapacity from a stroke of his more intelligent brother, Hamid, Suleiman became leader of the clan in spite of an unpromising past. He was no worse than his predecessor, perhaps, but he was no better, and corruption involving members of his family was an open scandal, which seriously marred the regime's image and its ability to deal with trouble when it came. In Frangieh's defense, he had inherited the Cairo agreement and the results of Black September in Jordan, and it is doubtful that any Lebanese president would have been able to deal effectively with the resultant problems. Frangieh was at least courageous and direct, and the collapse might have come sooner under Helu. The inherent weaknesses of the Lebanese system made it incapable of standing up to the pressures brought to bear from both inside and out.

I was not involved with Lebanon from 1964 to 1977, and the details of our errors and miscalculations during that period are largely unknown to me. The greater problem of our policy on the Arab-Israel question was a factor in the Lebanese collapse. Our failure to move more energetically to implement Resolution 242, or to press for Israeli withdrawal from the occupied territories and our unwillingness to talk to the PLO except via General Walters and the CIA, all contributed to the continuing crisis in Lebanon; but these were errors and omissions on a broader scale and not strictly Lebanese in scope.

On the Lebanese scene we made, or almost made, a couple of errors that perhaps gave rise to problems of perception and communications but which did not affect the basic strength of our position. Ambassador Dwight Porter reportedly urged that we arm the Kata'ib, or Phalanges, and apparently his attraction to that organization gave rise to some misconceptions about American sentiments and intentions. But these, while still bothersome by the time I came along, were something that could be countered. Perhaps more serious was the sniffing dog incident, in which an overzealous narcotics agent used a dog to inspect the luggage of President Frangieh and his suite when they arrived in New York on a visit to the United Nations. Frangieh was mortally offended and did not receive our ambassador, Mac Godley, for some time. In retrospect, Godley should have been withdrawn, because the lack of communications at the top was a serious handicap to our ability to deal with the crisis when it came. There were many ins and outs to that story, however, and I have no right to second guess.

My *amour propre* was also piqued at the thought of being selected for the difficult and dangerous task of ambassador to Lebanon, and by the thought that perhaps I could do something to help Lebanon out of its difficulties. I thought I knew the country as well, or better, than anyone in the service and I had a deep love for it. I could not say that about any other place I had served. As a cardiac patient, however, I was worried about the stress I would encounter and about my vulnerability in the event I was wounded, because I was taking a blood thinner. I adopted a fatalistic approach to this, however, and decided it was better to die while active and in full flower rather than to decay in old age, which I am now doing.

On arrival in Beirut we were met by a crowd of correspondents, and thus began twenty months of constant publicity and press coverage. I made a prepared statement to the effect that it was time to bind up the wounds and start the process of reconstruction; we were then whisked off in our armored cavalcade and a new life began. We were taken to the old DCM apartment in the Duraffourd building, a hundred yards down the corniche from the Embassy, to be briefed by our DCM, George Lane, and his wife Betsy, on the new rules. I would normally travel in an armored limousine with a guard car in front and in back. My personal bodyguard, David Marshal, whom we had picked up in Rome, would sit in the front seat; Bob O'Brien, the regional security officer, would ride in one of the other cars part of the time. Everyone was armed. Our total party, when fully staffed, was thirteen people. (We moved up to the residence at Yarze, near the presidential palace, late in the spring, glad to get out of the Duraffourd, which was confining and depressing.)

I called on Foreign Minister Fuad Boutros the following day and presented my credentials to President Sarkis on the 15th, which must be a speed record. Vance arrived on the 17th and was taken up to the presidential palace for a meeting and lunch. During lunch I was roundly berated by Phil Habib, in a most graceless way, for not insisting on being present when Vance and Sarkis met for a tête-à-tête, in which case it would not have been a tête-à-tête.

The essence of the message Vance was bearing was that we supported the independence and integrity of Lebanon, that we were prepared to support the central government politically and materially to this end, and that we also hoped to do something about the overall Palestine problem. Sarkis and Boutros were gratified, and Vance went off in a cloud of goodwill and optimism. Then the grind began.

Two problems in particular were posed at that point, and were still posed when I left and are still posed today: disarming the militias and the South. The most pressing of these on my arrival had been disarming the militias. The Syrians, who dominated the Arab Deterrent Forces, were poised to enter the Sabra and Shatilla camps on February 14 or 15 to start collecting arms from the PLO. Their tanks were moving into position, and a fierce struggle loomed. We and the Lebanese government very much wanted the Syrians to grasp this nettle, but we did not want it to ruin Vance's visit, so we asked them to postpone it a week. Meanwhile Arafat and others were urging that it be postponed indefinitely or canceled. The Syrians agreed to postpone it, and then lost momentum. As a result, arms were never collected. There was a farcical voluntary surrender of arms by all the militias some months later in which they got rid of some old equipment, but their real strength remained untouched. There undoubtedly would have been carnage had the Syrians proceeded into Sabra and Shatilla as scheduled that February, but it might have prevented a great deal more carnage five years later.

The other problem, the South, proved to be just as intractable, and it exposed the basic hollowness of our assurances of support to Lebanon—those assurances were valueless when they crossed purposes with Israel.

The story begins with Syrian efforts to move into south Lebanon to bring the Palestinians there under control in December 1976 (or January 1977). When they reached the village of Aishiya eight kilometers north of Nabatiyah, the Israelis sent word that they should move no further or the Israelis would react militarily; they had reached the Red Line. (There is a good deal of mythology about the so-called Red Line; Israeli writers in particular write as though it were in fact a line drawn on a map. I have never seen that map and do not know anyone who has.)

The negotiations over Israeli acquiescence in Syrian entry into Lebanon in 1976 were carried out through Kissinger. He and his sidekick, Peter Rodman, and some confidential clerks at CIA, should know what the agreement actually was; but as of 1985, Kissinger could not recall its terms and the State Department was unable to find a piece of paper setting them forth. My understanding of it at the time was that there were no lines on maps, that the Israelis had agreed to let the Syrians come into Lebanon provided they did not get too close to Israel or threaten Israeli access to Lebanese air space. The Syrians and Lebanese thought the Litani was the line. Nabatiyah is just north of that river and the Syrians had no hope of controlling the Palestinians if they did not control Nabatiyah. Prime Minister Yitzakh Rabin, commenting in an article by Naomi Weinberger in the Summer 1983 *Middle East Journal*, explained Israeli policy as follows:

> I believed that Syrian military presence along the Lebanese-Israeli border was much more dangerous to Israel in the long run than the presence of the PLO, which I did not consider as a military threat to the very existence of Israel....I will not deny [that], as a result of our limitations [of] the Syrians going beyond the "red line," practically we gave an umbrella to the PLO to run away from the Syrians to the southern part of the country.

Rabin's decision was understandable. It made sense in Israeli military terms, but it spelled death for Lebanon, because the Palestinian presence in the South led eventually to the Israeli invasion of 1982. This would not have happened had there been disciplined Syrian troops along the border, or even controlling the Litani.

Although the embassy in Beirut remonstrated with the department, and I believe officers in the department supported the same view, the Israeli action came on the cusp between the Ford and Carter administrations, at a moment of maximum disorganization. Kissinger was packing his bags, and Vance was not yet on board. Had Kissinger been staying, he might have had the strength to face down the Israelis, but I doubt that Vance would have even after he was firmly in the saddle. He was not a combative man, and what the Israelis really needed at that point was a swat on the head with a two-by-four.

So the South was left a no man's land, and two limping devices were seized upon to limit the resulting damage. The Israelis built up the forces of Saad Haddad, the renegade Lebanese major, and began efforts to form a *cordon sanitaire* along the border. Meanwhile the U.S. government began to concentrate on building up the Lebanese army with the hope that eventually it would be able to move into the area and police it. We also urged the Lebanese to send internal security forces, the gendarmerie, into the area, but that was baffled by the weakness of that organization, a weakness compounded by our inability to help it with so much as a single cartridge, thanks to the so-called State of Siege Law against our helping foreign police forces. Our efforts led eventually to the Kawkaba fiasco, discussed below.

Meanwhile, the South remained a festering problem. The Maronite militias, and particularly the Chamounists in the spring of 1977, were sending men down to the South via Israel to help Haddad and mounting attacks on Shia villages along the border in an effort to create a *cordon sanitaire*. They risked provoking a major outbreak of fighting, particularly after taking Taybeh, ancestral seat of the Asads, a leading Shia family of the South. One of my first efforts was to intercede with Camille Chamoun to get him to pull off his men before they provoked major hostilities. He reluctantly agreed, but as it transpired, regular Fath troops were brought up to help the Shia and evicted the Chamounists, with heavy losses. A little while later I tried to convince Bashir Gemayel of the dangers posed by his military cooperation with the Israelis and Haddad in defiance of his own government. He reported my remarks to Menachem Begin, who then complained to Sam Lewis, our ambassador in Tel Aviv. The working level of the department tried to support me in these efforts, but it was clear that there was no inclination at upper levels of our government to challenge Israeli assertion of a right of eminent domain in South Lebanon. Among my souvenirs is a newspaper cartoon showing me with South Lebanon hung around my neck. This was early in my tour, but it proved prophetic.

As sporadic fighting between Maronites and Palestinians continued in the South and Palestinian incursions occurred across the border, the Israelis retaliated from time to time with air strikes and limited military actions, with heavy civilian casualties when they struck at refugee camps. When this happened, frightened Shia, caught in the middle, would stream up to Beirut, exacerbating the already severe socioeconomic and security problems of that city and paving the way for eventual Shia dominance in west Beirut. Shia notables would plead that something be done to permit them to return to normal life, but nothing was. The PLO consolidated its position, and increasingly the area south of Beirut became its surrogate homeland—the only space the Palestinians really controlled, and neither Syrians nor Lebanese could gainsay them. Their only effective enemies were the Israelis and their puppet, Saad Haddad. He was effective only to the extent that he could call on Israeli firepower, but that threat gave him potential well in excess of his real strength.

Progress was being made on other fronts, however. It was spasmodic, and slow, but as Sarkis said, we were moving two or three steps forward for every one backwards. AID had moved expeditiously to erect some prefabricated steel warehouses in the port area at Beirut, while the Beirutis had cannily sold the scrap of the old, destroyed warehouses to the Romanians at a profit. A reconstruction council had been formed under Muhammad Atallah and was deeply engaged in planning. We had some housing experts out and were concerting with the World Bank on an offer to finance low-cost housing. Meanwhile various charitable agencies were operating reconstruction programs in rural areas, and economic life was gradually returning to normal. Property owners were repairing their buildings, airline flights were resuming, and a willingness to start anew reflected the perpetual optimism of the Lebanese. Unfortunately, progress was too slow.

In particular, the reconstruction council spent all its time planning and talking, with no evidence that anything was happening. The center of Beirut, which should have been a priority area for immediate work, was untouched, not for any lack of funds but for lack of agreement on what should be done. The Beirut property owners generally put their own interests before those of the community. When I called on Ahmad Daouk, for instance, in his capacity as a former prime minister, he explained that he opposed the proposed plans to rebuild downtown Beirut because they would have eliminated many of the market stalls his family owned in the suq. I said he presumably would be compensated for that, but he replied that the compensation would not be adequate. Besides, no one could really compensate you for real estate, which was the best investment. As he said this, his shops were in ruins and totally useless to him.

I don't think his attitude was any worse than that of his peers.

It was rare to find a Beiruti, or other Lebanese, for that matter, who had a thought for the commonweal before thinking of himself and his family. Few would clean up the refuse in front of their neighbor's place even though it might be polluting their own environment. I felt that Lebanon would be on the way out of its hole when I would see Beirutis caring for their neighbors' property. I never saw it. Aside from a few truly brave people in the public service and medical sectors, there was little evidence of public spirit, except where it was forced upon people at gunpoint, as happened in the areas controlled by the Kata'ib. That perhaps is the only way. Lebanese individualism is a hardy plant.

What was needed in 1977 was a charismatic leader—a man who was a natural politician, who would come on the television every night and tell his people what was going to happen, and who would be able to knock their heads together if need be. Sarkis was not that sort of person. He was shy and reticent and did not like public speaking. He was intelligent and honest, and I found him very likeable, but I also felt sorry for him. He was the wrong man in the job. I think the best comment on him was in Karim Pakradouni's book, where Sarkis, reflecting on his six years in office, says that he might not have done everything he should have, but at least he didn't do anything he should not have. That is the essence of the Chehabist philosophy, and while Sarkis's prudence was understandable in the circumstances, a more dynamic approach might have made Lebanon work. It was clear to me by 1978 in any event that the Sarkis approach would not work.

One day in 1978 Dany Chamoun called me at home in Yarze to tell me I must go to the presidential palace immediately. Sarkis had just resigned, and I must talk him out of it. If he left office there would be chaos. Although I did not take orders from Dany, or anyone else in Lebanon, I agreed with him that, whatever his faults, Sarkis would have to stay in office. I immediately walked over to the palace, which was about 300 yards away, and found the president upstairs in his living quarters. He was refusing to go to the first floor office and was receiving visitors at home as a sign that he had quit. Fuad Boutros was with him, and various other political figures were drifting in and out. His presidential aides were standing around with embarrassed smiles on their faces.

Sarkis had been brought to this pass by his inability to prevent Syrian bombardment of Beirut. How hard he had tried is not clear to me, but he had been in a blue funk about it for some time. He was also tired of the constant sniping and lack of cooperation from right-wing Maronites, and particularly the Gemayel family, whose Phalanges were the proximate cause of the trouble. The Chamounists were responsible, too, but to a lesser extent. At least one got sensible answers from Camille Chamoun. The Gemayels were beyond reason.

I sympathized with Sarkis and said I understood how he felt, but told him he could not leave or there would be chaos. Boutros said, "You see? Chaos!" Sarkis nevertheless said his mind was made up. He was tired, and he was leaving. I went back home and dictated a flash telegram (or did I telephone?) to the department, requesting an urgent message from the president or the secretary urging Sarkis to stay on. A message from Vance to Sarkis arrived a few hours later, and I delivered it in person. Meanwhile, every other ambassador of the Big Four had called in similar fashion, and so had most of the *aqtab,* or political leaders, of the country. By evening Sarkis had relented and announced his intention to stay on.

The whole affair was reminiscent of a similar abortive resignation by Fuad Chehab when he was president, and one by Henry Kissinger when he threw a tantrum in Vienna. There was inevitably a good deal of speculation that Sarkis was staging the resignation in an effort to gain support and silence his critics. If that was the purpose, it worked briefly, but his respite was soon over. I was never able to read Sarkis's mind and do not know for certain what he had intended; but I do know that he was tired and disgusted with the job and that if an impressive effort had not been made to dissuade him, he would have gone through with it. It was not a cynical political ploy.

In the summer of 1978 an IBRD (World Bank) mission under Maurice Bart came to propose a low-cost housing scheme for Beirut. This was something both we and the bank thought was vital to the future of Lebanon. While there was plenty of housing for the wealthy, the government's housing programs, which relied essentially on impersonal market forces rather than on any regulated effort to ensure social justice, were providing loans to people who could already afford housing. Nothing was being done, however, for the poor, whose concentration in Beirut provided much of the fuel for the civil war.

Housing experts from AID and the World Bank had worked out a modest building program to start the ball rolling, and the bank was proposing to finance a major part of it. We were also prepared to contribute. Maurice and his companions called on Sarkis in the morning, and I was to call on him in the afternoon. We met for lunch at the Residence in between to see how we were doing. We found Sarkis's approach surprising but, on reflection, purely Chehabian and therefore to have been expected. He said he wanted nothing to do with such housing, because he would have to decide who got it, and that would inevitably cause all sorts of problems. Whatever he decided, those who did not get chosen would attack him. In the Lebanese scheme of things, it has always seemed easier to let the market make the decisions, and that is one of the problems.

In spite of Sarkis's problems, we were making progress throughout 1977 and early 1978, until the incident at Fayadiyah in February 1978. The full truth of Fayadiyah will never be known. The following is my account. Others will differ, and I make no claim to have all the facts. On the other hand, I have no axes to grind.

For some time the Maronites had been complaining about the excesses of the Syrian occupation, about the behavior of Syrian officers, who were systematically stealing everything they could, about the rudeness and insolence of Syrian army personnel at road blocks, and about an attitude implying that the Syrians were planning to occupy Lebanon permanently. Our contacts at all levels of the Phalanges, including Bashir Gemayel, revealed the prevalence of very unrealistic ideas about Christian vs. Syrian military capabilities. The Phalangists in particular, but other Christians as well, were boasting of their ability to take on the Syrians and expel them from Lebanon. They were counting on Israeli and, to a lesser extent, American support, in this enterprise. Their illusions about the Americans were fed by Charles Malik. He had been received by Vance and reportedly returned saying that, Parker's preaching to the contrary notwithstanding, the American administration understood the Maronites' position and would support them against the Syrians. Whether this was in fact what Malik reported I do not know, but that was what one Christian contact (Karim Pakradouni) told us.

In December 1977 Bashir Gemayel had called on me one evening to say he was planning to take over the government. He was going to seize the presidential palace and institute a new order. I told him not to be foolish and that we would oppose any such attempt on his part. I did not tell Sarkis or Boutros of this conversation until it became clear, in a matter of hours, that Bashir had been talking in this fashion all over town and that Johnny Abdo, the G-2 intelligence man, had already told Sarkis. The president summoned Bashir and his father to the palace and asked what was going on. Bashir denied vehemently that he had ever had such ideas. I happened to be waiting in the president's outer office when Bashir and Pierre came out, Pierre looking grim as usual and Bashir looking his normal, smiling self. He was a consummate liar and dissembler. The truth was not in him.

Roughly two months later, on February 7, 1978, as we were puttering around the garden one weekend morning, we heard the sound of gunfire coming from the direction of Fayadiyah, the military academy just over the Hazmieh ridge. Our Lebanese guards quickly discovered that there was a firefight between Lebanese and Syrians on the Aley road, and several of them rushed off to do their part, shooting at God knows what. One of them returned to announce triumphantly that he had gotten three Syrians, and Ed Badalato, my defense attaché, reported that there was euphoria among the officers at Lebanese army headquarters up the hill. The Lebanese had given the Syrians a lesson they would not forget.

The incident reportedly was sparked by a dispute at a roadblock set up by the Syrians just below the academy. The Syrians, so the story went, had insulted some Lebanese soldiers, whose companions had thereupon come out of the academy and shot up a Syrian convoy coming down the hill, killing a large number of Syrian soldiers. The Lebanese operation had been under the direction of Colonel Barakat, commander of the academy, who was subsequently sent as military attaché to Washington and promoted to general. He was a notorious hardliner and his assignment to Fayadiyah, a sensitive post, showed very poor judgment on someone's part.

The Fayadiyah incident signaled a generalized campaign of

Maronite sniping and ambushing of Syrians. The Phalanges were the most prominent, but a notorious Chamounist thug, known as Hanash, or Snake, who dominated the Ain al-Rummaneh district, was reportedly responsible for some of the worst excesses, including the ambushing and burning of another convoy.

Though the Syrians were perhaps prepared to swallow the Fayadiyah incident, since there may indeed have been some reason for the Lebanese outburst, they wanted the perpetrators of the other incidents punished. Their way of exerting pressure to this end was to bombard east Beirut. We could stand on our terrace and watch the Katyusha rockets taking off from a launching site in Sin al-Fil. They made a tremendous noise. Damage was limited, but the psychological impact was severe. The Lebanese announced the formation of a mixed (Syrian and Lebanese) tribunal to try the perpetrators of the most flagrant of the ambushes. These occurred in Furn ash-Shubbak and involved known Phalangist gunmen, who had killed the occupants of a Syrian jeep in front of many witnesses. At Fuad Boutros's request, I went to see Pierre Gemayel to urge him to surrender the perpetrators to the tribunal. He gave me a long harangue about his inability to control the action of all the "cons" who were claiming to be in the Phalanges, and he did nothing. The tribunal never came to anything, the bombardment continued, and Lebanon went downhill most of the time thereafter.

Ghassan Tueni later told me there was evidence that the Fayadiyah incident, which we were certain at the time was a deliberate Phalangist provocation, was done in coordination with the Israelis. Given the general irresponsibility and stupidity of Israeli actions in Lebanon, I could easily believe it, but have seen no hard evidence and there is no need to invoke Israeli complicity to explain what happened. I suspect it was a purely Lebanese initiative, based on miscalculations regarding U.S. and Israeli support.

The spring of 1978 was violent. Brief periods of calm and hope would be broken without warning, usually by the Maronites but occasionally by the Syrians, who seemed to have only one reaction to provocation—bombardment. The Syrians also used kidnapping and assassination, but this seemed the work of dark and twisted minds with no coordinated plan for what they were doing. Sarkis, putative commander of the Arab Force, at one point tried to order the Syrians to stop, but they ignored him. I went to see him the day that happened and found him practically in tears, as shells fell on the city down below and around us from time to time. Syrian intentions were never clear, and probably never will be. As someone has pointed out, Hafez al-Assad belonged to a *batni,* or esoteric sect, and *batnis* are inclined to deserve their name. The destruction of Hama and Beirut are but two aspects of the same brutish mentality.

At one point, at the urging of Fuad Boutros, I managed to persuade a number of the *aqtab* to agree on a resolution to discuss the militias, the details of which have faded from my mind. My only record at the moment is a cartoon showing Pierre Gemayel, Saeb Salam, Camille Chamoun, and Kamel al-Asad disporting themselves bashfully on a stage while an unlabeled hand sticks a Parker pen through the curtain in the background. This was a considerable accomplishment, but it fell apart a couple of days later as someone started taking potshots at someone else, or was it the Israeli invasion?

In early May, Jeanne and I left for consultation in Washington. Heavy fighting had broken out a day or two before our planned departure, and it was not at all clear we would be able to make it to the airport. We managed to do so during a lull, however, and boarded the aircraft without incident. I was tired and nervous and depressed by the security precautions thought necessary to assure our safety, particularly because we had just learned that the group we thought had killed Ambassador Meloy had said it was going to get us. I counted thirty men armed with automatic weapons guarding the approaches to the plane. Settled in my seat, I was given a copy of that morning's *Herald Tribune,* which carried a front-page statement by President Carter saying Israel's security was our primary concern in the Middle East. It was the normal fatuous declaration one comes to expect from all administrations in Washington, and I should have ignored it, but it particularly irked me at that moment and I brooded over it all the way home. My first priority was our own safety, and that of other Americans, not the Israelis. They had shown scant concern for my safety or that of anyone other than themselves, and I really did not feel like sacrificing myself for them, or for a president who did not know better than to make statements like that.

On agreeing to go to Beirut in 1977 I had posed two conditions: that I be allowed to take Jeanne with me, even though dependents had not been allowed back, and that I would be allowed to leave after eighteen months if I had had enough. I had about decided to take up this option by the time we arrived in Washington. My resolve was strengthened by conversations I had with Mike Sterner, Hal Saunders, and Bill Crawford at the department. They made it clear to me that we had opted to go for a separate peace between Egypt and Israel, and that we were moving in a cynical way in that direction. I told the gentlemen in question I did not want to face the bloodshed that would result. I was quite angry.

When Sadat went to Jerusalem in 1977, he was talking in terms of a comprehensive as opposed to a bilateral settlement—of peace between Israel and the other Arab states as well as Egypt. The Israelis, however, were already talking in terms of a bilateral settlement as the only reasonable possibility. About a month later we received a circular telegram from the department asking for frank views as to whether we would be better off with a separate peace than none. The answer had to be "yes," because removing Egypt from the contest would lessen the chances for a major Arab-Israeli war and for great power confrontation in the area. It was clear to me, however, that the price for this would be paid in Lebanon, and I so wrote to Morris Draper.

Subsequently, there was a small chiefs-of-mission conference in Amman. Hermann Eilts refused to go, which was unfortunate. He sent Art Lowry in his place. Dick Murphy was there from Damascus, John West from Jidda, Sam Lewis from Tel Aviv, Mike Newlin from Jerusalem, and Atherton and Saunders from Washington. There was a lot of discussion about what sort of fig leaf Sadat would need to protect him in the event he concluded a separate peace, but we were still talking in terms of progress on the overall problem. The argument advanced by Atherton and Saunders then and subsequently, as I recall it, was that once the peace process started, it would create a "dynamic for peace" that would bring others along. This was based on assumptions about Israeli interest in wider agreements, assumptions that overlooked the essentially bloody-minded character of Begin and his associates. It might have been realistic to think in those terms with a group of enlightened labor Zionists in power, but not with a group of ex-terrorists in control. Furthermore, the argument assumed a willingness on the part of the United States to exert pressure on Israel, a willingness that faded rapidly, if it ever existed, as the 1980 election approached.

That circular telegram about separate peace, which I assumed was drafted by Mike Sterner, marked the beginning of the failure of the Sadat mission to affect an overall peace. Most of my colleagues in the field gave the usual cautious replies, and none of them, except Art Lowry, who was too junior to be effective, spoke out at Amman. The die had been cast, I feared, and if I had had any doubts, these were removed by the conversations I had in May.

Although I had been standing up well to the physical and mental stress of Beirut, thanks in part to venting my spleen frequently in telegrams to the department, there were limits to my supply of energy and stamina. I was getting tired and saw no hope for the future. I was prepared to die for my country, but not for a policy in which I did not believe. There were more peaceful places one could go, and I had had my share of danger, from World War II to Amman in 1955, to Yemen and Egypt in 1967, and to eighteen months in Beirut. I decided to bail out and accordingly went to Harry Barnes, the director general of the Foreign Service, and told him I wanted to leave Beirut in the next six months or so. He asked if I was serious, and I said I was. Thus began the process that took me out of Beirut on October 1, after I was appointed and confirmed as ambassador to Rabat.

I went back to DACOR Bacon House, where we were staying, and told Jeanne what I had done. She berated me roundly and said I would regret it. She was right, but I don't think she understood just how depressed I felt.

We returned to Beirut via a brief stopover at our Italian farmhouse and plunged back into the arena. I did not tell anyone except George Lane, who was about to go off to Yemen as ambassador, that I would be leaving.

In 1977, during the era when things were looking up, we had staged a very successful Fourth of July reception. It had been the first such occasion since 1975 to which people from all sectors of the city came. Every politician of any importance was there. Camille

Chamoun wore his white suit, which, as Halim Maamari pointed out to me, was a good sign, because he only did so on very special occasions. We had a large awning set up over the terrace outside the living room, lots of champagne and good hors d'oeuvres and everyone seemed to have a good time. It was widely heralded as a return to normal.

We resolved to repeat the performance in 1978, even though the atmosphere was tense and we had difficulty getting the men up the hill to fix the awning. We invited everybody. Heavy firing started a day or two before the Fourth, however, and we eventually decided we would have to cancel, which we did with newspaper and radio announcements on the morning of the Fourth. By then the situation was so bad there was not a car on the road. My staff and I were there and dressed, just in case someone came. We had one visitor, Antoine Jabre, the Maronite businessman (beer), who hadn't heard the word and who had driven over from the Matn. He stayed for a glass of champagne and reported that his ride had been very spooky. No one else had been on the road. He was unaware of the shooting going on all sides.

We managed to lead a fairly pleasant life for a while that summer. Firing would start every afternoon after about 2:30, when we could no longer stay out in the garden. We rarely went out at night, but the daytime was a time of feverish activity when the shooting stopped. The Israeli invasion had come and gone and provoked the creation of UNIFIL, the United Nations Interim Force in Lebanon, which was supposed to take the Israelis' place as they retreated but which was frustrated by the Israelis' interposition of Haddad and their refusal to let UNIFIL come to the border. We were all hopeful that UNIFIL would lead to peace in Lebanon, but it had become evident by June that this was unlikely and that the South was going to continue to be a problem.

Kawkaba

From the beginning of my tour in Lebanon, if not before, we had been urging the Lebanese to send their own troops south. Habib had made a particular effort to persuade them of this during the UN session in the fall of 1977; but Boutros, who was minister of defense as well as foreign affairs, and his Army commander, General Victor Khoury, were unwilling to do so because the army was so weak. Both men were innately cautious and prudent, and they had no illusions about how well the various sectarian elements would hang together if called upon to shoot at other Lebanese, as they would have to do if they ran up against Major Haddad and his men, which they were sure to do unless something could be worked out.

In the summer of 1978, we began to work out such an arrangement, ignoring to the extent we could the impractical suggestions coming from our UN mission in this respect and concentrating on the facts on the ground. In July, I was talked into letting Jim Leonard from USUN and Nat Howell from ARN/State come out to Lebanon and go to the South under UN auspices. At this point, or soon after, we had reached agreement with the Israelis that they would not object to the Lebanese army moving into certain positions in the South. Jim Leonard made a strong demarche to Boutros about the workability of this arrangement and the need for the Lebanese to grasp the nettle.

Meanwhile, the Lebanese had been working on another approach. They were trying to bribe Haddad to leave the South. They had sent a young officer from the Marjayoun area down to see Haddad and offer him a large sum of money, a passport to go anywhere he wanted, and guarantees that he would not be pursued or prosecuted as long as he did not return to Beirut. My recollection is that the amount to be offered was $25,000. When Boutros and G-2 Johnny Abdo told me this, I expressed surprise that Haddad would settle for such a piddling sum. Abdo, never one to lack confidence, assured me he would grab it and run.

In anticipation of the success of this effort, and of Israeli cooperation, the Lebanese were assembling a handpicked force in the Beqaa to march south along the eastern flank of Mount Lebanon. They were insisting on this route because they did not want to move under Palestinian sufferance along the coastal plain. There was a delicate task of coordination between Beirut, Damascus, and Tel Aviv. To facilitate things at the Beirut end, Johnny Abdo gave me a scrambler telephone to use for talking to him at any hour of the day or night. Almost as soon as it was installed in my office someone called to warn us that there were other people listening on that telephone and not to use it. I therefore confined myself to banalities most of the time, or sent a messenger.

By this time we were living in the Embassy downtown. The situation up at Yarze had become so bad that our security officer had convinced me I should vacate the Residence if for no other reason than that my personnel should not be exposed to the dangerous transit up the hill. This transpired the day after Jim Leonard and Nat Howell had come back from their ill-considered trip to the South. Jim and I were sitting beside the pool having a drink at sunset, and Jim had remarked on how pleasant it all was and how difficult it was to believe that, as the people in the department were saying, Parker was working under great stress.

That night we were awakened by shells dropping in the Residence grounds. One of the Marines had entered in his flak jacket and helmet and told us we must move down to the shelter, which was the pantry on the ground floor. We got up and dressed, I took a Golden Molson from the refrigerator, and we went into the pantry for an hour or two, where I reminded Leonard of his words. Our tension was heightened by the fact that one of my American bodyguards had almost been killed by a stray bullet at the entrance to our sleeping quarters. The round had parted his hair before lodging in the doorframe. When last I saw him he was wearing it on a gold chain around his neck.

Knowing that we were going to be moving in a few months anyway, I decided to pull out of the Residence entirely and move into the little pied-a-terre we had already fixed up in the Chancery. Jeanne was quite depressed by this, and so was I, but it seemed the wise thing to do at the time, and it was useful to be there during the Kawkaba operation, because communications were a good deal easier.

Thus, in the middle of the night before the troops were scheduled to move south from Shtaura towards Kawkaba in the southern Beqaa, we received an urgent message from Tel Aviv that there was no deal as far as the Israelis were concerned. They gave some disingenuous explanation about the troops in question being under Syrian influence. I called both Boutros and Abdo to inform them of this, and there was dismay on the other end of the line. They decided, however, that the operation was too far advanced to be halted. They had already announced it and would have to take their chances.

A day or two before this, it had become clear that the effort to bribe Haddad had not worked. The young officer from Marjayoun had been summoned by Bengal or Eitan on the Israeli side and given a terrible dressing down and sent home. Haddad's attitude was ambiguous. He had indicated an interest privately but had scornfully rejected the offer in front of the Israelis. He subsequently told a group of reporters that I personally had offered him $250,000, which he had refused. Like others in this affair, Haddad did not have great regard for truth.

The troops got as far as Kawkaba, where Haddad's men began lobbing shells at them. The column stopped promptly and eventually withdrew. The Israelis later offered to let the column be transported by helicopter to certain agreed locations, but this was unacceptable to the Lebanese both as to location and access. They rejected the offer as an insult.

"Parker's Panic"

When we moved back into town from our residence in the summer of 1978, I was alarmed by the number of heavily armed men to be seen on the streets of the Ain Mreisseh quarter at night. At the same time, CIA reports we thought reliable indicated that Bashir Gemayel was getting ready for an offensive in Beirut. For some time the department's security people had been making noises about the desirability of sending dependents out of Lebanon, where the situation had deteriorated well below the level at which we had let them return the year before. The number of people involved was small, about twelve, and I had discretion to order their departure whenever I felt the situation required.

After a full discussion of the problem with my staff, I decided to order the dependents home. In retrospect, it was unnecessary. We had overreacted to the intelligence reports, which proved wrong. Given the number of people involved, this would not have been a matter of public concern had we shipped them out quietly, as most other embassies had already done. Unfortunately, my officers had prevailed on me to advise the American community of what we were doing, otherwise we would be accused of sneaking out when we knew danger was coming. We ordered the Marines to begin telephoning people to tell them we were sending dependents home and advising all people who did not have a real reason for being in Lebanon to leave as well (we did not imagine there were many in that category but felt we must give advice to those who might be). By the time this had worked its way through the Marines and the telephone system, it began to sound like a rout, and there was a good deal of excitement within the community and among the Lebanese. I half-hoped that this would deter the Phalanges from doing something stupid, and perhaps it did, but I certainly would not claim it.

There was a good deal of snickering by other embassies, which, as indicated, had already sent their dependents home with no one outside being the wiser. My British colleague, Peter Wakefield, un-kindly referred to it as "Parker's panic," and I'm sure that many people who resented my prominence on the Lebanese scene took pleasure in my discomfort. (More will be heard about this later.)

We left Lebanon on October 1, arriving in Paris to learn that almost as soon as we left, Syrian shelling of the city had started in earnest and that it had been the worst day since the civil war began in terms of casualties. In my farewell speeches to Lebanese friends I had said that it was always my luck to do the groundwork and have someone else reap the product, and I was sure my successor would find a better Lebanon than I did. In fact, he did, but it took a while, and he had his problems too. I went back in 1983 and my friends all told me I had been there during the worst period other than the civil war, but they were premature. Lebanon continued to deteriorate, with no end in sight.

Postscript

January 31, 1986: I spent the day in the department reading my telegrams from Beirut. I was impressed by the number of them— perhaps eight hours' worth of reading. What leaps out at me when going through them is how often I saw the foreign minister, Fuad Boutros, and President Sarkis, how tenuous the situation was from the beginning, how often we urged the Lebanese to send troops to the South, and how cautious Sarkis and Boutros were about responding. In retrospect they were right. We couldn't get the Israelis to cooperate with UNIFIL, so in time we tried to throw the Lebanese into the breach, and it didn't work. We had a lot of blood on our hands before it was over.

16

Rabat II—Me and the King

In May 1978, while in Washington on consultation, I had indicated I wanted to leave Lebanon. Hal Saunders, assistant secretary for Near Eastern and South Asian Affairs, said two posts were going to be available in the NEA area: Rabat and Tunis. I said without hesitation that I would prefer Tunis. I had already served in Rabat and had no desire to deal further with King Hassan, whose unpleasant qualities were well known to me. This was agreeable to Hal and others at State. I returned to Beirut thinking Tunis would be my next post. We would leave Lebanon early in 1979, after completing two years there.

On June 30, however, Bill Crawford, senior deputy assistant secretary for NEA, wrote to say that NEA was making a strong case that I should go to Rabat to succeed Robert Anderson. Their purpose was to prevent Harry Barnes, the director general, from giving the post to an outsider, John Gunther Dean. Crawford made flattering statements about my qualifications for the post and said that if Rabat came through it would mean leaving Beirut in October, four months earlier than planned.

I replied on July 11 that, again, I preferred Tunis and was not really sure I was the man for the job in Rabat. I wrote a separate letter to David Newsom, the under secretary for political affairs, in which I said I did not want to go to Rabat "because of the excremental way Hassan treats ambassadors." I should have followed my instincts and refused to go, but that had not always gone well in the past. I decided to leave it up to my friends in the department.

I also thought that perhaps King Hassan would refuse my appointment. The Moroccans would remember my presence during two coup attempts in 1971 and 1972, which many Moroccans suspected had involved the CIA.

Agrément came through without trouble, however, and messages from Rabat indicated that the Moroccans were pleased with the choice. On the other hand, Rabat had been something of an ambassador's graveyard. For one reason or another, none of the three before me had a fully successful tour there. I was stupid to think I would do any better than they had. No one seemed to be a real success in Morocco, at least not since Henry Tasca, who left in 1970. There was a bittersweet character to American-Moroccan relations. The king did not like career officers, who often knew too much about his past and about the country. I don't know why I agreed to take the job, but the short answer is that I was flattered by the appeal to my team loyalty and *amour propre*. I was going to save the day for NEA. I should have had my head examined.

The first portent of evil times came when I was living alone at the Residence in Rabat just after presenting credentials in October 1978 and before leaving for the forthcoming visit of King Hassan to Washington. This visit had been the occasion that required my early departure from Beirut. One evening while I was sorting books in the study, Freddie, our aged fox terrier, who had bitten all our children's friends and was cordially detested by many people, fell into the swimming pool and drowned. It was one of the most depressing episodes of my life. We had debated whether to have him put away on leaving Beirut and had decided to let him die naturally. The thought of him paddling desperately around the pool, unable to get out, still haunts me. This tragedy set the tone for our second tour in Rabat.

Hassan's three-day state visit to Washington in November was less of a comedy than some, but was not a success. Hassan did not understand the need to be frank with the president and tell him what he needed. Reportedly, he thought statesmen should only talk about grandiose things and leave the grubby details to their subordinates. Thus, when we sat down around the table in the cabinet room at the White House on the first day of the visit, instead of bringing up the question of arms, which was turning our relations sour, he wasted everyone's time talking about a tunnel under the Strait of Gibraltar and about the Red menace in Africa, the leading element of which was Qadhafi of Libya. He also went on at length about his readiness to send a team to Iran to help the shah cook an election, which he said was a Moroccan specialty.

During the gathering in the family suite at the White House prior to the state dinner that evening, I had the misfortune to be standing with King Hassan and President Carter when the king began to complain about the American school in Rabat. Some of the royal children were in attendance at the school, which apparently did not respect the protocol requirements of the Palace. King Hassan wanted the children to perform certain ceremonial and academic functions at the Palace during school hours, and the school resisted letting them go. I subsequently realized that the problem was exacerbated because the American school, though mediocre, was academically better than the Palace school. I misunderstood his elliptic remarks as praise of the school and made an enthusiastic comment about how good it was. The king was annoyed with me and very quickly corrected my misapprehension. The president, of course, was mystified as to why the king would bother him with a petty detail like that.

The next day, CIA Director Stansfield Turner called on the king at Blair House. He was accompanied by Alan Wolfe, Near East director for the agency. Bill Crawford had urged me to join the meeting, as we were trying to break the king of his habit of dealing separately with the CIA instead of going through the ambassador. We called and cleared my presence with Turner, so I accompanied him through the door of Blair House and into the reception room on the left. The king appeared a moment later, with his protocol chief, Moulay Hafidn al-Alaoui, signaling me frantically to absent myself. I ignored him, but the king said, "M. l'Ambassadeur, this is a matter of intelligence we are to discuss and not a diplomatic subject. You will please excuse us." I had no alternative but to back away, but I knew this had been a faux pas on my part. It would not help me with Hassan. On the other hand, it was something of a declaration of independence.

On the second night of the visit, the king received Secretary of

State Cyrus Vance at Blair House. They talked principally about arms. Guedira, Boucetta, Saunders, and I had had a lively discussion on the subject during one of the breaks in the meetings between the two chiefs of state on the first day of the visit, but we had assumed the king would raise the issue with the president. He did not. President Carter was not going to raise the arms issue either, because the king was the *demandeur*. The arms problem was left to Vance.

Under the Carter administration, largely because of pressure from liberal members of Congress and Africanists in the department, we had begun to take a more restrictive position on the use of American-supplied arms in the Western Sahara. The Moroccans had occupied that territory in 1975 without regard for the various UN resolutions calling for self-determination by the local inhabitants. We did not recognize the area as sovereign Moroccan territory, although we did recognize Morocco's right to administer the territory under an agreement with Spain and Mauritania signed in 1975. The department's legal adviser had issued a *fatwa* that the arms supplied under U.S. military aid programs could not be used in the Sahara. This policy was blocking the sale of certain military items Hassan thought he needed to combat the Polisario guerillas, whose wide-ranging sweeps were beginning to threaten towns well within traditionally recognized Moroccan territory.

Hal Saunders had discussed this matter with Hassan some four months before. A particular issue at that time was the location of F-5 aircraft we had supplied well before 1975 and which the Moroccans were using to consolidate their hold over the Sahara. Saunders and his companions thought they had reached an understanding with the king, securing assurances that such arms would not be used in the Sahara. If I understand the record correctly, the F-5s were to be stationed in Mauritania so that at least we could say honestly that they were not based in the Sahara. Later that summer, however, the king's adviser, Reda Guedira, had told our ambassador at the time, Robert Anderson, that we had misunderstood the king. He would give no such assurance. Saunders had a subsequent discussion on the subject at the UN in October 1978 with Moroccan foreign minister Mohamed Boucetta, who seemed to think that some sort of deal was in the works under which the F-5s would be moved to

Mauritania, as Saunders had originally negotiated. He also said the Moroccans did not want to cause any problems with Congress, indicating his awareness of the congressional angle to the affair.

The king opened the meeting with Secretary Vance by saying he did not want to embarrass his friends. I came to realize that this was his traditional way of introducing a dubious proposition. What followed would always warrant close examination. He continued that he would give the secretary assurances that Morocco would not use American arms except in defense of Moroccan territory. Vance said that sounded like a reasonable proposal which we could accept. The arms problem was resolved, or so the Moroccans thought.

After the meeting, I asked Saunders if he thought the secretary realized the king included the Western Sahara when he said "Moroccan territory." We agreed to query the secretary in the morning. Before doing so I called Ali Bengelloun, the Moroccan ambassador, to confirm that the term "Moroccan territory," as used by the king the night before, included the Western Sahara. Bengelloun said of course it did. I informed him that I did not think the secretary understood this and would have to enlighten him. Bengelloun urged me not to and said it would be very unfortunate for me at the beginning of my Moroccan tour. We both knew he meant it would anger the king. I told him I had no choice. Not to do so would lead eventually to a major misunderstanding.

Saunders and I went to see Vance, who said he had not understood what the king meant. We had no deal. I communicated this development to Bengelloun and waited for the flak to hit.

That evening, as the king was riding out to Andrews with the secretary, he made some remarks about me that were a little obscure but clearly ominous. He said Vance should tell me not to talk too much to Lalla Lamia, Prince Moulay Abdallah's wife. She talked too much to her Lebanese friends on the telephone, which the king monitored. I had met with her about some modest U.S. government aid to a project to aid the blind when I was DCM in Rabat, and I had gone to the inauguration of the completed project shortly after presentation of my ambassadorial credentials. We also shared an interest in Lebanon; her father had been the first prime minister of independent Lebanon and one of the authors of the National Covenant. We had never talked politics.

The king further stipulated that I should beware of doing too much business with his ministers. Vance had an impression of unease and sent word through Hal Saunders that I should be careful.

I probably should have tried to get a seat on the royal aircraft back to Morocco in order to talk to the king, but I wanted to stay behind for a few days to visit our daughter Alison, who had just given birth to her first child and our first grandchild. I planned to spend Thanksgiving with the family and then return to Morocco. I also turned down the offer of a ride with Bill Crawford and Senator Robert Byrd, who were going out to Tehran by military aircraft, stopping in Morocco en route. After twenty months in Beirut, I wanted a rest and really did not care what it cost in career terms.

When I returned to Rabat some ten days after the king's departure, he had moved to Fes and there was no occasion to see him. Saunders, aware that I might have a difficult time, had said he would try to send me something attractive in the way of a message to deliver to the king, but none ever arrived. All I got were the usual fatuous messages about peace in the Middle East, and I was not going to disturb the king to deliver those. Besides, I was busy trying to restore embassy morale, making the customary required calls on diplomatic colleagues, and dealing with a number of serious problems, including Moroccan default on financial obligations. I found myself fully occupied.

The Search for Assurances

We nevertheless continued to look for some formula that would resolve the arms question. In particular, we were looking for a way around the problem posed by six Chinook helicopters the Moroccans had ordered from Augusta Bell of Italy. The aircraft had been ordered and paid for, I believe, in the spring of 1972. I remember the case well. Morocco's General Oufkir had tried to block the sale because a large bribe to the palace was involved. Oufkir had told us so, and we had informed Washington, but the king overruled Oufkir. A dispute over whether Morocco was Bell Aerospace's or Augusta Bell's market led the U.S. firm to attempt, unsuccessfully, to block its licensee's deal. I remember our Italian colleagues gloating that the deal had gone through despite what they saw as a U.S.

plot to stop it. Now, some six years later, the helicopters were ready for delivery, but the United States still had to clear their export from Italy. The aircraft had been manufactured there under U.S. license in accordance with our Mutual Security legislation and offshore procurement procedures. Given the department's legal ruling on arms use in the Sahara, we still needed some Moroccan undertaking that would satisfy our legal requirements yet not infringe on Moroccan sovereignty. Otherwise, the U.S. government would not license the helicopters' export.

Jim Bishop, the State Department's country director for North Africa, had been corresponding with me about formulas we might use. In late December he sent me some language in French, which I brought to Reda Guedira on January 12, 1979. I have long since forgotten what the formula said, but it sent Guedira into orbit. He reacted very strongly and said the U.S. position was incomprehensible and was destroying our relationship. Other suppliers were not imposing such conditions. This was the work of U.S. senators manipulated by Algerian agents. I replied that we wished to maintain our supply relationship but did not want to get in the middle of the Sahara problem. There were no senators in the pay of the Algerians or under their influence. Guedira maintained firmly that our proposal was absolutely unacceptable.

I went back to my office and sent a telegram to State. I said that at least we had a straight answer, something of an accomplishment in Morocco. I thought Guedira was serious and did not believe we would get the sort of assurances we wanted. I suggested we consider revising our policy.

The department responded in hurt tones and asked if the Moroccans did not realize that they were running the risk of having Congress mandate an arms cutoff, as it had with Indonesia and Turkey. Further, did they not understand our need to be careful with the Algerians, who were going through a delicate transition following the death of President Boumediene? I assured the department both answers were negative. The Moroccans thought our proposal was a plot and were concerned that the hawks would win the succession contest in Algiers.

On January 24, I heard from an American public relations consultant whose firm was working for the king. He said Guedira was fit to be tied over the piece of paper I had given him. Guedira thought we were asking the Moroccans to withdraw the F-5s from the Sahara. I said that had not been the intention at all. There must have been a misunderstanding. I received a similar report from former ambassador Robert Neumann, who went to Marrakesh and was given an earful about the proposal by one Moroccan colonel.

One Sunday evening, I received a call from royal protocol telling me to be in Marrakesh at ten o'clock the following morning, January 28. I arrived at the palace in Marrakesh to find my Italian colleague and friend, Francesco Mezzalama, alighting from his car. He too had a 10:00 a.m. appointment with the king. We went in together to find the king with Guedira, Boucetta, Chief of Staff Colonel Achabar, and Chief of the Royal Air Force Colonel Kabbaj. We sat on two couches facing each other. The king on one, Mezzalama and I on the other.

The king said his real business was with Mezzalama. He had asked me along as an observer because the United States was indirectly involved. He then told Mezzalama that the Italians must either deliver the helicopters or face a suit in the tribunal of the International Chamber of Commerce in London. The Moroccans had already paid for the aircraft and insisted on having them. Mezzalama compared himself to a man who walked out of his house and was hit by a falling roof tile. He responded that the Italians had taken the Moroccan order in good faith, had manufactured the helicopters, and were prepared to deliver them. Unfortunately, their hands were tied. The Americans would not give them license to deliver.

The king then turned to me and delivered a long, scolding lecture on how the deficiencies of American policy in this matter threatened the whole fabric of our relations. I said we had domestic political problems. He said that was nonsense. If we wanted to help the Moroccans badly enough, we would say to hell with Congress and issue the license. It was a question of priorities. In fact, he was right, but I demurred and said we did indeed have a problem. I suggested that since the helicopters were to be based at Rabat-Salé, could we not agree on some informal oral assurances that would satisfy our requirements? The king made clear that where the helicopters were based was none of our business. Such an arrangement would make me a high commissioner, supervising Moroccan military deployment. That was totally unacceptable. He then went off to another meeting, leaving the six of us to hash something out.

Then Guedira took up the cudgel. He lambasted me for half an hour with a diatribe about the stupidity of American policy. His remarks were rude and offensive, and I was tempted to tell him to shove it and just leave. I decided not to, because I was not a free agent. When the king returned, he resumed his own attack and concluded that if we did not license the helicopters, military cooperation between us would cease. We would not get permission to use the old SAC base at Ben Guerir for a satellite tracking station, a proposition he had agreed to in principle in Washington. In the end, he got the helicopters, but we did not get the tracking station. The king was never much for keeping his word.

It was a trying experience. The other Moroccan officials present had been uncomfortable with the rudeness of Guedira's remarks and the sharpness of the king's tone. When I had the temerity to disagree with the king about our political problems, Colonels Achabar and Kabbaj exchanged looks indicating they thought I was being foolhardy. I probably was. The king did not tolerate dissent. Mezzalama, who stayed throughout, agreed that it had been an extraordinary performance. I had been chewed out by bullies in the past but had not encountered anything quite so offensive in a long time, even from Phil Habib, that master of intimidation.

I sent three separate telegrams reporting this exchange. I had telephoned a brief report to Peter Moffat, our DCM in Rabat, and composed a longer version on the three-hour ride back from Marrakesh. The next day, on rereading these first two reports, I sent a third telegram to assure the department that I was not exaggerating the extraordinary resentment displayed by Hassan and Guedira. I suggested that we forget about assurances and authorize the Italians to export the helicopters right away. Two days later, I received a telegram authorizing me to inform the Moroccans that approval had been granted. I conveyed the message to the foreign minister immediately. Unfortunately, I got no credit, because he had already heard the news from the Moroccan ambassador, to whom it had been leaked by one of the cretins in NEA.

Although I had only served as the vehicle to convey the royal wrath, I had been instrumental in turning American policy around on this issue. The Moroccan military realized this, but I got no credit with the palace. The king was an ingrate as well as a liar and a cheat.

The Shah

Shortly before my encounter with the king, the recently deposed shah of Iran had arrived in Marrakesh from Egypt en route to exile. He was accompanied by the empress and a large retinue. The party was transported in two aircraft: Iran Air Force No. 1 and a smaller plane called the *Shahin* (meaning "falcon"), owned by the shah personally. It was our understanding from press reports that he would spend three or four days in Morocco and then proceed to the United States. My first question was whether, in accordance with diplomatic custom, I should arrange to be at the airport when he departed for my country, given the increasing criticism of our identification with him. I sent a query to the department and was told not to go to the airport. Meanwhile, I had called the chief of royal protocol, Moulay Hafidh al-Alaoui, and asked him about the shah's travel plans. He said he did not know; it was not his affair. The shah was the personal guest of the king, and all questions should be addressed to the Iranian ambassador, Farhad Sepahbody.

Sepahbody was in Marrakesh with the shah and hard to find. I eventually reached him and learned that the shah's plans for the future were indefinite. I also learned that the former Iranian ambassador to Washington, Ardeshir Zahedi, had come to Marrakesh and told the shah that he would be unwelcome in the United States. This had caused the shah to hesitate. When I was summoned to Marrakesh on January 29 for my berating from the king, former ambassador Robert Neumann was in Marrakesh at the king's invitation. So was Vernon Walters, former deputy director of the CIA, who had some sort of contract with the Moroccans, the details of which I never learned. Various representatives of the world press were also on hand. Everyone was lounging around the pool of the Mamounia Hotel waiting for a summons from one royalty or another.

Walters had been a frequent visitor to Morocco ever since Henry Kissinger sent him there secretly and, I gather, without telling Neumann, to meet with the PLO in the midseventies. I assumed on this occasion he was on a commercial rather than political mission. I could not imagine the Carter people enlisting him. We exchanged a few words of greeting, and Walters looked at me appraisingly, as if he knew I was in trouble with the king. I have always wondered whether he played any role in what followed.

During a brief conversation with Neumann, I learned that the previous night Zahedi had been trying to convince the shah to return to Iran and stage a military coup. The Iranian generals were allegedly ready to fight and awaiting his command. The shah's response was that he did not want a bloodbath on his account. Neumann was perplexed as to how he should report this. It had been given to him in confidence, but he felt the U.S. government should be aware of what was happening. I believe we decided to convey the information to Washington without indicating the source.

About a week later, I was summoned back to Marrakesh to meet with the shah and King Hassan. The shah was staying at the king's new Moroccan-French provincial-style palace in the palm groves. I was ushered into a room in which both men were seated. The king explained that the shah was very concerned about his family in the United States and particularly about his son, who was in flight training at Lubbock, Texas. The shah wanted assurances that, first, his family would be protected and, second, the prince would be allowed to finish his training course. The king asked me to call the president or the secretary of state, pass on the shah's concerns, and get some assurances from them.

I did not bother to explain that my chances of reaching either of those gentlemen were rather remote, but went to another room and eventually managed to get Hal Saunders on the line. He, while holding me on one line, spoke to Secretary Vance on another. He relayed back to me the message that the prince would be allowed to graduate from Lubbock. We would provide such security as we could for the shah's family, but the burden on us was very heavy, and the Iranians would have to hire some private guards to help out.

I rejoined the king and the shah, who had been joined by the empress. She was very elegant but exceedingly nervous and sat next to me cracking her knuckles. I reported that the prince would be allowed to finish his training but that our resources for providing security were limited. We would be expecting the Iranians to provide some of their own. This did not seem to bother the shah, who appeared pleased by the news about his son and spoke of him as any proud father would. He turned to the king and said the prince had just received an "outstanding," did Hassan know what that was? The king said of course he did; it meant very good. At that point the prince had some six weeks of scheduled attendance at Lubbock remaining, but the miracle of an Air Force time warp accelerated it to ten days. He was graduated in record time, enabling us to keep our promise and still get rid of him quickly. The shah did not complain, at least not to me, but must have thought it was a pretty cheap trick.

During the course of the conversation, I asked the shah about his travel plans. He gave a response that implied he was dubious about his welcome in the United States. I knew that at that moment his former CIA case officer had come out from Washington to see him and was waiting for a summons. I decided to leave the question of welcoming messages up to him and made no comment.

On February 20, sixteen days after my meeting with the king and the shah, Ambassador Sepahbody came to see me to discuss the shah's plans. He said the shah was upset that the United States had let him down. He was unsure of his welcome in the United States, and his entourage was shrinking. Air Force 1 had returned to Tehran and so had the *Shahin*, with some twenty staff personnel on board. I had the feeling from these remarks that the shah's ship was beginning to sink. Ayatollah Khomeini had returned to Iran on February 1, and the Bakhtiar government had collapsed, leaving Khomeini largely in control. I told Sepahbody that while I was sure our government would continue to welcome the shah, Khomeini was talking about extradition. That could cause problems. The shah should hurry and make up his mind where he wanted to go before we changed ours.

Two days later, Sepahbody returned and said he was coming at the shah's request to ask officially about going to the United States. He had decided to do so within the next week or so but had heard conflicting reports about whether he would be welcome. He also

wanted advice about where he should go in the United States. I
tried to assure Sepahbody that the administration would do the
honorable thing, but he regarded this as my personal opinion. They
needed an official response. The shah was not worried about protocol but about security.

I immediately sent a telegram reporting this conversation, and
the department responded the same day. The United States was not
retreating in any way from the assurances of welcome it had given
earlier. The response added that we had no extradition treaty with
Iran and therefore that risk did not arise. Our readiness to receive
the shah was repeated in a second telegram sent to Rabat that week.

I passed these assurances to Sepahbody. He thanked me but
said the shah needed something warmer and had asked that I come
see him on Monday the 26th. I reported this to the department and
said that whether or not I went to see the shah—and Hassan would
be angry if I did not—it was evident the shah felt the need for a
personal message from the president or the secretary. I noted that
Barbara Walters was nosing around, trying to wriggle her way in
to see the shah. He might decide to go public about the tepidity
of his invitation to the United States. If he did so, he would find a
ready sounding board in the press. As I recall, I was told the answer
would be given via the CIA case officer again.

That Friday, Sepahbody returned to say the shah was making
contact with people in the United States, but he was still vacillat-
ing. Meanwhile, his retainers, like Hannibal's troops before Capua,
were succumbing to the earthly delights of Morocco. They had
shrunk to about twenty in number, mostly domestic staff and a few
courtiers. They were enjoying themselves and were in no hurry to
leave. They were urging the shah to stay. So was King Hassan, who
told him he was welcome to stay as long as he wished. Meanwhile,
Sepahbody was receiving daily messages from Moulay Hafidh, the
king's chief of royal protocol, telling him that the continued presence of the shah was an embarrassment to the king and please to
move him on.

Indeed, public criticism of the shah's presence was increasing.
There were reports of demonstrations in Casablanca, where the students had shouted and carried placards reading, "*Le chien* [Hassan]
reçoit le chat [the shah]." Pro-Khomeini graffiti was appearing on

walls around the country. Even students at the Tangier American School, not previously known for their political involvement, were picking up pro-Khomeini cries. The demonstrations in Casablanca were not massive, and these manifestations of public displeasure hardly threatened the monarchy, but the king was nervous about his situation. He may also have grown tired of the bother and expense of having an imperial guest.

On Sunday, a senior State Department official, Under Secretary Newsom, told PR consultant Don Agger and his sidekick, former Senator Robert Goodell, that the shah was still welcome, but we hoped he understood the problems we faced with regard to the safety of our personnel in Tehran. He mentioned the possibility that they might be taken hostage by some armed group. I wonder, if we knew this so early, why was our embassy so scandalously unprepared when it came? Agger and Goodell were going out to Morocco at the king's request to help him with the problem of the shah.

Later that week, Agger and Goodell came to see me in Rabat. They gave me my first detailed description of the security problem the shah's entry into the United States would pose for our embassy in Tehran and of the debate within the administration about the wisdom of honoring our commitment. The State Department had been less than informative in this regard; and while I could well imagine in general terms what the problem might be, I did not have details of our chargé in Tehran Charlie Naas's warning of the dire consequences. He said he needed thirty hours' advance warning of the shah's departure to the United States in order to evacuate all personnel from the Embassy in Tehran, which he feared would be burned and its occupants killed. I immediately sent a telegram that if we wanted the shah to go elsewhere, we should get to work right away.

The following Saturday, Reda Guedira told Agger that the shah had definitely decided to go to the United States. The Moroccans were stepping up their efforts to get him to leave. Agger saw the shah later in the day and again was told that he had firmly decided to go to the United States. The shah said he had been told that President Carter had said he was welcome. He noted, however, that he had no explicit invitation.

On March 14, I followed instructions to visit the king to request his support for the recently signed Camp David Accords. I delivered an oral and written message from the president on the subject. Reda Guedira was also present, the two of us sitting face to face in front of the king's desk. The king said that of course he would support the agreement—in fact he did not—but his ability to do so would be much enhanced if we could help him with his own problem, the continued presence of the shah. The situation was weakening his hand with the other Arabs. He said, *"Me debarrassez du shah"* ("rid me of the shah"). It was important that this be done by March 30, when a referendum on an Islamic republic was scheduled in Iran. After the vote, the shah's status would change from absent monarch to fugitive from justice.

I said we had reaffirmed our welcome to the shah on several occasions, but we were facing severe difficulty with maintaining the security of our personnel in Tehran. The Moroccans should be familiar with this issue. They had already abandoned their own Embassy there. The king replied that the United States was in a better position than Morocco to respond to such threats. The problem of the shah was too big for Morocco. They needed President Carter's personal help, and the king wanted that message conveyed to him.

I reported this conversation by telegram immediately and in the evening received a call from the department, by secure telephone. The response was going to be negative, but I would not have to deliver it. I understood this to mean a special emissary, perhaps the CIA case officer, would be sent out with it. According to Newsom, the assignment went to Vernon Walters, who refused to go. The next day, however, the department sent me a telegram the essence of which was that we appreciated the king's generosity in receiving the shah and that we had hoped the shah could come to the United States; but the deteriorating situation in Tehran posed new threats to our personnel there. The president had reluctantly concluded that the time was not propitious. We would try to help the shah find a haven elsewhere. I asked for and received additional language that took note of the king's frankness and then asked for an audience to deliver the message. Royal protocol told me it should be delivered to Guedira. I went to see him on Friday the 16th and conveyed the message. I said I was sorry to have to deliver it but was only a soldier in the service of my commander. I would be delivering the same message to the shah that afternoon. Guedira indicated that he understood my situation.

By this time the shah had moved into Dar al-Salaam Palace, across from the golf course south of Rabat. I met with him there for about an hour and a half. He was wearing a tweed sport jacket and slacks and looked tanned and healthy, but he kept wandering off the subject. I gave him the message orally and told him we were looking for alternatives. South Africa and Paraguay were both willing to receive him. Mexico and Argentina were possibilities. We were looking into both places. We were not the only people making inquiries. King Hassan told me during the meeting on the Camp David Accords that Constantine of Greece had asked Queen Elizabeth about his going to England; she said she would like to have him but her government would not. Prince Rainier of Monaco said he had security problems. I also heard that the Swiss and Spanish had both turned him down.

The shah took the news calmly. He did not lose his temper or reproach me or my government, but rather seemed resigned to the answer he had received. He said that in many ways South Africa was an agreeable place, but he had sad memories of it because his father had died there in exile. He might have been willing to go there, but the empress apparently vetoed it emphatically. He would not go to Paraguay and would not discuss it. He recalled a rather pleasant resort in Argentina in the mountains, and he talked about that for awhile, but then said that if he could not go to the United States, Mexico would be best. It would be close to his mother, who had left for the United States in January. I promised to inform Washington of his views and did so by immediate telegram. This whole ordeal had been, I felt, one of the most painful tasks of my career.

The following Monday, March 19, I wrote to Under Secretary Newsom, who had been directing the department's responses — such as they were — to most of my messages dealing with the shah. I indicated that delivering such bad news was what ambassadors were paid for, but that I disliked being the bearer of such tidings. I concluded, "If Hassan has any doubts about my being a bird of ill omen, they would have been resolved by now....I have yet to have a positive message for him." Newsom responded that the president appreciated the way we had handled this matter. Newsom also hoped to have something good for me to say. It never came.

Two weeks of often obscure maneuvering followed. We heard no more from King Hassan, except that he summoned Agger and reiterated the need to get the shah out of the country by March 30. Unfortunately, the shah did not want to deal with Agger, and he and Goodell were able to do little. Soon thereafter, David Rockefeller got into the act. The first indication we had of his involvement was a call from his longtime aide, Joe Reed, in New York. He said cheerfully that they were working on the problem, and all was not lost. I was grateful for that, because the department was telling us nothing.

It was largely through Joe Reed's efforts that a temporary refuge was found in the Bahamas. This required, I later learned from Reed, the bribing of very senior Bahamian officials. For their part, the Moroccans let it be known that they were readying an aircraft. They would take the shah to South Africa on March 30 if no other place were found. Meanwhile, the king continued to tell the shah he was welcome to remain as long as he liked, explaining to Agger that he could not tell a royal guest to leave. Someone else would have to do it. I was later told that the palace bagman, M. Freij, was still carrying such messages to the shah in Nassau, telling him he was welcome to return when he wished. I suspect Hassan hoped eventually to get his hands on some of the shah's money, regarding which wild rumors were flying about.

After nearly two months of maneuvering, the shah finally left Morocco for the Bahamas on the morning of Friday, March 30. A large bodyguard and a small civilian retinue accompanied him. Sepahbody, who remained loyal to the shah to the end, despite imprecations from Tehran, left soon after for the United States. He and his wife left with us a large can of caviar, which we ate when our own turn came.

In early April, Secretary of Commerce Juanita Kreps came to Morocco on an official visit to discuss ways of increasing U.S.-Moroccan trade. The Department of Commerce staff handling the visit was somewhat new to North Africa and became increasingly disturbed by our inability to pin the Moroccans down to precise arrangements in advance. They wanted a detailed agreed-upon program, in particular assurances that Mrs. Kreps would be received by the king. This sort of commitment was rarely given, and certainly not to someone of Mrs. Kreps's relatively junior rank. We kept assuring Commerce that the Moroccans would do their duty and see to it that the visit was a success. This Commerce was unwilling to accept. At one point they talked of canceling the visit. I was told that this reflected Secretary Kreps's own sense of insecurity. I made strenuous efforts by telephone and cable to calm these fears, while the department, in the person of AFN country director Jim Bishop, issued several doses of gut stiffener to Commerce.

The trip finally got underway. The visit went well, as anticipated. The king did receive Mrs. Kreps, who was given all the hospitality she could have asked for. The crowning event, in my personal view, was the dinner we gave for her at which various Moroccan ministers stood up and said what a great job I had been doing in improving U.S.-Moroccan relations. Earlier the same day, however, when Mrs. Kreps had an audience with the king, I had been excluded from the meeting at the last minute. This was not the first time that sort of thing had happened, but I was upset. I almost walked out of the palace and turned in my suit, as I had earlier considered in Marrakesh. I regret not having followed my instincts, because at least I would have had the satisfaction of showing my contempt openly. One can rarely do that and remain at post, however. Diplomats do not have that luxury. As it was, I let the incident pass. It seemed to me the king gave me a particularly venomous look when I was called in at the end of his meeting with Mrs. Kreps for an exchange of banalities. We went on with the program, and the next day Mrs. Kreps had what seemed to me a warm farewell.

About a week later Jim Bishop telephoned to say the secretary wanted to see me. Travel orders for both Jeanne and me to come to Washington would be forthcoming. I asked what it was about, and Jim mumbled something vague about U.S.-Moroccan relations. I discussed this with Peter Moffat, the country director, and said it sounded ominous, but he thought I was overreacting.

We left a few days later, stopping in Madrid for a pleasant couple of days with Terry Todman and his wife and with the Ulrich Hayneses from Algiers. We had wide-ranging discussions of Maghreb-Spanish relations and U.S. policies in the area, did a little shopping, had a nice meal or two, and went on our way with no sense of impending doom.

On arrival in Washington I was told that the secretary could not see me but had commissioned David Newsom to do so. Newsom began by saying that the hard jobs were always given to him and then said that the king had complained to Mrs. Kreps about me. He showed me a report of the conversation. The king had made the following points:

(1) U.S.-Moroccan relations would not improve as long as I was in Rabat. There were three specific problems:
    (a) Ambassador Bengelloun had seen a message from me to Washington saying the Moroccan government was not interested in receiving Secretary Kreps. I might note that of course there was no such message.
    (b) I had lost my nerve in Lebanon, causing the unnecessary evacuation of the American community. I can thank my diplomatic colleagues in Beirut for that, I guess.
    (c) I had served previously in Rabat as DCM and had known many people. Unfortunately, many continued to think of me in my previous capacity. Ambassadors had to act with more discretion. The secretary must have overlooked the fact that I had been DCM before, because it certainly was not normal to assign someone as an ambassador in such circumstances. This is nonsense, of course, but Warren Christopher, the deputy secretary of state told me after it was all over that he felt the same way.
(2) The king was less certain of other facts, but he had heard that I had been a friend of General Medbuh, who had led the Skhirat coup attempt in 1971. The suggestion had been made that I therefore must have been aware of the coup in advance. This is ironic; I was one of the few diplomats in Rabat who did not play golf and who therefore never met Medbuh, whose principal responsibility was the royal golf courses. I never knowingly laid eyes on him.
(3) The king did not want to embarrass the president by requesting my recall and hoped that the secretary would see to it that this was not necessary.

Newsom said there seemed to be no alternative to my leaving Rabat. Unfortunately, no other post was available that was suitable for me. Perhaps I could go somewhere as diplomat in residence, or I might wish to consider retirement. This is the standard formula with which one is ushered out. While by this time I had no desire to remain in Rabat, I was stunned by the message. I went back to DACOR house, where we were staying, and told Jeanne what had happened. Thus began one of the most difficult periods of my life.

From the beginning, I had known that I started off on the wrong foot with Hassan and that our relations would never be warm. I felt, however, that I had done him a favor in reversing the U.S. policy on the supply of arms, and the Kreps visit had gone well. I enjoyed widespread recognition in Rabat, where Moroccans knew that I had been working diligently to resolve outstanding problems between our two countries. In retrospect, I think the king believed the shah's assertion that we had dropped him like an old slipper and decided that I was the agent chosen to do the same to him. He may have been influenced by the myth that I had been the *éminence grise* in Cairo and Beirut. I suspect that my delivering the disinvitation to the shah was the final straw. The king's remarks about my numerous contacts, on the other hand, make me think perhaps I met once too often with someone the throne considered an enemy. Perhaps Sadiq al-Glaoui, son of the former pasha of Marrakesh, who came to see me several times about his son, who was in the Tangier American School. Or the doctor with whom we had lunch and a frank talk in Meknes at the urging of the head of the Peace Corps contingent. Combing my memory, these are the only two occasions I can recall that might have excited suspicion. But perhaps it was neither of these. Perhaps it was nobody.

Jim Bishop had a conversation with Ali Bengelloun that tends to support my impression about the *éminence grise* factor. Bengelloun said the problems with the Kreps visit were the fault of the Moroccan officials doing the coordinating. He then commented that relations between the king and me had not gone well from the beginning. We did not enjoy the degree of personal rapport that had existed between Hassan and my predecessors. The king had agreed to my appointment without realizing that I had served previously in Rabat. He had intended to speak to Secretary Vance about this on the way to the airport the last night of his visit, but it had slipped his mind. Speaking personally, Bengelloun said the king might have been superstitious about my presence because I had been there during the 1971 and 1972 coup attempts. Bengelloun offered to and later did speak to the secretary on my behalf. Vance told him I was leaving Morocco and that was that.

After consulting Hal Saunders and others, I decided there was no purpose to be served in trying to ride out the storm, although Hal did offer that alternative. Rather, I decided the king's laundry list of complaints should be seen as liberating me from a career that was becoming less and less pleasant. The Foreign Service had changed as the role of the ambassador dwindled while that of the security officer grew. I had long planned to leave the service around 1980 anyway and thought I should start looking for new employment. One of the first people I called was retired NEA hand Luke Battle, who always seemed to know what jobs were coming up, although he never came through with one for me. We agreed to have lunch at the Metropolitan Club.

I was walking down the corridor of the department en route to meet him when I suddenly had an attack of vertigo of the sort I had been suffering since 1972. Margery Ransom of USIA, who was accompanying me out the door, helped me back to Jim Bishop's office. We called the medical division, which sent up a doctor with a portable EKG machine to take a reading. I subsequently met with the department's cardiologist, who suggested that I would be wise to return home so that I could be followed more closely. He did not seem to think it was urgent, though, and I don't think he was suggesting that I curtail my tour in Rabat. These attacks seemed to be related to stress, however, and I decided that I wanted someplace quiet for a while. The department made some effort to place me and made me two or three offers. I eventually settled for the job of faculty adviser at the Air University at Maxwell Field, Alabama.

In the meantime, we returned to Rabat, where I announced to my diplomatic colleagues that I was leaving for health reasons, and the embassy put out a press release to that effect. No one believed it, of course. I had told the full story to my senior staff, and they may have leaked some of it. Even if they did not, no politically sophisticated observer in Rabat would have accepted such an explanation unless I had been carried out on a stretcher with an intravenous feeding tube attached to my arm and my wife dressed in mourning black. The one Moroccan to whom I told the truth was my physician, Abdeslam Tazi, who promised that he would tell people I was *fatigué*, something he always said every time I went to see him anyway. Our departure was not unnoticed, but there was no great to-do about it. I gather the diplomatic corps buzzed with rumors for a while, and there were a few speculative press comments, but the *Washington Post* and *New York Times* barely noticed. On June 28, a week after our departure, the *Washington Post* (p. A17) carried a brief item under the heading "Mideast Violence Imperils Peace Effort," which said in part:

> Kissinger is to finish his tour in Morocco, where he is to see King Hassan II. Kissinger is close to the Moroccan monarch, whose relations with the Carter administration have been uneven and who earlier this month abruptly demanded the recall of Ambassador Richard Parker, according to US officials.
>
> These officials said they were not sure how Parker had angered Hassan, but speculated that the move was a show of the king's displeasure with the State Department's opposition to increased arms sales to Morocco and with what Hassan sees as the department's favoritism toward Algeria. Parker has previously served as ambassador to Algeria.
>
> The administration has kept the king's action secret and is moving to replace Parker quickly in contrast to its handling of a similar rebuff from Iran's revolutionary government last month. Then the State Department disclosed Iran's refusal to accept Walter Cutler as ambassador and said that a replacement for Cutler would not be sent to Iran.

The department in fact kept the post in Rabat open for five months. On June 29, the *Baltimore Sun* carried a correspondent's dispatch, which read in part:

> Relations between the Kingdom of Morocco and the United States are badly strained, the poorest they have been in many years, American and Moroccan officials here agree. Prospects for easing the resentment felt by the North Afri-

can nation of 18 million persons were not improved any by the sudden departure last week of US Ambassador Richard Parker.

Mr. Parker, an Arabist who had written about Islamic monuments in Morocco and lived in the country previously, only became ambassador in October. Just two weeks ago he announced he would be giving up his post for health reasons. However, many officials here suspect that discouragement over the tense U.S.-Moroccan relationship and frustration at not being able to do anything to improve it contributed to his decision to leave.

Of more interest was an item by Davis Humphrey, described as an American freelance writer who had long observed events in North Africa, in the October 23, 1979, *Christian Science Monitor*:

In recent years US diplomacy regarding Morocco has been less than brilliant. This strategically positioned, longtime friend is calling for support at a time when the US has failed even to supply adequate diplomatic ties.

The one recent American ambassador in whom King Hassan had confidence was Robert Neumann, who held the post from 1973 to 1976. Mr. Neumann, who had a deep understanding of Moroccan interests, was "done in," so to speak, by two other US diplomats, the ambassadors to Spain and Algeria, because of his pro-Moroccan attitude after the takeover of the Spanish Sahara in November 1975. Mr. Neumann was removed over Hassan's objections and replaced by crusty Robert Anderson, who immediately put himself in the king's disfavor by demanding that Morocco cease the use in the Sahara of arms and aircraft bought in the US. By mid-1978 the King asked that Mr. Anderson be replaced.

The next US ambassador, an able Arabist, had been posted previously in Morocco, and had ironically been the ambassador in Algeria who helped cause the dismissal of Mr. Neumann. Again the king failed in his request for US helicopters and aircraft parts, many of which had been bought but whose shipment was blocked by the State Department's

Munitions Control Board. He requested the removal of Mr. Parker.

Neumann himself sent me a clipping of this item and said, "As far as Stabler [who was ambassador to Madrid in 1976] is concerned, he is right, but there was more to the story than that. At any rate it's water under the dam [*sic*]...."

I wrote back to say I hoped he didn't believe I had anything to do with his removal from Rabat.

He replied on November 26 saying, "I never suspected you seriously, but I cannot say the same of Stabler. I do know that he conspired against me with the first Franco [*sic*] Foreign Minister Cortina. As Cortina also conspired against his ambassador in Rabat, it was par for the course."

I have not pursued the matter further with Neumann or Stabler, but knowing Stabler well I find the story most improbable. It is true that Neumann and I held opposite views on the Sahara issue, and we had some lively exchanges as a result, but I had a high personal regard for him and certainly had nothing to do with his departure from Rabat. That was due rather to his running afoul of Kissinger. He tried to go around Kissinger by getting in touch with friends in the White House in an effort to reverse the department's restrictive policy on military cooperation with Morocco. Henry found out about it and sacked him. Or, at least that is the story I was told. Neumann did have a conspiratorial bent.

At about the same time there was an article in some publication I cannot identify, having only a photocopy of the article itself, with no attribution, but which comes under the rubric News in Perspective:

American sources in Algeria are worried that the Carter administration may be influenced by the need to "persuade" Morocco's King Hassan to give greater support to the Egypt-Israel peace treaty and that this could lead Washington to abandon Algeria and give its full backing to Morocco.

This seems unlikely, however, for US Congressman Stephen Solarz, who just visited the region, is advising caution. Moreover, although the US agreed to remove Dick

Parker because King Hassan held him responsible for the failure of the talks in Washington last October, he is not being replaced by a more sympathetic figure. The US accepts Parker's essentially correct analysis that the king was losing ground in the Sahara, and the post is being left vacant....

I suspect the source of this particular story was Rick Haynes in Algiers. The last sentence does not make much sense, either internally or in relation to its context.

We departed Rabat at the end of June, spent some time in Paris and Monterubbiano, and reported to my new post at Maxwell in early September. On September 21, the State Department announced it would award me the Distinguished Service Award, its highest nonvalor decoration. Given in recognition of my services, the nature of which was rather vaguely defined, this was designed to make me feel better. It also sent a message to the Moroccans that the government held me in high regard and did not take kindly to King Hassan's cavalier treatment of me.

The department decided that it should not waste another career officer on Hassan for a while and took its time about selecting a replacement. Eventually it sent Angier Biddle Duke, former chief of protocol and ambassador to Spain. As a person with money and social position whom the king could trust, he was an inspired choice. He got along very well, but I don't think he found Rabat very exciting. Neither had I. I once heard that in Rabat one should think of one's self as being in a French provincial capital, where the king was the prefect. Everything revolved around him, and nothing else was of interest.

I was subsequently told that my trouble in my final post was as much with Deputy Secretary of State Warren Christopher as it was with the king. Bill Crawford described him as having an anal personality and no sense of humor. Some of my telegrams from Beirut displeased him, and he went so far as to ask Tony Ross, an old friend, to do a study of my reporting to see whether or not I was a serious person. Ross reportedly told him after examination that indeed I was serious but under considerable stress. I gather that my fall from grace in Rabat confirmed Christopher in his view. I was told that he had blocked my consideration for a number of senior posts for which colleagues had proposed me. In retrospect, that was probably just as well. I had had enough.

17

Over and Out

As I mentioned earlier, Hal Saunders had offered to let me stay in Rabat to see if we could overcome the king's dislike of me, but I knew that would be awkward and demeaning and declined the offer. I wanted to leave. Harry Barnes, the director general of the Foreign Service, suggested several possibilities that would allow me to remain in the service. One was the Economic and Social Council job at the United Nations, then held by a woman who was leaving. I regret not taking it, but I had heard that Andrew Young, our permanent representative there, was a difficult man to work for and I was concerned about the stress that would result. The second was as a special assistant to former secretary Dean Rusk, who was at the University of Georgia. I also regret passing up that experience. The third was a faculty adviser job at one of the war colleges. I eventually opted for this, figuring it would give me maximum opportunity to look for a job on the outside.

We left Rabat in June, having told people I was leaving for health reasons, which was not totally untrue. We went to Saint-Germaine-en-Laye for the wedding of Jeanne's niece Catherine Jaccard to Gilbert Souchier, and then on to Monterubbiano for the summer. After arrival there I was offered the job of faculty adviser at the Air University at Maxwell Air Force Base at Montgomery, Alabama, which was advertised as giving the greatest scope for traveling around the country and looking for other possibilities. I decided to accept it. We arrived at Maxwell in late August or early September and realized immediately that it was a mistake.

It was not the people, it was the place. The Air Force people were admirable—kind and helpful and one could not fault the reception we had. We liked all of them. But both Montgomery and Maxwell were isolated from the main currents of American thought. There was no decent bookstore in town and not even an indecent one on the post. The *New York Times* was not delivered there, and the intellectual climate of the Air University and its War College was strictly professional. There was little serious interest in or knowledge of what was happening on the ground in the Middle East or elsewhere abroad, and we did not receive the classified mail that I had been reading every day for years. Because of its operational environment, the Air Force is much more isolated from events on the ground than the Navy and the Army and consequently thinks it can afford to ignore them or pay them scant attention. Air Force lieutenant generals would arrive talking about Eye-ran and Eye-raq, just like George W. Bush, and nobody knew enough to correct them.

We were given quarters on the generals' circle, where I was outranked only by the president of the university, Lt. Gen. Stan Umstead, a good fellow. The quarters were nice—a four-bedroom masonry structure put up during the building campaign of the 1930s that transformed places like Ft. Bliss and Ft. Sam Houston, too. Our rent was $800 a month, and there was no housing allowance from the Department of State.

I was given a large office with a pleasant and competent secretary (Dot Dean) and given free rein to do whatever suited me. I would be expected to give an occasional lecture and participate in a seminar or two and to participate in periodic rituals, but other than that I was free to fly around the country and learn about the Air Force. But it really made no difference if I did nothing. I was a ceremonial figure. The job was what we called a turkey roost. And I was a turkey.

I began looking for something else almost as soon as I decently could. The Hoover Institution offered me a post as successor to George Rentz, a famous Saudi expert who had been the librarian. They were only offering $25,000, housing was extraordinarily expensive, and I was no librarian. The director of Central Intelligence, Stansfield Turner, offered me an appointment as a national intelligence officer, a prestigious position. I was tempted, but it would have been a comedown. At the same time I was offered the position of diplomat-in-residence at the University of Virginia. It came with a historic house but no salary. I said that would not do. Ruhi Rama-zani, head of the department of government and politics, agreed to pay me $10,000 a semester to teach one course. which I tentatively accepted. Meanwhile, the Middle East Institute offered me a job as editor of the *Middle East Journal* at $25,000 per year. After deciding that I could handle both jobs simultaneously, I accepted and retired from the Foreign Service on June 1, 1980.

We moved to Charlottesville immediately, passing by Durham, North Carolina, for Richard's graduation from Duke, and then took off for Monterubbiano, via a gourmet trip from Nancy to Lyon with our dear friends Bill and Marie-Ange Underwood. We went on from Lyon alone, stopping for memorable overnights and dinners at the Pyramide in Vienne and the Beaumanière at Les Baux, where we decided we'd better stop eating for a while.

We spent two years at Charlottesville. It was a pleasant place. My students were polite and reasonably good about staying awake in class and doing the readings, but I encountered no signs of ge-nius among them. Perhaps my course—"The Modern Diplomatic History of the Middle East"—did not sound all that attractive to the brightest students.

Our rent-free house was very comfortable. It had the distinction of being the only historic house at the University not designed by Thomas Jefferson. A large, ungainly structure in a large garden off the main campus, it had been built in the early 1800s by a professor of natural history who wanted a place where he could keep ani-mals, which he could not do on the Lawn. Its name, Morea, referred to mulberry trees, which he tried to grow for food for silkworms. The experiment was not a success.

I would spend the first three days of the week at the university and take the bus up to Washington on Thursday morning, arriving at the Middle East Institute in time for lunch, and return to Char-lottesville on Friday afternoon. Jeanne sometimes accompanied me when there was a special occasion, such as a New Year's Party, or a conference. We were given a bedroom on the top floor of the MEI as a temporary residence.

We seriously considered staying in Charlottesville permanent-ly, but the diplomat-in residence appointment was supposed to be only transitional. In the spring of 1982 Ruhi Ramazani said an assistant professorship was all that could be considered for me beyond two years, and the way he said it made me think he would not seriously pursue it—he made no offer and no attempt to recruit me. I had the impression, perhaps wrong, that he did not really want any competition in the field of Middle Eastern studies. We would have to give up Morea at the end of two years in any event. and that was a serious disincentive to sticking around. Nevertheless, we did some serious house-hunting with a local agent. We saw some nice houses, including some we could afford to buy, but there was very little going on with regard to the Middle East at Charlottesville while a great deal was going on in Washington, and eventually we decided to return to that city.

We notified our tenants at 6640 32d Street, the Koppers, that we were returning and wanted the house back. We left Charlottesville for Monterubbiano as soon as school was out and returned to Washington in September, traveling via North Africa. The Council on Foreign Relations had asked me to write a book for the general reader on the region, and I had chaired a working group of people thought knowledgeable about it who were supposed to help me decide what to write. I was paid no money for the book, but the Council did pay for our travel through North Africa. The book was published by Praeger in 1986 under the title *North Africa—Regional Tensions and Strategic Concerns*. It was a good book and was reasonably well received. It did not break any records, but a second edition was published in 1988. The Council has since resisted efforts by various people to bring out a revised edition, and the book is far out of date today.

We moved back into 6640 32nd Street on a very hot day. I went to take a shower, and the water was cut off in the middle of it. The Koppers had left with an unpaid water bill of some $600, and I had to go downtown and pay it in order to get the water turned back on. I eventually sued them in small claims court and got a fraction of the money back. A very irresponsible couple. May God pardon them and the District Maryland Realty Company that was handling the rental. That company is no longer listed in the telephone directory, so I assume it has closed.

I now began working four days a week at the *Journal*. The Middle East Institute was a Dickensian sort of place—threadbare and cluttered, with seven full-time employees. The president, L. Dean Brown, was a retired Foreign Service officer who had served in senior positions in the department and had been ambassador to Jordan. He knew nothing at all about the Middle East, but had been something of a troubleshooter. Kissinger had sent him to Lebanon in the spring of 1976, for instance, to see what could be done there, before we sent out Frank Meloy as ambassador. (I do not know whether Brown had anything to do with that tragic appointment.) He had a drinking problem and was very quick with his answers. He asked me to jazz up the *Journal,* and left me alone. I never felt at ease with him.

My predecessor at the *Journal,* Bill Sands, was an alcoholic who managed to get through the day thanks to a loyal staff, especially Kathleen Manalo, who called herself the "publisher," and Suzy Pratt, the secretary. The *Journal* was very unexciting, and I knew no one who read it. I had never subscribed and had never belonged to the Institute, which was supported in a hand-to-mouth state by modest donations from oil companies and dues from a membership of 2,000. The *Journal* was a respectable, peer-reviewed quarterly, however, and publication in it was sought by academics.

Academic journals are usually dull, reflecting the qualities of their contributors. Making their writings readable was often a challenge, and much of my time was spent copy editing. We also gave the *Journal* a face lift, hiring a professional to design a new cover and improved typeface. I did my best to select articles that were timely and interesting. Unfortunately you can only do so much with Turkish economists and political scientists and sociologists of all stripes and origin. At least some people liked my changes, and we got subscriptions up to 5,000. (They are at about 3,000 as I write this in 2006.)

The editorship was also a handy perch from which to watch and participate in the creation of what passed for the common wisdom. I was a frequent participant as moderator and panelist at conferences and seminars and appeared on all the TV networks, including C-SPAN and CNN. I reviewed books, wrote articles, and was a model pundit of the Third Class. I was paid to pontificate on my area of presumed expertise but not enough to live on.

There are three classes of pundit. The first, or ayatollah, class is allowed to pontificate on anything at all. The ayatollah does not actually have to know much about the subject. He is well paid and is listened to by people in the government. Walter Lippman was such a pundit.

The second, or *hojat al-Islam*, class is allowed to pontificate on anything, does not have to know anything about it, is well paid, but no one serious listens to him. George Will is such a pundit today. There was a time, however (when Mrs. Reagan was in the White House), when he was first class.

The third-class pundit is poorly paid, is allowed to pontificate only on a subject about which he has managed to persuade people that he is knowledgeable, and nobody listens to him.

We continued to go to Monterubbiano every summer and for several years were able to spend three months there. It had developed into a comfortable home, and we enjoyed it thoroughly. We wished that our children would come more often but understood why they did not. Meanwhile, we knew many people in the village, had a small group of American and Italian friends, and felt very much at home.

At the same time we had been making improvements to 6640 32nd Street—enlarging the kitchen, adding air-conditioning, enclosing the porch, and making the place more habitable. Still, it seemed too modest for me. The ceilings were too low, and it was far from the center of cultural and political activity. From time to time we had looked at houses in Georgetown in a casual sort of way and never found anything that we both liked and could afford. Meanwhile, the value of 6640 was rising. From its original $40,000 it had risen to $300,000 by September 1986, when we sold it and bought 3317 P Street NW in Georgetown, for $310,000. (As of February 2006 its assessed value for tax purposes was $1,047,9900.)

Meanwhile, earlier in 1986, Steve Low, director of the Foreign Service Institute (FSI), our diplomatic training academy, approached me about becoming founding president of ADS, the Association for Diplomatic Studies (later renamed ADST, the Association for Diplomatic Studies and Training), a new organization he had conceived to enhance FSI. It would create an alumni organization, promote the study of diplomatic history, create a museum of diplomacy, and support projects at FSI that would not find official funding. All of this was directed at creating a collegiate atmosphere at the new campus the FSI was to occupy at Arlington Hall, a former girls' school the Army took over during World War II.

The salary would be modest, but I would only have to work two days a week to start with and could walk to the FSI in Rosslyn across Key Bridge once we moved to Georgetown. Steve had received a generous donation from Lloyd Miller, a friend and former noncareer ambassador, that would provide initial funding, but I would have to raise a god deal more money as we went along. We thought, erroneously, that the Council of American Ambassadors, an association of noncareer ambassadors who were thought to be anxious for the legitimacy we could give them, would support the organization. They turned out not to realize how illegitimate they were. In any event, I accepted Steve's offer and for a while had two jobs.

In the fall of 1986 Dean Brown retired from the Middle East Institute, and I was encouraged by Georgiana Stevens, a longtime supporter of the Institute, to put my name on the list of candidates to succeed him. (I had been offered the job in 1971 but had declined.) I put my name in, and even wrote a letter of resignation from ADS. The job went instead to Luke Battle, who had told me earlier that I was his candidate. He took over in January 1987. At that point, to everyone's surprise, Kay Manalo, my number two, was accepted into the Foreign Service at the age of 50-plus, and Luke would not hire the young woman I wanted to replace her. He insisted on someone older that I did not want. After six years I was getting tired of reading journal articles, was finding two jobs onerous, and thought I should be spending more time at the FSI. So I quit the *Middle East Journal*, turned the job over to Jean Newsom, and began to spend four days a week at ADS.

I thought that spending four days a week on the job would give me time to do some serious fundraising, and I set about learning the folklore that is associated with that trade, attending a conference of the association of fund-raising executives and trying to apply the principles and tactics they said were effective. I struck out, however, and gave up after three years. I did get the organization up and running and helped to set up the oral history program that has been its most promising activity. I also helped set up an annual awards program for language teachers at the FSI that has continued to the present. My successor, Tom Boyatt, had little more success than I at fund-raising, and the same can be said of his successors, but over the years the organization has taken on some weight and has built a base of support that will, I hope, keep it in business. The oral history program in particular has been a great success, thanks to the efforts of its director, Charles Stuart Kennedy.

For some time I had hoped to escape from all executive and administrative responsibilities and do what I really wanted to do in retirement, which was to write a book on miscalculation, a permanent aspect of our Middle East policy. To that end I applied to the Woodrow Wilson Center for International Scholars at the Smithsonian Institution for a grant to spend a year there writing my book. I was accepted in 1989 and formally retired for the second time in the spring. I was 66.

We spent the summer in Italy and then returned for a pleasant, unstressful year of research. A trip to Moscow for more research on the origins of the June War followed. We spent a pleasant three months in London as the John Adams Fulbright Fellow, which involved speaking on U.S. foreign policy at universities throughout Britain, including Oxford and Cambridge.

I tend to think of the Fulbright Grant as my last remunerative employment, but in 1992–1993 we spent an academic year at Lawrence University in Appleton, Wisconsin, where I was the Stephen Scarff Distinguished Visiting Professor, teaching a couple of courses on the Middle East and working on the final phase of my book on miscalculation. Jeanne worked on her non–cook book (a collection of recipes she refused to call a "book"). Lawrence was not very exciting, but people were friendly and the students were polite. It was an agreeable sojourn and we paid off the mortgage at 3317 P with the salary.

Six months later, after our return home, I taught a semester-long course on conflict resolution with Bill Zartman at Johns Hopkins School of Advanced International Studies (SAIS). That really was my last employment. Aside from some minimal book royalties and an occasional speaking engagement, we have had no income other than my pension, Social Security, and a couple of miniscule annuities. It has been enough to live on in reasonable comfort (our adjusted gross income in 2005 was $114,275).

A few side excursions have been left out of the above account, however. The most important was my appointment in late 1982 as adviser to the U.S. Businessmen's Council on Reconstruction in Lebanon, presided over by Louis Preston of the Morgan Bank. Formed at White House request, its members represented major companies like Westinghouse and General Electric. They were ready, at least in theory, to invest in reconstruction projects following Israel's 1982 invasion and the imagined resolution of Lebanon's civil war. I was hired as a counterweight to a woman named Joyce Starr, who had been appointed as secretary of the Council by Peter McPherson, the administrator of AID, which had a poorly defined role in the Council's formation. Preston was concerned that Joyce was too closely identified with the Israelis and would reflect their views in the Council's deliberations.

I went to Beirut for three weeks in late January—early February 1983. It was a strange experience. I was almost the only guest in the large Carleton Hotel, yet there seemed to be a noisy wedding party every other night. I talked to many old friends, called on all the appropriate cabinet ministers and President Amin Gemayel, went to numerous dinners and luncheons with various personalities. I returned persuaded that: (1) I could make a lot of money if I stayed in Beirut but would be shot by someone before I could enjoy it. 2) While it was a good time to reconnoiter, it was too early to put any serious money in the place. Nothing had been settled, and the civil war was not yet over.

Joyce Starr, on the other hand, relying on her conversations with Israelis and Maronites, maintained that the forces of order had the situation well in hand and this was the time to jump in and seize the opportunities for investment.

The Council agreed with me, and Preston fired Joyce. An interim report was prepared by John Law, and Preston and I were to go to Beirut in May to present it to President Gemayel. The blowing up of our Embassy in April, however, persuaded us that it was no time to go to Lebanon, and that was the end of that.

In 1984 I took three journalists on a tour of Jordan, Syria, Israel, and the Palestinian territories on behalf of UNRWA (United Nations

Relief and Work Agency for Palestinian Refugees). In 1985 I did a speaking tour of the Gulf and Jordan for USIS, and in 1989 did one of Algeria, Egypt, Yemen, Jordan, and Syria. In 1989 I represented USIS at a conference in The Hague on Arab-Israel peace, where I confidently predicted that there would be no initiatives for peace under George Bush and Secretary of State James Baker.

We also had some entertaining touristic experiences during this period. In 1986, Jeanne and I were paid to escort a group from the Philadelphia World Affairs Council across the Atlantic by ship from San Juan Puerto Rico to the Azores and on to Lisbon, Cadiz, Majorca, Collioure, and Villefranche, where we got off. The "group" turned out to be a single couple named Lopata from St. Louis. We were amazed to discover that of the four couples at our dinner table, we were the only ones on our first marriage. We felt out of date.

In 1987 we took a group from the World Affairs Council of Northern California across North Africa by bus—from Rabat to Tunis. That was a lot of fun. In 1994 I took another group from Northern California on a bus tour of Morocco.

In between, Jeanne and I had several trips as resource persons on small cruise ships around the Mediterranean. While they were very comfortable, and Jeanne enjoyed not having to do any cooking, my role was really a bit demeaning. There was no time to listen to my lectures. The ship companies evidently decided that they did not want me any more, perhaps because I suggested ways they could improve the voyages.

The last scheduled trip, a tour of Morocco for a New York TV station slated for the fall of 2001, was canceled after September 11 and never revived.

My long-awaited book, *The Politics of Miscalculation in the Middle East,* was published by Indiana University Press in 1993. A reviewer in *CHOICE,* the librarian's journal, called it one of the outstanding academic books of the year. It received favorable reviews and is often referred to by writers for its description of the origins of the June War. It is still available, in paperback, from Indiana University Press. With its publication, I began to work seriously on what became *Uncle Sam in Barbary,* a study of American diplomacy in North Africa in the period 1785–1815, but it was often put on hold while I dealt with other projects—the conferences on the June and October wars and the Joel Barlow memorial.

In 1989, Brian Urquhart, former assistant secretary general of the UN, who knew about my work on the June War, suggested to Edgar Bronfman of Seagram's that I was the man to arrange and direct a conference on the 25th anniversary of that war that the Samuel Bronfman Foundation was considering funding. A local representative of the Bronfman Foundation came to the Smithsonian to see if I was interested in such a project and led me to believe that the sky was the limit as far as money was concerned. He and I went to New York and met with Bill Friedman, a personable young man who was working for Bronfman and who was very positive. I asked why they did not pick a nice Jewish boy for the job instead of an old Arabist like me. He said they had looked me up and understood that I had my views but was OK.

Urquhart had been inspired by the Soviet-American discussions of the Cuban missile crisis of 1962, which had revealed that we had come closer to a nuclear exchange than we had realized at the time, and thought a similar exchange about June 1967 would be useful. I began building castles in the air and sketching plans for whom to invite, and where to hold the meeting. Time passed, and I heard no more from the Bronfmans; I then heard from Friedman that they would not be needing me. By this time I had become interested in the project and Bob Keeley, who had succeeded Luke Battle as president of the Middle East Institute, agreed that the Institute would sponsor (meaning lend its name to) such a conference if I could raise the money for it. Starting with $5000 in seed money from the late Tim Childs, an MEI board member, I raised some $40,000 from various places, and the conference was held at the Foreign Service Institute in Rosslyn in June 1992. The participants—Israelis, Soviets, Egyptians, and Americans–were all former government officials who had participated in the crisis in some capacity or other. It is described in detail in *The Six-Day War, a Retrospective,* published by the University Press of Florida in 1996. We did not make any discoveries of the magnitude of those discussed in the Cuban Missile Crisis talks, but we produced an authoritative and balanced account of what happened as seen by the parties to the dispute. The book is an edited transcript of the proceedings, with commentary by me and the panel chairmen. Bill Friedman, to whom I sent a copy because Bronfman had given us $5,000, said he found it a page-turner. It is a standard reference text today.

I raised over $90,000 for a somewhat grander conference on the October or Yom Kippur War, held at the Cosmos Club in 1998. It is described in *The October War, a Retrospective*, published by the University Press of Florida in 2001. It is perhaps most useful for its discussion of the American airlift of arms to Israel during the war.

Although I received a modicum of administrative and secretarial support from the MEI, and from the FSI for the first conference, and I had help from Bill Zartman of SAIS and Bernard Reich of George Washington University with drawing up the programs and deciding whom to invite, I did all the work of fund-raising and inviting, of chairing the conferences, and of editing the books.

Meanwhile, my research on Barbary had awakened me to the story of Joel Barlow, who played a major role in the resolution of the hostage crisis with Algiers, our first, in 1796. He lies buried in the churchyard at Zarnowiec, a village near Krakow, Poland, where he died in 1812 while en route back to Paris from an abortive effort to see Napoleon in Vilna. The precise location of his grave is unknown, but I raised $10,000 to erect, with help from our consulate general in Krakow, a small monument to him in the churchyard. It was dedicated in June 1998. Jeanne and I attended, traveling by train from Paris to Prague, Krakow, Warsaw, Berlin, and back to Paris.

While all this was going on I was working slowly on *Uncle Sam in Barbary*. At Carl Brown's suggestion, I chose it as a retirement project with a view to seeing whether an area specialist could add anything new to the subject. The story had already been told a number of times, but the tellers knew very little about North Africa. Did that make a difference? Some, I guess, but not all that much. It was probably more important to have a diplomat look at the story. I think I have made an important contribution to our diplomatic history.

I also found it fun to do, and it was a useful raison d'être. In 2004 it was awarded the American Academy of Diplomacy's C. Douglas Dillon Prize for a book on the practice of American diplomacy, which brought with it a check for $5,000. I don't expect to duplicate that, but my next project is a study of why Thomas Jefferson apologized to the Bey of Tunis for the behavior of our Naval commander in 1805. (I have yet to work up the energy needed for that.)

In May 2004, after a trip to Redding, Connecticut, Barlow's home town, to publicize him and my book, and attempt (so far unsuccessfully) to promote an exchange of correspondence between the students at Joel Barlow High School in Redding and the high school in Zarnowiec, I suffered a brain hemorrhage (a subdural hematoma) and was *hors de camp* in the hospital and hospice for four months. I am lucky to be alive, but am not up to much these days. As of the summer of 2007 what energy I have is largely devoted to taking care of Jeanne, who after taking care of me for long months has developed troubles of her own. It has been a long and largely successful voyage, and we both wonder how much more it will last. Meanwhile, we are grateful for the many friends who have been solicitous for our welfare and whose company we have enjoyed over the years. They have been very important to our enjoyment of life. I am afraid to list them for fear of hurt feelings.

Index

www.ingramcontent.com/pod-product-compliance
Lightning Source LLC
Chambersburg PA
CBHW020656270326
41928CB00005B/151